FileMaker® Pro
Design & Scripting

FOR

DUMMIES®

FileMaker® Pro Design & Scripting

FOR DUMMIES®

by Timothy Trimble

Wiley Publishing, Inc.

FileMaker® Pro Design & Scripting For Dummies®

Published by
Wiley Publishing, Inc.
111 River Street
Hoboken, NJ 07030-5774
www.wiley.com

WILEY

About the Author

Timothy Trimble is a professional computer geek, writer, and software developer with over 25 years of industry experience. He started as a video game developer and worked his way into the PC and PDA software development markets on various commercial, corporate, and vertical market applications. He currently exhibits his geekish tendencies as a FileMaker developer at SolutionMakers, Inc. (www.solutionmakers.com) in Woodinville, WA.

Timothy has written a multitude of articles for various industry publications and wrote a book on flight simulation. He maintains a blog on the Art of Software Development at www.timothytrimble.info. Although he has significant publishing credits in the computer industry, he dreams of some day having his science fiction work published as well.

When Timothy is not cranking away at the keyboard, he likes to be with his family, entertain his friends by singing and playing guitar, and door-to-door to tell others about his faith. Feel free to contact Timothy with your comments on this book by e-mailing him at fmp4d@timothytrimble.info.

Dedication

To the WhoWeAre Band. Two CDs, the House of Blues, and a wonderful, nine-year ride that I'll never forget!

Author's Acknowledgments

First of all, my loving wife and soul-mate, Denise. You continue to love and support me on this adventure of life. And to the pride and joy of my life — my boys Alex, Andrew, and Sam — proof that the nuts don't fall far from the tree, though they hate to admit it. I love you all dearly.

A special thanks goes to Dennis Cohen for his pulling up the tail end of the edits on the book during crunch time and to the staff at Wiley Publishing: Tiffany Franklin for nudging me when I needed nudging; Rebecca Huehls for putting up with my strange writing style while she taught me *For Dummies* style; Nancy Stevenson for helping me through my first chapter; and of course the unsung heroes at Wiley who handle the layout, printing, and awesome cartoons.

To my buddy, spiritual brother, fellow musician, and strangely enough — my technical editor, Mark Hammer. You're one of the reasons that I decided to take such a serious look at FileMaker. So, how big is the stage now?

A special thanks to Marco and John, for giving me the initiative to dive back into the FileMaker world.

A very special thanks goes to my agent at Waterside Productions, Carole McClendon. Not only am I impressed that such a prominent agent is willing to handle my stuff, but she has a gift for turning my proposals into real work. Thank you, Carole!

A heartfelt and warm thanks and appreciation to the Flowers family for helping my family and me through a very challenging period in our life. Because of you, this book could be written.

No acknowledgments would be complete without a special thanks for the things that got me through this book: Red Bull and Monster for getting me through the late nights of writing; Eve-online and my fellow pilots in Codito Ergo Sum for providing the brief moments of computer recreation when the diversion was needed; and iTunes for the constant flow of music while madly typing away.

Of course a thank you goes to the FileMaker, Inc., organization for making FileMaker Pro the product that it is today, and for promoting what is truly an Art in Software Development.

Lastly and most significantly, thanks to Jehovah for blessing me with the gift of words and the ability to grasp technology, and for allowing me to know all the people I mentioned above.

Publisher's Acknowledgments

We're proud of this book; please send us your comments through our online registration form located at www.dummies.com/register/.

Some of the people who helped bring this book to market include the following:

Acquisitions, Editorial, and Media Development

Project Editor: Rebecca Huehls

Acquisitions Editor: Tiffany Ma

Copy Editor: Heidi Unger

Technical Editor: Mark Hammer

Editorial Manager: Leah P. Cameron

Media Development Specialists: Angela Denny, Kate Jenkins, Steven Kudirka, Kit Malone

Media Development Coordinator: Laura Atkinson

Media Project Supervisor: Laura Moss

Media Development Manager: Laura VanWinkle

Editorial Assistant: Amanda Foxworth

Sr. Editorial Assistant: Cherie Case

Cartoons: Rich Tennant (www.the5thwave.com)

Composition Services

Project Coordinators: Tera Knapp, Adrienne Martinez

Layout and Graphics: Andrea Dahl, Denny Hager, Barbara Moore, Barry Offringa, Lynsey Osborn, Alicia B. South

Proofreaders: Leeann Harney, Dwight Ramsey, Techbooks

Indexer: Techbooks

Publishing and Editorial for Technology Dummies

Richard Swadley, Vice President and Executive Group Publisher

Andy Cummings, Vice President and Publisher

Mary Bednarek, Executive Acquisitions Director

Mary C. Corder, Editorial Director

Publishing for Consumer Dummies

Diane Graves Steele, Vice President and Publisher

Joyce Pepple, Acquisitions Director

Composition Services

Gerry Fahey, Vice President of Production Services

Debbie Stailey, Director of Composition Services

Contents at a Glance

Table of Contents

Introduction

*W*ith over 10 million units of FileMaker software sold around the world, FileMaker has become the diamond in the rough when it comes to creating and managing data. After over 20 years of use, today's FileMaker Pro 8 has matured from its humble beginnings to become the hottest cross-platform database-development environment available.

Though I hate to admit it, when I first took a look at FileMaker in the early '90s, I wasn't impressed. The database tables were flat (no relationships), and aside from being able to quickly throw together some forms, I couldn't see how or why this application had any appeal. Needless to say, I was blinded by my experiences with dBASE and Superbase. Yes, I was being narrow minded. I took another look with version 5.0, and though I was impressed with the improvements to the database structure and the ability to write programming scripts, I still felt that it was underpowered as a software development tool.

Then FileMaker 7 came out, and I was blown away! My socks rolled up and down! I was impressed with the ability of FileMaker to be utilized as a full-blown application development tool — not only for Mac OS X but Windows as well. Now with the release of version 8 (the current version as I write this book), the FileMaker folks have provided a serious, relational database design and development system. After being in the computer industry since 1982 (yeah, I'm showing my age), I am finally excited about a programming environment again. By the time you get through this book, you'll be excited too!

About This Book

I wrote *FileMaker Pro Design & Scripting For Dummies* for all types of FileMaker users. Whether you're just starting out in developing applications or have experience in database design but are new to FileMaker, this book can help you get custom applications up and running.

You can select individual topics from the book to aid in gaining a deeper understanding of the power of FileMaker, or you can start at the beginning and cover each chapter in sequence. How you use this book is up to you, but regardless of your current FileMaker experience, I hope that you find out something new about this incredible product.

Because FileMaker is a cross-platform tool, this is a cross-platform book. Whether you work on a Mac or a PC, you find the pointers you need.

Foolish Assumptions

This is where I usually get into trouble — especially with my wife, when I assume that she knows what I'm thinking or when I assume that I know what she's thinking. Fortunately, with this book, I can make only some basic assumptions about you as the reader.

- ✔ First of all, to get to this spot, I'm assuming that you have a computer (either a Mac or a PC), you know how to use it, and that FileMaker Pro is already installed on it.

- ✔ To keep the focus on design and scripting, I also assume that you're fairly comfortable with the basics of using FileMaker. If you need more general information about working with FileMaker, check out *FileMaker Pro 8 Bible* by Dennis R. Cohen and Steven Schwartz (Wiley Publishing).

- ✔ I *don't* assume that you have any programming knowledge, or that you have done any database development before. It should be easy for you to grasp an understanding of these topics by reading this book.

How This Book Is Organized

This book is organized in a manner that allows you to quickly find what you're looking for. While a complete understanding of FileMaker Pro design and scripting could fill several books with thousands of pages, my intent with this book is to give you enough information to make you productive as a beginner.

Part 1: Getting to Know FileMaker Pro

To kick off Part I, Chapter 1 introduces why FileMaker is such a great tool for application development, helps you choose the right version, offers tips for setting up FileMaker, and gives you a quick tour of the interface. In Chapter 2, I explain how you begin building your database, and Chapter 3 helps you tap into the power of scripts.

Part II: Building the Perfect Beast

Part II begins with one of my favorite chapters of the book, Chapter 4, which guides you through the process of designing a good FileMaker application. Here, you discover the fundamentals of database design, layout design, and what makes a good software program.

The remaining chapters in this part help you fine-tune your creation, and a sample application called Hey, Look at Me! is provided as a workbench. Chapter 5 explains how to make your database layouts look good while adding more functionality to your database application. Chapter 6 offers tips and tricks for adding searching and sorting capabilities to your application. And in Chapter 7, you discover how to assign functions to objects on the layout, use lists and menus, and more.

Part III: Taking Control with FileMaker Programming

This is where you get to be geeky! Chapter 8 digs deep into the logical processing power of the Calculation Editor so that you can enhance your programs. And you'll get a nice, dice-rolling application out of it too! Then in Chapter 9, I share the programming tools I've put together over the years so you can start creating a toolbox of templates and organization tricks all your own.

Part IV: FileMaker Exposed! Sharing and Protecting Your Database

This very important part of the book deals with sharing your data — making sure you share it only with the people who should have access to it. In Chapter 10 you find out how to move data in and out of your database, by importing data from common sources, such as Excel or comma-delimited files, or exporting it to other formats when you need to. This chapter also explains how to make your FileMaker database available for others on a network. And because others will use your database, you find out about security and how to create and manage user accounts and Privilege Sets in Chapter 11. Then no discussion of sharing data would be complete without a chapter on how to put your database on the World Wide Web (Chapter 12).

Part V: The Part of Tens

In Chapter 13, find out how to apply your newfound knowledge to the amazing capabilities of FileMaker. You find ten cool things you can do with FileMaker, beginning with hiding buttons and including discovering how to launch another application on your computer. Chapter 14 wraps up this part with an introduction to great add-ons that help you extend FileMaker's capabilities.

Appendix: Scripting Reference

Be prepared to come back to this part of the book on a regular basis. This section is a reference for the FileMaker Pro scripting language. Not only do I show you the syntax and options of various script steps, but I also give some examples on how to use those functions in your FileMaker programs.

Icons Used in This Book

The Tip icon draws your attention to tips on how to use FileMaker to its full potential.

Remember when you used to tie string around your finger to help you remember something? Well, now we all use PDAs and smartphones. Anyway, this icon indicates something that you should remember when using FileMaker.

The Warning icon alerts you to very important information that you should be aware of. Ignoring this information could lead to very undesirable results.

If you're feeling geeky or would like to have a little more technical knowledge about FileMaker, the computer industry, terminology, or just geeky stuff in general, feel free to read the items marked with this icon at your leisure.

Downloads for This Book

In many places throughout this book you're directed to files that you can download as examples and workbenches for steps in the book. These locations are:

✔ www.timothytrimble.info

✔ www.dummies.com/go/filemakerprodesign

Where to Go from Here

If you're an experienced FileMaker user, you might want to just skim the table of contents and determine what's of interest to you. You might be amazed to discover that there are some areas of FileMaker that you haven't found out how to utilize yet. However, if you're just getting started with FileMaker, dive into Part I, follow each chapter in sequence, and be prepared to have your socks knocked off!

Part I
Getting to Know FileMaker Pro

The 5th Wave   By Rich Tennant

SNOW GLOBE DATA STORAGE

Okay let's shake this thing and see what we come up with.

In this part . . .

You take the first steps toward building your own application in this part. Chapter 1 introduces application design the FileMaker way by explaining what you can do and what version you need to do it, and taking you on a crash course of the interface from a developer's perspective. Chapter 2 shows you how to create the foundation of your application — the database that will hold the data. And Chapter 3 gets you started with building calculations in the Calculation Editor and adding them to your database. If you're new to development, this may seem like a huge undertaking, but FileMaker (and these chapters) make it easier than you'd think.

Chapter 1

Introducing FileMaker Pro

- -

- -

*H*ow many times have you heard the phrase "information is power"? The ability to keep and manage information accurately is indeed powerful, especially when that information is vital to your business or personal life. FileMaker places that power in your hands by giving you the ability to easily create, manage, and view vital (and sometimes not so vital) information. The good news is that a certificate from High Tech U is *not* required to tap into all that power!

Why Use FileMaker?

Yes, you can choose from a lot of products designed for keeping track of information. Just off the top of my head, I can think of Microsoft Access, Oracle, Microsoft SQL Server, Acius 4D, FoxBase, MySQL, and dBASE (Yes, it's still around). So, with all these other products out there, why should you use FileMaker? Here are just some of the reasons:

- Through the use of layouts, FileMaker provides a point-and-click interface for designing databases without requiring you to have prior database experience.

- FileMaker allows for cross-platform databases for Microsoft Windows and Mac OS X. You can design your database in one environment and run it on both platforms.

- You can publish your database to the Web in just a few clicks, which means that users on any platform with a compatible browser can use your database — even Linux users.

✔ FileMaker lets you save data as an Adobe PDF, a Microsoft Excel spreadsheet, an XML document, and many other formats for importing and exporting data.

✔ FileMaker comes with 30 Starter Solutions databases that you can put to work right away, or you can examine their script code, layouts, and databases to find more about FileMaker development.

✔ You can easily use FileMaker for storing and showing pictures and movies, playing sounds, and linking with many different multimedia file types.

✔ FileMaker provides full, multiuser support for up to five users without requiring the user to add any additional licenses or patches. (FileMaker Server supports up to 250 users.)

✔ FileMaker has a powerful point-and-click script programming environment for creating sophisticated applications, while it preserves an easy-to-use list of robust functions that can be assigned to buttons and layout objects.

With over 10 million licensed copies sold, FileMaker is a significant database design and development tool for use by novices and seasoned developers.

Common uses for FileMaker

Now that you have the power of FileMaker in your hands, what are the types of things that you can use FileMaker for? Here are some common databases that have been designed with FileMaker:

✔ **Contact management:** That's a fancy way of saying *an address book*. This is one of the most prevalent uses for FileMaker. In fact, one of the sample applications that comes with FileMaker is named Contact Manager. It's perfect for tracking your personal and business contacts.

✔ **Inventory control:** Need a place to track all your products? Many developers design inventory control applications with FileMaker. And with the integration with e-mail, you can use FileMaker to automatically e-mail your vendors when your products on hand are getting low.

✔ **Project management:** This is another great example of the type of things that people are doing with FileMaker. They track their projects, tasks associated with the projects, and the people assigned to handle those tasks and projects.

✔ **Time and billing:** This is one way my employer and I use FileMaker. As we do projects for our customers, we keep track of how much time we put into a project. Then FileMaker generates invoices and reports for billing our customers.

✔ **Tracking newspaper ads:** This is how the USA Today folks use FileMaker. They keep track of all the newspaper ads in the newspaper, their locations in the paper, and the date they are to be included in the print run. Plus, the information is shared with their AS/400 computer via SQL. Now that's power!

Picking the Version That's Best for You

The full range of FileMaker products is designed to fit the needs of any database, but you most likely want FileMaker Pro or FileMaker Pro Advanced. Although FileMaker Pro is the base version of FileMaker, don't think that it lacks power. It provides all the tools necessary for creating, customizing, and managing databases for use as stand-alone, multi-user, or Web-based databases.

However, FileMaker Pro Advanced comes with extra features that you'll find especially useful in database design and scripting. Along with the features of FileMaker Pro, FileMaker Advanced supports tooltips, custom menus, advanced script debugging with data viewing, a built-in calendar control, and the ability to create runtime FileMaker applications. Tooltips make it easier to blend seamless hints and reminders on using your database application. Custom menus let you tailor a database solution to your particular clientele, eliminating unnecessary menus and providing menus and menu items specific to your solution and client. Although FileMaker Pro's scripting is one of the easiest-to-use programming environments around, scripting is still programming and the ability to step through a script to ascertain why it is doing something you don't expect (or not doing something you do expect) is very helpful in getting your scripts just right.

A version to suit every purpose

In addition to FileMaker Pro and FileMaker Pro Advanced, you can get FileMaker in a few other ways, too. The following versions suit more specialized uses of FileMaker:

✔ **FileMaker Mobile 8** helps you extend your FileMaker databases to the Palm OS and Pocket PC PDA devices, and it lets you synchronize your data with all the FileMaker 8 products. In this hand-held world, you and/or your clients are prone to be tethered to a PDA. Being able to access your FileMaker Pro data from your PDA is an obvious step.

✔ **FileMaker Server 8** is used in larger, multi-user environments. It offers support for up to 250 users, along with the necessary tools for security, automated backups, and remote administration. If you develop for a corporate or institutional user, five simultaneous users just won't cut it. Deploying your solution via FileMaker Pro Server is the next step up.

✔ **FileMaker Server 8 Advanced** has the same features as FileMaker Server 8; plus, it supports up to 100 Web-based users, 50 ODBC/JDBC users, and 250 FileMaker 7 and FileMaker 8 users. The top rung on the FileMaker Pro ladder is for those of you with really heavy usage requirements.

The Happy Modes of FileMaker

The word *mode* makes me think of the word *mood.* I guess I'm just weird that way. However, notice the following similarity. The mood of your spouse, friend, or coworker can determine what you're going to ask for, just as the mode that FileMaker is in dictates what you can ask it to do. I'm just glad that all the modes of FileMaker are happy modes. Each of the four modes helps you get something done by offering different types of functionality. If you're new to FileMaker, I'm happy to introduce them:

- **Layout** is the mode where you'll spend much of your time because it's for designing the layouts and reports your customers see and employ (in the Browse and Find modes) when entering, perusing, and searching for data.

- **Browse** mode is for browsing and editing the data in the database. This is the mode where you can check out your final product, and it's the mode that your users will likely use most often.

- **Find** mode is for searching for specific data within the database. This is where your customers search for records in your database, so you should make sure to design layouts that facilitate searching.

- In **Preview** mode, what you see is what you get! It's for previewing what the printed layout or report will look like before your customer actually prints it.

So, where will you spend most of your time? Initially, if you're designing a database application, you do most of your work in Layout mode as a developer. After you complete the application, you spend most of your time in Browse mode as an application user with an occasional jaunt into the Find and Preview modes.

To move in and out of the different modes, you can use the Tool palette. Although most of the tools on the palette change as you move between the modes, you always see the following buttons, which you click to move to a different mode:

    Browse mode

    Find mode

    Layout mode

    Preview mode

Dealing with data in Browse mode

I was in a bookstore a little while back, and one of the store clerks asked if they could help me find anything. My reply was, "No thanks. I'm just browsing." Then it hit me. I was standing in the middle of a huge database in browse mode. Every book was a record in a huge, physical database. And as I moved around the store, I was changing my view and stepping through different records in the database. FileMaker Pro mimics that real-world process with the Browse mode. When you design your layouts and create your scripts, keep in mind that your customers will be using them to facilitate this browsing, so make them easy to navigate and use. Cluttered layouts are like a store whose aisles form a maze — they frustrate the customer.

Browse mode is primarily for viewing, editing, sorting, hiding, and deleting database records. Figure 1-1 shows a sample application (the FileMaker Contact Management example) in Browse mode.

Slider

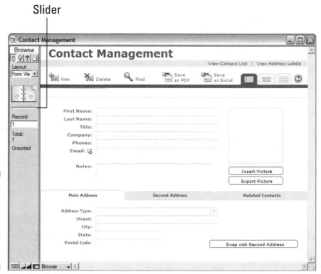

Figure 1-1:
Viewing the database in Browse mode.

The Tool palette in Browse mode is simple and easy to use. Here's what each tool does:

- **Layout drop-down list:** Shows a list of available layouts. Select one to view and use that layout. Some layouts might be designed for data entry, some for reports, and still others for searching; so name them appropriately for their purpose.

- **Book icon:** Navigates a database page by page. Click the left page to go to the previous record, or click the right page to go to the next record.

- ✔ **Slider:** Navigates a database more quickly than the Book icon. Use this to slide through multiple records in the database instead of clicking through each record with the arrows on the Book icon.
- ✔ **Record:** Shows the current record number. The user can go to a specific record by typing the record number in this box (but he usually doesn't know the number because it varies based on search criteria and sorting order).
- ✔ **Found:** Displays the number of matching records resulting from a Find (not shown in Figure 1-2).
- ✔ **Total:** Shows the total number of records in the currently active table.
- ✔ **Sorted/Unsorted:** Shows the current sort state of the active table.

Searching in Find mode

"Finders, keepers. Losers, weepers!" It's amazing that this phrase from my childhood can have so much of a correlation to searching for data. It's true! When you know the data you're looking for is in the computer among thousands of records, trying to find it can sometimes be a frustrating experience. FileMaker presents an easy-to-use approach to help you find data. It's called the Find mode.

The FileMaker Find mode, shown in Figure 1-2, presents a layout view of the table fields. By entering what you want to search for in any of the presented fields, you can search for data. The tools in the Tool palette can also help you track down the data you're looking for.

Here's a brief explanation of each tool, which I explain how to use in more detail in Chapter 6:

- ✔ **Layout selector:** Shows a list of available layouts. Select one to view that layout.
- ✔ **Book icon:** Navigates a database page by page. As in Browse mode, click the left page to go to a previous record, or click the right page to go to the next record. This icon isn't active until results are returned from the Find request.
- ✔ **Slider:** Navigates a database more quickly than the Book icon. Use this to slide through the records in the database. The slider isn't active until results are returned from the Find request.
- ✔ **Request:** Displays the ID number of the Find request that you are currently working with.
- ✔ **Total:** Displays the total number of records in the result of the Find request.

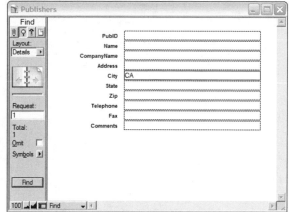

Figure 1-2:
Search for
data in
FileMaker
Find mode.

✔ **Omit:** Tells FileMaker that you want to omit an item from the search. Activate this feature by clicking the Omit check box. See Chapter 6 for more information.

✔ **Symbols:** These are logical relations (for example: greater than, not equal, and so on) that you can employ when specifying your search criteria. See Chapter 6 for more information.

✔ **Find:** Executes the Find and then places FileMaker in Browse mode.

Taking a look in Preview mode

Isn't it nice when you order something and you get exactly what you ordered? In FileMaker, the Preview mode, shown in Figure 1-3, is a great method for taking a sneak peek at a report before you print it so that you can make sure you get the printout you asked for.

As in the Browse and Find modes, you see the Layout drop-down list and the Book icon for navigating through pages of your review. The Page text box displays the current page number, and Total shows how many pages are in your preview.

Laying out the layouts in Layout mode

The Layout mode is the primary mode for designing the layouts (dialog boxes) used in FileMaker. In Figure 1-4, you can see that the Tool palette has some icons that also appear in the other modes. The Layout drop-down list lets you select a layout, and you can use the Book icon to navigate to the next or previous layout. You also see the layout number in the Layout box and the total number of layouts in the current database.

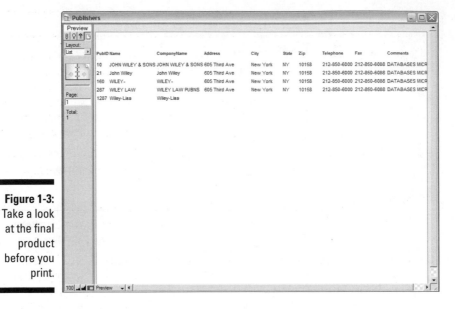

Figure 1-3:
Take a look
at the final
product
before you
print.

You might notice that Layout mode offers a lot more tools than the other
FileMaker modes — all of which are quite easy to use, as I explain in Table 1-1.
You find out all the details about creating great custom layouts in Part II.

Figure 1-4:
Choose the
look of your
project in
Layout
mode.

Table 1-1	Tool Palette Tools in Layout Mode	
Icon	*Name*	*Description*
	Selector tool	Select objects on the layout. By holding down the Shift key while using the Selector tool, you can select multiple objects. Or you can select multiple objects by dragging a box around them.
	Text tool	Insert text labels on the layout.
	Line tool	Draw lines on the layout. Lines can be used for borders, or as separators between areas on the layout.
	Box tool	Create boxes and rectangles on the layout. Boxes can be used for making borders or visually sectioning off areas of the layout.
	Round Box tool	Create boxes with round corners (so you don't hurt yourself). Round boxes make good borders and visual sections.
	Circle tool	Draw circles and ellipses.
	Button tool	Create buttons. You'll be using this one a lot when designing layouts. You assign a function or a script to the button, which executes when a user pressed the button.
	Tab Control tool	Create folderlike tabs on your layout to group data fields that you can hide when they're not needed.
	Portal tool	View data from a related table by using the sub-form that this very powerful tool provides. See Chapter 8 for more information.
	Field tool	Place a field from the current table onto the layout. See Chapter 6 for more information.

(continued)

Table 1-1 *(continued)*

Icon	Name	Description
Part →	Part tool	Add a new part to the layout. The layout can be divided into parts (sections).
	Fill controls	Set the fill color, pattern, and the object effects for the currently selected object(s) on the layout. This set of tools is grouped with the paint bucket that lies just above them, left-justified. The first tool on the left is the Fill Color tool.
	Pen controls	Set the pen color, pattern, and the pen (or line) effects for the currently selected object(s) on the layout. These tools are grouped with the Pen icon.

What's on the Menu?

Like almost any application, FileMaker has a number of menus along the top of the application window, and each holds commands to help you use this powerful program. Unfortunately, there's no Chinese menu among them for those nights when you're up late designing a database and get hungry. But this section introduces the many menus, so that as you're creating layouts or scripts, you know what tools are available and have an idea of where to find them. I point out the tools that are especially useful for creating layouts and scripts along the way.

If you don't like using a mouse, you can use keyboard shortcuts for opening menus and executing commands. These keyboard shortcuts vary slightly from PC to Mac.

On a PC, holding down the Alt key reveals underscored letters on the main menu bar. You can open a menu by pressing Alt and the underscored letter. Alt+F opens the File menu. Likewise, you can choose an item *within* the menu by pressing Alt and the key that's underscored. For example, you can choose New Database in the File menu by pressing Alt+N. If a particular menu item doesn't have an underscored letter, that means that menu item doesn't have a keyboard shortcut.

So, you see that when you choose a menu option, you might be presented with more choices. But, for now, I give you an overview of the primary menus.

- ✔ **File menu:** The primary purpose of the File menu is to help you manage the current FileMaker database file with commands for starting a new database, opening a database, printing, importing and exporting records, and more.

- ✔ **Edit menu:** The Edit menu offers the standard cut/copy/paste/find features along with the ability to edit FileMaker application settings. I'm still waiting for the Edit Weather function, which should help my golf game.

- ✔ **View menu:** The View menu provides functions specific to the current mode. For example, in Figure 1-5, you can see how the menu changes in Layout mode versus Browse mode.

For the most part, this menu offers check mark options that you can select or deselect, depending on the options you want to view. Similarly, when you see the black dot, then that menu option is currently active, and the other menu options it is grouped with are not. And if you see a little can of Red Bull, then you've been up too late. Quit working and go to bed!

- ✔ **Insert menu:** Like the View menu, the Insert menu's options change depending on FileMaker's current mode. In Layout mode, you can find a more varied selection of items to insert — such as field controls, buttons, and pictures — than in other modes. Outside of Layout mode, you can insert the date, time, and username. Part II of this book covers how you use the layout options in more detail.

Figure 1-5:
The View menu in Layout mode and Browse mode.

✔ **Format menu:** Anytime I see the word *format,* I have flashbacks to the time when I accidentally reformatted my hard drive when I thought I was formatting a floppy disk. (Shiver!) Don't worry though — nothing that dangerous here. The Format menu provides the ability to *format* (or make orderly) the current layout objects.

✔ **Records menu (Browse mode):** The functions within the Records menu enable you to navigate and manage the database records. This menu is available only in Browse mode.

✔ **Requests menu (Find mode):** The functions within the Requests menu help you search for data within the records. This menu is available only in Find mode.

✔ **Layouts menu (Layout mode):** The functions within the Layouts menu are for navigating and managing the layouts. This menu is available only in Layout mode.

✔ **Arrange menu (Layout mode):** I, personally, use these functions a lot when designing and editing a layout. You find that you'll soon have the shortcuts memorized. The functions within the Arrange menu, shown in Figure 1-6, provide functions for arranging the placement of objects on the layouts. This menu is available only in Layout mode.

✔ **Scripts menu:** There's only one static item on this menu — ScriptMaker. ScriptMaker is the editing environment for creating and editing FileMaker *scripts* (programs), and its shortcut is Ctrl+Shift+S (⌘+Shift+S on a Mac). If other items appear on this menu, they are scripts that have been written and provided as part of the FileMaker database. Those are easily selected via Ctrl+ the index number of the script (or ⌘+ the index number on a Mac). You can find more information about the ScriptMaker in Chapter 8.

✔ **Tools menu (FileMaker Pro Advanced only, in Layout Mode):** The Tools menu is basically the menu for all functions and tools that don't really fit anywhere else — kind of like that old, rusty, red toolbox that I keep next to the garage door, with the tools that I use the most. On this menu, you find script debugging tools and developer utilities, among other things.

Figure 1-6:
You get to know the Arrange menu very well as you edit layouts.

Getting Help in FileMaker

I always need help of one type or another. In fact, my wife says I need help — but I think she means in a different way. At least FileMaker has an extensive help system.

You can access FileMaker Help in various ways. The initial way to get into FileMaker Help is via the F1 key (Windows), the Help key or ⌘+? (Mac), or by selecting FileMaker Pro Help from the Help menu.

One of the most common methods of using the FileMaker Help system is to drill down into the topic that you want to see. Just click any linked topic to see that topic's help page.

You can print the topic by clicking the Print button on the toolbar (Windows) or choosing File⇨Print (Mac).

If you're using the Windows version and you find yourself referring to a specific topic often,

you can save it as a favorite. Click the Favorites tab at the top of the left pane. Click the Add button at the bottom of the left pane to add the current topic to your Favorites list. Now, when you want to revisit this topic, just go to the Favorites tab, select the topic that you want to see, and then click the Display button at the bottom of the left pane. (Mac users can use the Integrated Spotlight functionality to quickly find anything in the FileMaker Help contents.)

Personally, I like using the Search feature of FileMaker Help. It allows me to find topics when I don't quite know how to find the topic via the drill-down process. To use Search, click the Search tab at the top of the left pane. In the Search box, enter a topic that you want to search for and click the List Topics button. You can then select topics that appear in the results

- ✔ **Windows menu:** The Windows menu helps you place and view the windows on the FileMaker desktop.

- ✔ **Help menu:** When all else fails, use the Help menu, which provides help and general information about FileMaker. I cover your resources for help in more detail later in this chapter.

The Right Toolbar for the Job

I'm a very visual person. In fact, I think most people are. That's why toolbars are such a good idea. Finding a picture that represents what you want to do is easier than looking through a bunch of menu items. (Though I'm sure my menu guide makes this a lot easier.) FileMaker Pro has the following four sets of toolbars:

- ✔ Standard
- ✔ Text Formatting
- ✔ Arrange
- ✔ Tools

To view or hide any of these toolbars, simply choose View⇨Toolbars and select or deselect its name from the Toolbars submenu. The following sections introduce each toolbar.

The Standard toolbar

The Standard toolbar is the most common set of tools in just about any software product. Some of the tools — such as New Database, Open, Print, Copy, and Paste — may be familiar to you already. Others are unique to FileMaker and change depending on FileMaker's mode. Figure 1-7 shows the toolbar in Layout mode.

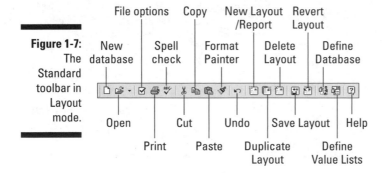

Figure 1-7: The Standard toolbar in Layout mode.

The Text Formatting toolbar

In the beginning there was Text. The Text was readable and everyone was pleased with the Text. Then a Text Artist came along and created Fonts, Styles, Sizes, and Colors. The world was thrown into a state of panic and chaos. The greatest minds in the world got together and created the Text Formatting toolbar. And once again, the world was at peace.

Yes, the Text Formatting toolbar serves a great purpose by helping you manage the many different combinations of text formatting. Take a look at the toolbar in Figure 1-8. Later in this chapter, you find out how to set preferences for default fonts and more.

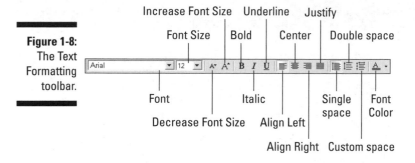

Figure 1-8:
The Text
Formatting
toolbar.

The Arrange toolbar

What do florists and software developers have in common? They both like to make arrangements. Well, in this case, FileMaker provides a toolbar for arranging the objects on a layout form. Therefore, the Arrange toolbar is available only in Layout mode. You can see it in Figure 1-9.

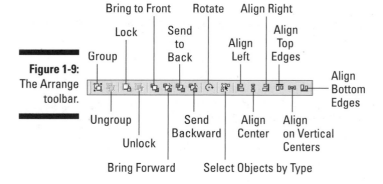

Figure 1-9:
The Arrange
toolbar.

The Tools toolbar

The "Tools toolbar"? Isn't that kind of like a double negative? Shouldn't it just be "The Toolbar"? But then, it would be just a blank toolbar. Which would then be called, "The Bar." And that's where one goes for drinks. Anyway, in FileMaker Pro, it's the Tools toolbar. This toolbar, shown in Figure 1-10, is a duplication of the tools that are available on the Tool palette when in Layout mode.

This toolbar works a little differently, however, in the sense that whichever tool is selected becomes the active tool controlled with your mouse.

You may not be familiar with some terms that FileMaker uses. A *control* is a generic term for an interface element such as a check box, radio button, or text box; a *portal* is FileMaker's term for a subtable; *part* is a layout feature such as a header or footer. I introduce all these elements in more detail in Part II, which explains the ins and outs of designing a FileMaker layout.

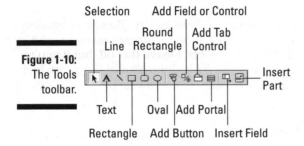

Figure 1-10: The Tools toolbar.

Configuring Your FileMaker Installation

Come on! You know you want to tweak your installation of FileMaker Pro.

If you think that you can just install FileMaker and then start cranking out databases, then — well, I guess you can. However, you would be missing some of the really cool features of FileMaker that you wouldn't normally see with the default installation.

To see what some of these features are, just choose Edit⇨Preferences to open the Preferences dialog box. The options are organized into five tabs, and the following sections describe the options available on each one.

Setting general preferences

On the General tab, you find the following options:

  ✔ **Allow Drag And Drop Text Selection:** When selected, provides the abil-
    ity to drag and drop text from other FileMaker fields or from other appli-
    cations. I leave this on (the default), but if you don't like drag and drop,
    feel free to turn it off.

✔ **Show Templates In New Database Dialog Box:** Did you notice that, when you first started FileMaker, the opening dialog box had a list of predefined templates? If you don't want to see this list, just uncheck this check box. Then when FileMaker loads, it automatically displays the Open File dialog box. I turn this off, but the default is to leave it on.

✔ **Show Recently Opened Files:** In the File menu, in the Open Recent option, a list of recently opened files is listed. This selection allows you to set how many of the recently opened files you want to see in the list. The range is from 1 to 16. Personally, I would like to see 42 — but that's just me.

✔ **Enlarge Window Contents To Improve Readability (Windows version only):** When selected, this makes the text on the layout easier to read by increasing the size of all the layout objects. I leave this off, but if you're vision-impaired or your database layouts include a lot of fine print, feel free to turn it on.

✔ **Reset Dialog Sizes And Positions:** One of the nice features about FileMaker is that all the dialog boxes that appear can be resized, and FileMaker remembers what size you used and keeps that size. However, if you decide that you want to reset all the dialog boxes back to their original sizes, you can click the Reset button.

✔ **User Name:** This is the default username that you want to use with FileMaker. Mac users can choose their system login name or specify another.

✔ **User Interface Language (Windows only):** If you want to change the default language that FileMaker uses for the interface, select the language that you want to see. *Capisca?* Mac users handle this via the OS X Language tab of the International System Preferences pane.

✔ **Font Smoothing Style (Windows only):** This allows you set the style of font smoothing for making the fonts look better. What you choose here depends on your personal preferences and the type of display you're using (CRT or LCD). Mac users make this setting in their Display System Preferences.

Choosing your layout preferences

On the Layout tab, you have the following choices:

✔ **Always Lock Layout Tools:** Select this option to make your tool choice stick; otherwise, the Select (arrow) tool will be reselected after any tool is used. I leave this off because double-clicking a tool locks it, and I tend to use the Select tool to reposition layout objects after I create them.

✔ **Add Newly Defined Fields To Current Layout:** When selected, FileMaker automatically adds fields to the current layout when they are added to the database table. The default setting is on, and that's how I leave it.

✔ **Save Layout Changes Automatically (Do Not Ask):** When you're making changes to the layout, your changes are automatically saved if this check box is selected. The default setting is off, and that's probably safest.

✔ **System Subset (88 Colors):** If selected, FileMaker provides an 88-color palette for color selections. The 88-color palette is a subset that the graphic artists and user-interface folks at FileMaker think makes a good base set. This is the default choice, and I usually leave it there.

✔ **Standard System Palette (256 Colors):** This sets the color palette to the system-standard 256 colors (which is different between Mac and Windows). In addition to the platform differences, it is sometimes difficult to tell the difference between one shade of a color and another when trying to match a previous selection.

✔ **Web Palette (216 Colors):** If you want your application colors to be common for both the Windows platform and the Mac, select this option. This option isn't as useful in this day of thousands or millions of colors as it was when 8-bit color was the norm (early to mid '90s), but if you're going to deploy your solution on the Web and you think some of your users might be employing older operating systems and browsers, the Web palette is a safe baseline.

Practicing memory control

Controlling how memory is used in FileMaker probably won't make you feel like a mad scientist attempting mind control. (You can decide for yourself whether that's a good thing.) But tweaking these settings can definitely make you feel better about FileMaker's performance — and about not losing your data, if you're worried about those things. You find the following settings on the Memory tab:

✔ **Attempt To Set File Cache To:** While you work in FileMaker, it temporarily keeps track of your changes in cache memory. As a default, this is set to 8MB. You can enter a different value to see if it improves performance. When you change this setting, it takes effect after you restart FileMaker. The larger the cache, the more data is memory-resident, resulting in fewer disk accesses. However, increasing the cache takes memory away from other tasks and setting it higher than the amount of data in your file doesn't gain anything.

✔ **Save Cache Contents:** The default is to save during idle time. However, if you want to save your cached changes more often, select the Every radio button and enter the time segment. The shorter the duration, the less likely you are to lose data in the event of a power failure. If you're using a laptop and are concerned with battery life, setting a higher time segment reduces the drain on the battery.

Plugging (and unplugging) plug-ins

A *plug-in* is a module that provides additional functionality to FileMaker. For example, one plug-in allows you to launch a script file at a specific time. You can get plug-ins from FileMaker, from third-party software companies, or from your friendly neighborhood C++ programmer. Plug-ins can be developed in the C or C++ programming language and with FileMaker Pro Advanced.

Any plug-ins that you see in the list are plug-ins that are installed. (See the instructions that come with the plug-in for installation.) When the check box is selected, that plug-in is available for use. When highlighted, you can see a brief description of what that plug-in does. And if the Configure button becomes active, you can set configuration options for that plug-in. Check out Chapter 14 for examples of some plug-in sources.

Fiddling with fonts

On the Fonts tab, FileMaker lets you make a few choices about which fonts you prefer and how you like them to behave:

✔ **Default Font For Each Input Type:** You can select the type of font that you want to use for each language input type (in case you are working with Cyrillic, Kana, Simplified Chinese, or some other language and its related, data-input methodology). Just select the Input Type that you want to change, and then select the font that you want to use in the Specify Font list box.

✔ **Synchronize Input Method With Font On Field Entry:** When selected, the font shown when users enter data is the font that has been defined specifically for the field. (To define that font, you use the field's Field/ Control, Behavior option when in Layout mode.) Synchronization is off by default.

✔ **Use Font Locking:** This is an interesting option. When selected, if you have a character in a field that doesn't have a corresponding character in the selected font, the character continues to be displayed in its original font. This is specifically handy when you are supporting multiple languages, such as Japanese and Roman, in the same field. Font Locking is selected by default.

Chapter 2

Creating a Database

● ●

In This Chapter

▶ Creating a database

▶ Using field options for more control

▶ Making relationships between tables

▶ Using the relationship graph

● ●

Say you've got a zillion, colored, sticky notes all over your office, and you're thinking, "I need FileMaker to help me keep track of all these molecular composition formulas stuck everywhere!"

Of course, FileMaker is designed just for those types of special needs, and this chapter helps you get started. Here, you find out how to create a blank database, set up fields and tables so they're ready for data, and sort out your parent-child relationships (among tables of data, of course). I also guide you through the important field options FileMaker has to offer — options that enable you to build a real solution for a real need.

Speaking of real solutions. . . . I want to use an example database for this chapter that you, personally, can use. Almost everyone, at some point in her life, is faced with the situation of having to search for a job. If you have ever gone through the job-search process, you know what I'm talking about. So, you can follow along in this chapter to create the Hey, Look at Me! example database either for getting the hang of using FileMaker or for finding that next, high-paying job. Just don't tell your boss! But you can also use the information in this chapter to build whatever custom database suits your needs.

 To build a good database solution, you first need to know what it is that you want to keep track of. So, before you even open FileMaker, make a list of all the pieces of data that you want to track. For the Hey, Look at Me! database, the categories reflect whatever you need to keep track of for potential jobs. To find details about the groundwork for a well-designed database, see Chapter 4.

Starting a Custom Database from Scratch

To begin creating a custom FileMaker database, you need to start with a blank database. The following steps demonstrate how to create a new database and the initial database table for tracking the job prospects:

1. **Launch FileMaker.**

   Figure 2-1 shows the New Database dialog box, which appears when you launch FileMaker.

Figure 2-1: Start with the New Database dialog box to create a custom database.

2. **Select the Create A New Empty File radio button, and click OK.**

   The Create A New File Named dialog box appears.

   Because this is a new, *custom* database, you don't need to use any of the FileMaker templates.

3. **Use the Save In drop-down list (or pop-up menu on Mac) to browse to the location where you want to save your FileMaker database.**

   Having a bunch of files saved in a single folder can get confusing. If you haven't done so already, I recommend creating a new folder specifically for your FileMaker projects. Simply click the Create New Folder icon in the top of the dialog box (or click the New Folder button at the bottom left of the dialog on a Mac) and give your new folder a name, like oh . . . FileMaker Projects.

4. **Type your database name in the File Name box at the bottom of the dialog box (or the Save As box at the top of the dialog on a Mac).**

   For my example database, I type **HeyLookAtMe**.

   If you look in the Save As Type box, you'll see that FileMaker 8 uses a file extension of .fp7 and not .fp8, as one would assume. (So, please, no e-mails about how you found a typo in my book.) The reason behind this is that FileMaker Pro 8 database files use the same format as FileMaker Pro 7 database files and thus share the extension. FileMaker Pro 7 can open and operate on FileMaker 8 files, although some features, like layout tab controls, aren't supported.

5. **Click the Save button.**

   The Define Database dialog box appears. FileMaker has already created a table called HeyLookAtMe and is now waiting for you to define the table's fields, as you can see in Figure 2-2. But first, you should rename that table because you generally want your table names to be more specific than your database name, especially when your database consists of multiple tables. See the next section for details on renaming a database table.

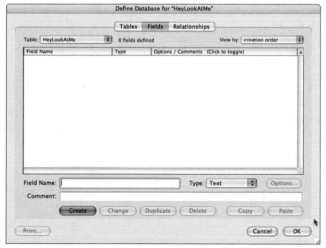

Figure 2-2:
A table appears after you create the database.

Adding and Renaming a Table

Tables are collections of records consisting of multiple fields. For example, an address table might consist of the following fields (or more): last_name, first_name, street_address, city, state, postal_code. Each record in the table consists of data in the various fields. (Although a particular field can be empty, it's still present in the record.)

To add a new table to your database, click the Tables tab at the top of the Define Database dialog box. When the Tables pane is present (see Figure 2-3), type a table name in the Table Name box and click Create.

After you create a new, custom database, FileMaker adds a table for you that has the same name as the database. You should give the table a different name so you can distinguish it from other tables in your database. Of course, if you have a very simple database that consists of just one table, you may (and probably do) want to leave the name alone. The following steps show you how to rename a table:

1. **Click the Tables tab at the top of the Define Database dialog box.**

   This dialog box shows a list of all the tables associated with the database. So far, there is only one table, currently called HeyLookAtMe, as shown in Figure 2-3. Because this custom database application eventually utilizes more than one table, it's important that we give each table a distinctive name.

2. **Type the table's new name in the Table Name box, and then click Change.**

   Now that the name of the table is more descriptive, you can get on with adding the fields to the table.

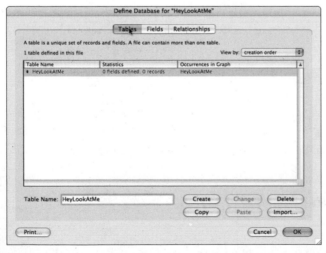

Figure 2-3:
Change a table's name on the Tables tab in the Define Database dialog box.

Playing the Field: Adding Fields to the Table

The *fields* of a database table are the most important components of a database. The fields hold the data! The rest of the pieces and functions of a database all revolve around the data. So, it's very important to make sure that the definitions of the fields for a database table are distinct and descriptive.

Records in a database table are kind of like people, in that they all need to have their own sense of identity. A record without an identity is just another jumble of non-unique data. It's very important to make sure that each record is *unique*. For example, in a contact manager database, you might have two records where the contact name is John Smith. These two contacts are (in real life) two different (unique) individuals with the same name. But the database sees both of them as the same person. What can you do to avoid that problem? Using a unique identifier helps you distinguish one database record from another. I explain the importance of unique identifiers in more detail in Chapter 4. In the sections that follow, I explain how to add these identifiers to a table and how to choose options for adding all kinds of other fields.

Adding an identifier field

Did you hear about the farmer? He's a man outstanding in his field! Because it's important to have an outstanding field — a unique identifier associated with each record in the table — the first field you create should be an *ID field* (also called a *primary key*).

The following steps explain how to add an identifier field:

1. **On the Fields tab of the Define Database dialog box, type a name for the unique identifier field in the Field Name text box.**

   Create a field name two to four characters in length, and make the name distinct enough that you'll remember what you're using the field for. In this case, I use JTID (Job Table Identifier) as the unique identifier field name.

   As a default, FileMaker assumes that the field is a Text field. However, make a unique identifier a Number field.

2. **Choose Number from the Type drop-down list (or pop-up menu on a Mac), or press Ctrl+N (or ⌘+N on a Mac) and click the Create button.**

Notice that FileMaker adds the field to the Field Name list for the table and activates the Options button. Just using the Number field type for this field is not enough. You need to make sure that the number is unique, and thus, establish a sense of identity.

3. **Click the Options button to display the Options dialog box, as shown in Figure 2-4.**

4. **Select the Serial Number check box.**

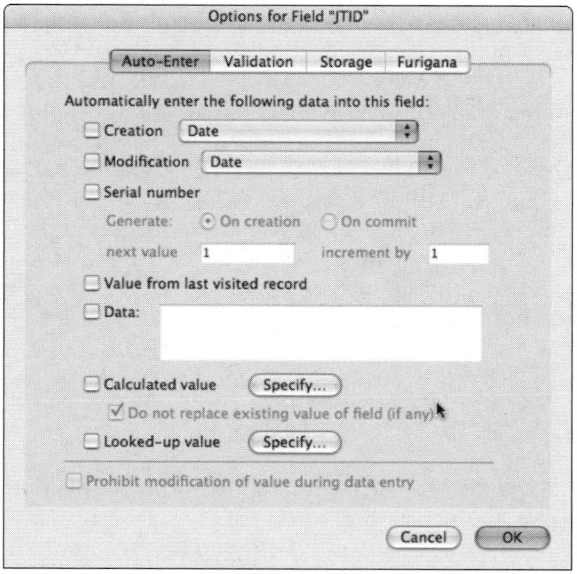

Figure 2-4:
Tell File-
Maker to
auto-enter a
unique
serial
number for
each
record.

The Serial Number option for this field tells FileMaker that you want to create a serialized number in this field. As a default, the On Creation radio button is selected, and the Increment By value is 1. This tells FileMaker to automatically create this serialized number whenever the record is created and to increment the number by 1 for each new record. So, when you add the very first record to the table, the JTID field holds a value of 1. When you add the next record, the JTID field for that record is 2.

5. **Select the Validation tab, and select the Unique Value check box.**

This ensures that a user of this database can't change the value to coincide with an already existing value.

6. **Click OK to save these field options for the JTID field.**

The Fields tab on the Define Database dialog box now shows that the table contains a field called JTID, with the options of Auto-Enter Serial and Unique.

When using a field name that is a little cryptic (resulting in significant head scratching when others see the field name), it's a good idea to use the Comments feature for describing the purpose of the field. You might know what the field is right now, but if you've slept for six months before coming back to working on the table (or if someone else works on the table), you (or your coworker) might need a little reminder.

7. **In the Comment text box (below the Field Name text box) type** Unique ID **as shown in Figure 2-5, and click the Change button.**

You can toggle the display of the Comments or the field options by clicking the Options/Comments column title bar.

Figure 2-5:
The JTID field is now complete.

Adding the fields that hold the data

After you create an identifier field, you're ready to add the fields that will hold the important data — the data you want FileMaker to organize for you. The process is somewhat similar to adding the identifier field, but you vary the type of field depending on what kind of data that field will hold.

Just because a field contains numbers doesn't necessarily mean that you have to use a Number type for the field. A good guideline to follow is: If the field might be involved in an arithmetic calculation, use a Number type; otherwise, a Text type works fine. Data such as phone numbers and zip codes are good examples of numbers that can (and probably should) be stored as Text types. Storing a zip code as a number would cause leading zeroes to not display (this would irk residents of places like Paramus, New Jersey, whose zip code is 07652). FileMaker Pro also allows you to specify that a field is a Date, Time, Timestamp (combined Date and Time), Container (catchall for things like graphics, audio, or movies), Calculation (a formula that gets evaluated), or Summary (Totals and Averages of values in your records are examples of Summary fields).

Perform the following steps to add a field to your table:

1. Double-click in the Field Name text box.

This highlights the previously entered field name. This is okay because you're adding a new field.

When you start typing in the Field Name text box, the Create button is highlighted. So, when you finish typing your field name and/or selecting the field type, just press the Enter key (Return key on a Mac) to save the new field. FileMaker automatically highlights the Field Name text box in anticipation of getting the next field name that you want to create.

2. Type the field name in the Field Name text box.

If you're following along to create the Hey, Look at Me! database, you can create any of the fields listed in Table 2-1.

3. Select the appropriate Field type. If you have a Comment, enter that as well.

Just as with any other FileMaker dialog box, you can use the Tab key to move from one option to another in the dialog box when entering the Field settings.

Sometimes you might have a comment from a previous field that you no longer need. You can just highlight the comment and delete it or type over it.

4. Click the Options button to add validation, set automatic data entry settings, or apply other settings.

Yeah, I know — there are so many options available for table fields that it makes your head spin! Because I don't want you to walk away dizzy, I'll fill you in on what all those options are in upcoming sections. They're actually very useful, and they save a significant amount of time and effort compared to how other database environments work.

5. Click Create to add the field to the table.

Don't worry if you make a mistake while entering the new field. You can go back and make the necessary changes, and then click the Change button to save your changes. When you're done adding and editing fields, the Define Database dialog box looks something like Figure 2-6.

Table 2-1	**Field Definitions for the Jobs Table**	
Field Name	*Field Type*	*Comments (If Needed)*
JobTitle	Text	
JobType	Text	Management, Technical, and so on
JobTerms	Text	Full time, Part time, Contract, and so on
JobDescription	Text	
ContactName	Text	
CompanyName	Text	
JobAddress	Text	
JobCity	Text	
JobState	Text	
JobZip	Text	
JobPhone	Text	

(continued)

Table 2-1 *(continued)*

Field Name	Field Type	Comments (If Needed)
JobFax	Text	
JobEmail	Text	
JobURL	Text	
JobSkills	Text	
JobPay	Text	
JobNotes	Text	
JobStatus	Text	Active, Closed, and so on
AvailableDate	Date	
HowFound	Text	Newspaper, Internet, and so on

Robotic table field data entry

Well, not really robotic — but pretty close. The Auto-Enter options for table fields tell FileMaker to generate the data value based upon the options you've chosen. Refer to Figure 2-4 to see what kind of Auto-Enter options are available. The following list explains what each of the options is for:

- ✔ **Creation:** Select this option to enter the data associated with the creation of the record. The various options are:

  - *Date:* The date that the record was created

  - *Time:* The time that the record was created

  - *Timestamp:* The date and time the record was created

  - *Name:* The username of the person who created the record

  - *Account Name:* The name of the account used when the record was created. I discuss accounts in detail in Chapter 11, but (basically) FileMaker Pro is similar to your Windows or Mac operating system, where each user has an account by which they log into the system.

- ✔ **Modification:** This is similar to the Creation option, only it records information on *changes* made to a record. The same Date, Time, Timestamp, Name, and Account Name options are available.

- ✔ **Serial Number:** As I mention in the previous "Adding an identifier field" section, when selected, the Serial Number option generates unique numbers based on the Next value and the Increment By values. In most cases, you want to start with 1 for the Next value when creating a new database table, and usually you'll increment by 1. The On Creation option enters the number when the record is created. The On Commit option enters the number when the record is saved (committed). Whether you choose one or the other depends primarily upon whether you allow your users to modify the auto-entered value, in which case it should be On Creation so that there is a value for them to modify — if you choose On Commit, the auto-generated value replaces whatever the user entered when she entered the data.

✓ **Value From Last Visited Record:** This unique option provides the entry of data selected from the last viewed record. This can be really handy for copying data from one record to another when you know that the data needs to be repeated.

✓ **Data:** This is where you define what data is entered into the field every time a new record is created. Whatever you put in the box is entered into the field as the default content. For example, you might enter *Jones* in a family address book for the Jones family. Then you would replace those few entries where the names have been changed through marriage or some other action.

✓ **Calculated Value:** This very powerful feature tells FileMaker to perform a calculation on existing data or predefined values and then place the result of the calculation in the field when the record is created. When you click the Specify button, you see the Specify Calculation dialog box shown in Figure 2-7. Back on the Auto-Enter tab, you can also tell FileMaker not to enter new data if the field already contains data; just select the Do Not Replace Existing Value For Field check box. (See Chapter 3 for more details about the Specify Calculation dialog box.)

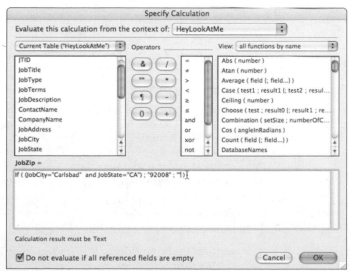

Figure 2-7:
Calculating
a zip code.

✔ **Looked-up Value:** This is another powerful option, which tells FileMaker to retrieve data from an associated field in a related table, and enter that data into the current field. When using the Looked-up Value option, you can also select the Prohibit Modification Of Value During Data Entry check box. Doing so prevents the user from changing an automatically entered value.

In Figure 2-8, for example, this lookup grabs the Action Type from the Actions table and puts it in the Status field of the Jobs table.

✔ **Prohibit:** The Prohibit Modification Of Value During Data Entry option, if checked, prevents the user from changing an automatically entered value.

Figure 2-8:
Selecting a
Lookup
value.

> **Lookup for Field "JobStatus"**
>
> Use a lookup to copy a value from a field in another table based on the relationships defined between these tables:
>
> Starting with table: Jobs
>
> Lookup from related table: Actions
>
> (When a new entry is made in the field "JTID", this lookup will copy the value from the first matching related record in the table "Actions".)
>
> Copy value from field:
> - ::AID
> - ::JTID
> - ::ActionType
> - ::ActionDate
> - ::ActionNotes
>
> If no exact match, then:
> - ⦿ do not copy
> - ◯ copy next lower value
> - ◯ copy next higher value
> - ◯ use [   ]
>
> ☑ Don't copy contents if empty
>
> (Cancel) (OK)

Automatic garbage detector

Ever hear the phrase, "Garbage in — garbage out"? It means that if you put garbage data into a computer, the computer is most likely going to spit garbage out. *Garbage* thus referring to bad data. Or my favorite way to put it is, "User error! Replace user and try again!"

A good database design prevents the entry of bad data. For example, you wouldn't want to allow the entry of **grizcybops** into the zip code field. This is why the Validation options for fields are so important. Via the use of these options, shown in Figure 2-9, you have the ability to enforce how the data is entered into the database.

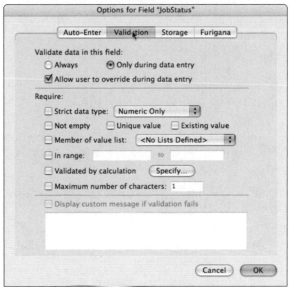

Figure 2-9:
The
Validation
options.

For example, in the Hey, Look at Me! database example in this chapter, I set validation for the following fields:

- ✔ JobTitle
- ✔ JobTerms
- ✔ JobDescription
- ✔ JobStatus
- ✔ HowFound

With validation, I made these fields required and enabled the user to override automatically entered values if needed. I also added a message that displays when the user makes an error so he knows when he needs to correct a mistake.

The following list describes what each of these Validation options is and how to use each one:

- ✔ **Validate Data In This Field:** It's important to define just when you want the data to be validated. The available options here are:

  - *Always:* With Always selected, FileMaker spends a lot of additional time checking the field to make sure it is valid. If you're automatically entering data into this field from some other source, use this option. Otherwise, avoid it.

  - *Only During Data Entry:* In just about all cases, you are going to want your data validated only during data entry.

- *Allow User To Override During Data Entry:* I'm not quite sure why this option defaults to always being selected. It basically defeats the purpose of making sure that your data is valid. Deselect this option to prevent the user from overriding and entering invalid data.

✔ **Strict Data Type:** Selecting this option enforces that the data entered can be only one of the following types:

  - Numeric Only

  - 4-Digit Year Date

  - Time Of Day

✔ **Not Empty:** If you never want the field to be empty, check this; FileMaker prompts the user to correct the situation.

✔ **Unique Value:** If you never want the field to hold data that has been previously entered, check this. This is especially useful for enforcing the use of unique serial numbers.

✔ **Existing Value:** This is the opposite of Unique Value. This ensures that the data entered has been entered previously in the database. Now, you may think, But what about when there's no data in the database yet? Good question. Usually, you wouldn't want to turn on this option until you have established some data in the database.

✔ **Member Of Value List:** This handy feature enforces that the data entered comes from an existing list of values. As an example, the most common list used is a Yes/No list, which contains two values — Yes and No. Selecting Define Value Lists from the drop-down list (pop-up menu on a Mac) brings up an editor for creating and editing value lists, as shown in Figure 2-10.

Chapter 7 covers how to use drop-down lists (pop-up menus on the Mac) and the Value Lists editor in more detail.

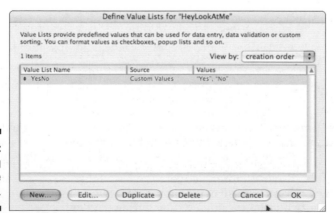

Figure 2-10:
Configuring
the value
list.

✔ **In Range:** You can enter the beginning and ending values of any specific range of dates, letters, numbers, or times to enforce that the entered data is within the specified range. Sorry, but entering **Empty** and **Full** doesn't work — I tried already.

✔ **Validated By Calculation:** This very powerful feature provides the ability to perform a calculation on existing data, predefined values, or the entered data itself and determines if the result is valid. Even if you're not a programmer or a math wiz, with geek blood running in your veins, the Specify Calculation dialog box is easy to work with, as you find out in Chapter 3.

✔ **Maximum Number Of Characters:** You can enforce how many characters can be entered.

✔ **Display Custom Message If Validation Fails:** This is one of my favorite features — though I've yet to get a project where the customer would let me use, `Whoops! You entered the wrong data. Try again!` as the custom message. Anyway, whatever message you put in here is what displays when the data entry fails the validation. A good error message should tell the user exactly what is wrong. For example, if a Numeric field's value (suppose the name of the field is Percentage) must lie within a specific range, such as between 0 and 100 (inclusive), a message like `The value in Percentage must be between 0 and 100.` would be more helpful than the `Whoops` message suggested earlier in this paragraph.

The bit bucket: Setting Storage options

Actually, the Storage options tab for the field is kind of a catchall for other options. Although these are the orphan children of options, they are very powerful options that you shouldn't ignore — they tell FileMaker where and how to store the field's values in the table. Figure 2-11 shows the options as they appear on the Storage tab.

The following list describes the storage options and how they are used:

✔ **Global Storage:** This is a really cool option! Or a least it used to be. This option provided the ability to use the field as a global storage container. Whatever value you place into this field is available for referencing from any other form, database, or script file in FileMaker. Now, the reason I state that this *used* to be a cool option is that FileMaker 8 now has a new feature, called global variables, which provides the same functionality without having to tie up a database field.

However, on occasion, you may still want to use a database field for storing a global value. Chapter 5 covers the use of global storage and Chapter 7 covers the use of global variables.

Options for Field "JobStatus"

| Auto-Enter | Validation | Storage | Furigana |

Global Storage

A field that uses global storage contains only one value that is shared across all records. A global field can also be used as a temporary storage location (for example, in scripts).

☐ Use global storage (one value for all records)

Repeating

Maximum number of repetitions: [1]

Indexing

Indexing improves performance for some operations like finds and supports functionality like relational joins and field value uniqueness at the cost of increased file size and time spent indexing.

Indexing: ⦿ None   ◯ Minimal   ◯ All
☑ Automatically create indexes as needed

Default language for
indexing and sorting text: [English ▾]

[Cancel] [OK]

Figure 2-11:
Storage
options.

Think of a *global variable* as a database field without a table. It's basically just a storage container in memory that holds a value. You give it a name, such as MyShoeSize, and then you store a value in it — such as 10.5 wide. Then whenever you want to look up your shoe size within FileMaker, you just check the value of MyShoeSize. Or if you've grown a little, you can always change the value later. The ability to use global variables becomes very important when you start to write FileMaker scripts (programming).

✔ **Repeating:** This powerful feature provides the ability to turn the field into a repeating field. For example, if you want to store a list of car colors in the field and you have 10 different car colors, you could have this field repeat 10 times. When used in combination with the Global Storage option, this provides a way to keep a list of values in memory.

However, with the use of table relationships, it is also just as easy (and less confusing) to create a subtable with all the needed values.

✔ **Indexing:** Indexing is an important option, especially when you're dealing with databases with a lot of records. By turning on indexing, you can improve the speed of searching through the database. The cost of using this feature is an increase in the size of the database and a possible increase in time used for adding new data to the database or changing data. The available options for indexing are:

   • *None:* Creates no indexes.

   • *Minimal:* Creates indexes for Text fields and Calculation fields that use text.

What is Furigana?

The final Options tab available for the field is called Furigana. I get all tongue-tied just trying to say it! It is specifically for supporting the use of Japanese characters in the database. By turning on this option and selecting the target field, you are allowing the use of Japanese characters in that database field. This is necessary because Japanese requires more data space for storage than English.

- *All:* Builds an index of all field data types, including dates, numbers, time, text, and so on.

- *Automatically:* Creates an index on the field if the user performs a search with the field or if the field is used in a table relationship.

- *Language:* Selects which language is utilized for building the index.

Sometimes you can resolve the performance issue by using faster computers and disk drives. A good rule is that if people use the database mostly for performing searches and lookups, it's a good idea to turn indexing on for the most-searched fields. If people use the database mostly for data entry and updating, you may prefer a smaller amount of indexing.

Indexing uses some very sophisticated calculations for creating a subset of the existing data, with pointers (maps) to the data. For example, if you have a contact manager database and the Last Name field is indexed, FileMaker creates an additional set of data with pointers to the data. This allows FileMaker to perform searches on the Last Name field much faster than if it wasn't indexed.

Connecting Tables with Parent/Child Relationships

Oops! Did you just stumble into a book about the social relationships between parents and children? Well, kind of! Not in the sense of individuals, but in the sense of parent database tables and child database tables.

When you design your database, you group the information into separate tables so that your database minimizes duplicate entries and runs more efficiently. (I explain this in more detail in Chapter 4.) When you separate tables like this, you need to set up *parent and child relationships* so that the data in the various tables is interconnected. The use of a subtable associated with another table is called a *child* table. And the table that it is related to is called a *parent* table. Here are a couple of examples:

- ✔ In the example Contact Manager database, the parent table is Contacts. The child table contains all the phone numbers. Therefore, each contact in the Contact table could have multiple child records in the Phone table.

- ✔ In the Hey, Look at Me! database example in this book, the Jobs table is the parent for all the jobs you've applied for. But each application involves a number of steps. First, there's the initial contact — usually, sending your résumé with a cover letter. Then there's the follow-up via e-mail or phone call. Next comes the interview and sometimes even two or more interviews. If you're going through all these steps while pursuing multiple jobs, it gets pretty confusing to keep track of what you did for which job. An Actions child table can help you keep track of all the steps (or actions) you've completed for a particular job application.

A database that provides the ability to establish relationships between tables is called a *relational database*. In earlier versions of FileMaker (before FileMaker Pro 3), the database model was called a *flat file* database — no relationships could be defined between tables. Being able to define a relational database in FileMaker 8 provides a new level of database sophistication and power that far exceeds early versions of FileMaker.

In the sections that follow, I explain how to set up a child table and define a relationship to its parent in FileMaker so that the information is clearly connected in your database. After walking you through a simple example, I explain the key features you find in FileMaker's Relationships Graph, which lets you set up table relationships visually — a wonderful shortcut for those who just want to keep their data organized without acquiring all the skills of a professional database administrator.

Setting up a child table

Creating a child table is much like creating a regular table except that you need to add extra fields to associate the child table with the parent. For example, the Action table in Hey, Look at Me! keeps track of the steps you have gone through for each specific potential job position. Here are the Data Categories this new table holds:

Table 2-2	Required Data Categories for the Action Table
Category	**Description**
Action Type	What type of action was taken?
Action Date	When was this step performed?
Action Notes	Any comments about this step?

As you can see, there's not much to this table. But remember that you need a unique identifier field to help keep each record unique, just as you did in the Jobs table. (See the "Playing the Field: Adding Fields to the Table" section earlier in this chapter for details.) Each Action record should have its own ID field.

There's another field that this table needs as well so that FileMaker knows which Job these Actions belong to — a field containing the JTID (Job Table Identifier). So, you also need to add the following two Categories to the table definition:

Table 2-3	Additional Categories for the Action Table
Category	**Description**
Action Identifier	Unique identifier for each action.
Related Job ID	Which job is this action for?

To add a child table to your database, follow these steps:

1. **If it isn't already open, open the Define Database dialog box by choosing File➪Define➪Database (or ⌘+Shift+D on a Mac).**

2. **Click the Tables tab.**

3. **Type a name for your child table in the Table Name text box, and click Create.**

4. **With the new table selected, click the Fields tab.**

5. **Add the fields and comments to the table, as I explain in "Playing the Field: Adding Fields to the Table" earlier in this chapter.**

   If you're following along to create the Hey, Look at Me! database, add the following fields to the child table:

Field Name	Type	Comments
AID	Number	Action ID, a unique identifier
JTID	Number	Foreign key relationship to the Jobs table
ActionType	Text	Resume, Phone call, and so on
ActionDate	Date	
ActionNotes	Text	

When adding a field to a table that contains the unique identifier from another table, this is called a *foreign key*. Because the unique identifier is assigned in the parent table, there is no need to have it generated in the child table. It is used as a reference back to the parent table. Right now, you just need to add the field; I explain how to associate the two in the next section.

The AID field is a unique identifier field for this table. Configure field options as Auto-Enter, Serial, just like I showed you with the JTID field in the Jobs table.

6. **Select the unique identifier field, and click the Options button. On the Auto-Enter tab of the Options dialog box, select the Serial Number check box, and click OK.**

See "Adding an identifier field" earlier in this chapter for more details.

After you've added the fields, the Define Database dialog box looks something like Figure 2-12.

What you have now is an orphaned table. The child table doesn't know who its parent table is. Will you be getting a visit from the local authorities for child abandonment? Not in this case — with FileMaker you can easily define the relationship between the parent and the child. See the next section for details.

Defining the table relationships

Unlike the complexity involved with the real-world relationships between a parent and their child, FileMaker table relationships are actually quite easy to define. And there are no temper tantrums if you don't get it quite right.

Figure 2-12:
Fields for
the Actions
table.

The following steps explain how to define a relationship between a child table with a foreign key in FileMaker:

1. **Click the Relationships tab at the top of the Define Database dialog box.**

   This screen is called the *relationship graph*, which you can use for viewing and managing the table relationships. Currently, just the two tables have been created for the Hey, Look at Me! database — the Jobs table and the Actions table.

2. **Resize the Jobs table by grabbing the bottom of the table and dragging down until you can see all the fields.**

3. **Drag the unique identifier field from the parent table, and place it on the Foreign Key field in the child table.**

   For Hey, Look at Me!, you drag the JTID field from the Jobs table and place it on the JTID field in the Actions table.

   Notice that as you're dragging the field from Jobs to Actions, the connector line changes to a single connection on the Jobs table and multiple connections on the Actions table, as shown in Figure 2-13. This connector shows that the relationship between the two tables is a One- (the single connection on the Jobs table) to-Many (the multiple connections on the Actions table) relationship. Which means that you can create multiple Actions records and have them associated with a single Jobs record. Jobs is the parent table, and Actions is the child table. Now that they're joined, they'll get along together just fine!

   4. Save your database by clicking OK.

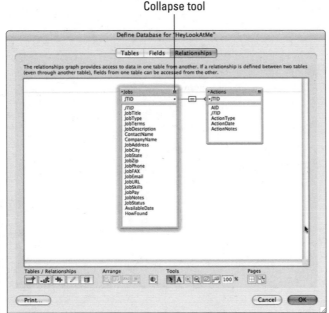

Collapse tool

Figure 2-13:
An
established
relationship
between
Jobs and
Actions.

Exploring your options in the relationships graph

I don't know about you, but relationship quizzes in the back of magazines scare me. But the relationships graph in FileMaker isn't scary at all! It provides a lot of powerful features for managing the relationships between tables in a FileMaker database.

The FileMaker developers have done a great job of taking the normally complex process of managing a relational database and have designed a simple interface for making this task easier. Lets admit it — not everyone (me included) has enough pocket protectors to be considered smart enough to become a DBA (database administrator), who normally has the task of designing databases and table relationships. So, having the FileMaker relationships graph is like having a built-in DBA!

Aside from using the relationships graph for the Hey, Look at Me! database, a lot of other features are available. The following list describes the various features of the relationships graph:

- ✔ **Select Table(s):** You can select a table or a group of tables several different ways. Here are some of them:

  - Clicking on a table with the mouse selects it.

  - Holding down the Shift key and clicking on multiple tables in sequence selects all the clicked tables.

  - Holding down the mouse button and dragging a box around multiple tables selects those tables.

- ✔ **Source Table:** By placing the mouse pointer over the curved arrow next to the Table name, a box appears which shows the names of the Source Table and the Source File, as shown in Figure 2-14. This is handy if you are using tables located in a different FileMaker database or in some other external database.

Figure 2-14:
Checking
the source
table.

- ✔ **Collapse:** The Collapse tool collapses the table, showing only the fields that are used in the relationships. Clicking it again collapses it even further by not showing the relationship fields. A third click restores the table. (Refer to Figure 2-13.)

- ✔ **Add A Table:** The Add A Table button is for adding existing tables to the relationship graph. When you click the button, the Specify Table dialog box appears, as shown in Figure 2-15. The table can be a part of the current database, or it can be a table in a different database.

- ✔ **Create A Relationship:** This button is for creating a new relationship between two tables. As shown in Figure 2-16, you can define the rules for the relationship. If you select Delete Related Records In This Table under the Actions table, this enforces that if the parent record is deleted from the Jobs table, all the associated records in the Actions table are deleted, too.

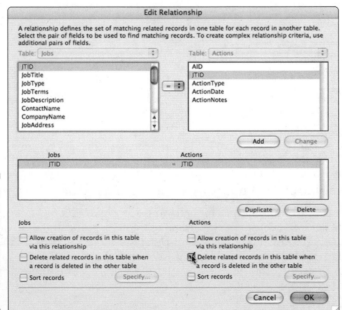

Figure 2-15:
The Specify
Table dialog
box.

 ✓ **Duplicate Selected Objects:** Being able to duplicate a table in the relationship graph is very handy for creating new relationships without cluttering the original table. Note that it doesn't actually create a new table in the database — just another table object in the relationship graph. Simply select the table or tables you want to copy, and click this button.

 ✓ **Edit A Selected Object:** The Edit button brings up the appropriate edit dialog box for the current object. If you select a table and click this button, an edit dialog box for the table properties appears. Or for a relationship, the relationship properties appear.

Figure 2-16:
Specifying
that deleting
a master
record
deletes all
related
records.

✔ **Delete Selected Objects:** Poof! All gone! But don't worry! FileMaker will ask you if you're sure first.

✔ **Arrange Objects:** This set of buttons (refer to Figure 2-13) is for arranging the positions and alignments of the objects on the relationship graph. When you have two or more objects selected, these buttons become available. By clicking any button, you'll see a list of alignment or positioning options. Just select the one that you want to use. This is a great way to make the relationship graph neat and tidy — for those impressive database relationship printouts to hang above the fireplace.

✔ **Change Color:** Want to make your relationship graph pretty? You can use the Color tool to select a new color for any of the selected objects.

✔ **Select:** This is the default point-and-click tool.

✔ **Text Notes:** This is a great tool for adding notes to the relationship graph, as shown in Figure 2-17. In the Edit Note dialog box, shown on the left, you can select the font, font color, font size, and even the background color that you want to use for the note, shown on the right side of Figure 2-17. I know a few DBAs that would kill to have this feature for their SQL databases!

✔ **Zoom:** Can't get it all to fit on one page? The Zoom-In and Zoom-Out tools let you resize the relationship graph between 1% (microscopic) and 100%. The size indicator tells you what your current zoom level is.

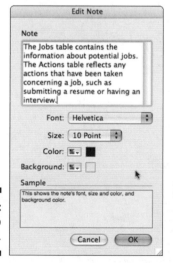

Figure 2-17:
Add notes to
your graph.

✔ **Return to 100%:** If you're zoomed down to 1% and your clicker finger is tired, you can use this button to bring the view back to normal.

 ✔ **Select 1-Away:** This tool allows you to select all the tables with the same source, or select all tables with 1-Away relationships (Parent to child). Just select a table to begin with, and click the Select 1-Away tool. Then you can select which option you want (1-Away or All Same Source).

 ✔ **Show Page Breaks:** If you have a large relationship graph that spans multiple pages, this tool is handy for showing where all the page breaks are. Then you can move the objects around to fit nicely within each page of your graph.

 ✔ **Show Print Setup:** This tool displays the Windows Print Setup dialog box (or Page Setup on the Mac).

Chapter 3

Calculation Programming: You Have the Power!

I can think of lots of reasons for using calculations in your FileMaker database application. Maybe you need an application that automatically adds up the hours of work that you have performed for a customer and then calculates how much to charge your customer for that work. Or you might need to use a comparison calculation to determine how many of your customers have ordered products during the past three months. When examining the power of scripts and calculations within FileMaker, you start to realize that FileMaker is not just for storing data. The real power of FileMaker is in its ability to manage, manipulate, and provide information about the data — which requires performing calculations on the data.

In this chapter, you find out how to tap into this powerful feature. After a quick introduction to the Calculation Editor, I explain how you can decide where to place calculations — in the database or in a script. You also discover the basics of working with ScriptMaker. In addition to walking you through the basic steps, I walk you through several examples to whet your appetite and get you well on your way to creating calculations and scripts of your own.

Introducing the Calculation Editor

When I was in high school, I took an algebra class. Fortunately, I had a knack for math and got good grades. However, one day, I approached my teacher and asked him, "What good is this going to do me in real life?" I couldn't understand why all these formulas and algorithms matter in the real world. How can a/b=a(1/b) apply to buying new parts for my car? My teacher just smiled at me and said, "Trust me. You'll be using this a lot!" Later, when I was introduced to computer programming, memories of my algebra class flooded back to me. My teacher was right! I was using algebra in my programming.

Now, don't close the book and walk away just because I brought up the topic of algebra! Although it's good to know some algebra for doing programming, you don't have to be a math wizard in order to write programs in FileMaker. That's the beauty of the Calculation Editor in FileMaker; it makes including calculations and functions in your Script code easy.

The Calculation Editor, shown in Figure 3-1, is a wonderful tool for assigning values, doing comparisons, and performing calculations. Here's a quick overview of the different areas in the Specify Calculation dialog box:

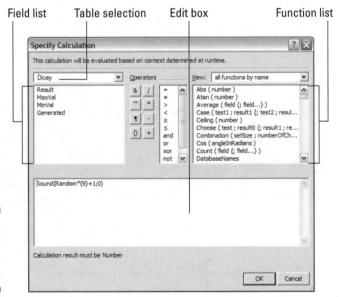

Figure 3-1:
Using the Calculation Editor.

✔ **Table selector:** This is the drop-down (pop-up menu on a Mac) list in the top left corner of the dialog box. Use this to select the table that contains the field in which you want to add a calculation, or use this to define new database field definitions.

✔ **Field list:** When a table is selected from the table selector drop-down list (pop-up menu on a Mac), the available fields in that table appear in this box. This is where you select which field you want to perform the calculation with.

- ✔ **Operators:** Operators perform math and/or comparisons with data, values, and variables. When selected, the operator is added to the edit box. I explain what each operator does later in this chapter.

- ✔ **View:** The view drop-down list (pop-up menu on a Mac) is for selecting how the list of functions is displayed. For example, if you want to see functions for trigonometric operations only, you can limit your options by choosing Trigonometric Functions from the view drop-down list (pop-up menu on a Mac). With all the functions FileMaker offers, this can be a helpful timesaver.

- ✔ **Function list:** This is a list of available functions for performing calculations. When you double-click a function name, the function you select appears in the edit box. Many of the functions have parameters that you specify, basically enabling you to tailor the way the function works for your specific needs. For example, Abs (absolute value) takes a numeric argument.

  The Calculation Editor has about 140 functions that you can choose from. And then there's the infamous Get function, which has 85 different options! Actually, that's not bad. Many programming languages have more than a thousand different functions and commands.

  So, where do you go to find out more about the various functions within FileMaker? Well, for starters, the appendix of this book has an extensive reference section on the scripting and calculation functions in FileMaker. Plus, the online help for FileMaker has a lot of information. Within the FileMaker online help, just do a search for "Functions reference," and then grab a big cup of coffee and start experimenting! For a quick review of how to search in help, see Chapter 1.

- ✔ **Edit box:** This is where you make selections to build a calculation formula, or you can type directly into the edit box if you know the correct syntax for the calculation.

Understanding the basic syntax

Among the buttons in the Calculation Editor, you find buttons that add punctuation marks — as though you might use it for writing your novel as well as building calculations! The real reason you find quotation marks, parentheses, and carriage returns, however, is that — like most prose — calculations and functions need some pointers so that FileMaker can read them correctly. Programmers call this *syntax*. (But yeah, it looks like grammar.)

Because you don't want to just make calculations — you want to make calculations and functions that work — here's the essential syntax you need to know:

✔ This button places a set of double quotes (" ") in the edit box. You use these to indicate the text is, well, text. If you don't use quotes, FileMaker thinks you're referring to a field name or that a symbol is part of some operation. For example, `"Italian" & DinnerSpecial` would return `Italian Meatballs`, if `Meatballs` were the value of the `DinnerSpecial` variable.

✔ This button places a carriage return in the edit box. Use it when you want text values to appear on multiple lines. For example, `"Italian¶ Meatballs"` would appear as:

```
Italian
Meatballs
```

✔ This places a set of parentheses ( ) in the edit box. The parentheses are used for grouping functions and calculations. For example, the parentheses in the equation `((4+8) * 27)` tell FileMaker to add 4 and 8 first and then multiply the result, 12, by 27.

Operator, could you please connect these values?

Operators make calculations spring into action, telling FileMaker how you want to connect two values so that you can add up orders, find values within a specific date range, test whether an expression is true. . . . You get the idea. You might be familiar with many of them, such as greater than and less than symbols. But because they're so important to creating calculations, Table 3-1 offers a brief refresher on the operators that you find in the Calculation Editor.

Table 3-1	Operators in the Calculation Editor	
Operator	*What It Does*	*Example*
&	Concatenates one text item to another.	`"My " & "name."` generates `My name.`
/	Divides.	`6/2 = 3`

Operator	What It Does	Example
*	Multiplies.	`4 * 5 = 20`
-	Subtracts.	If you don't know how this works, you need more help than I can give you in this book.
+	Adds.	
=	Indicates equivalence.	
≠	Compares two data items.	`(5 ≠ 4)` is `True` and `(5 ≠ 5)` is `False`
>	Tests whether one value is greater than another.	`(4 > 8)` returns `False`
<	Tests whether one value is less than another.	`(4 < 8)` returns `True`
≥	Tests whether one value is greater than or equal to another value.	`(5 ≥ 5)` returns `True`
≤	Tests whether one value is less than or equal to another value.	`(6 ≤ 3)` returns `False`
and	Compares two values. If both values are `True`, the result is `True`.	`(UserOn="Y" AND MyField="")`
or	Compares two values. Returns `True` if one or both of the values is `True`.	`(LastName = "Smith" OR LastName = "Jones")`
xor	Returns `True` if one value is `True`, but not if both values are `True`.	`(sky = "blue" XOR grass = "green")` is `False`, but `(sky = "blue" and grass = "red")` is `True`.
not	Changes the `True` value to `False` and the `False` value to `True`.	`NOT (MyValue = "No")` returns `True` if `MyValue` is not `"No"`.
^	Raises the first value to the power of the second value.	`2^10 returns 1024`

Deciding Where to Put a Calculation

Most developers use the Calculation Editor in two significant places — in the Database Definitions and in the ScriptMaker. How do you determine where to use the Calculation Editor?

- ✔ **When defining databases:** If a field in your database relies on a specific calculation, you can include the calculation in that field. This is a great feature because most programming environments require that you perform all calculations outside of the database, thus requiring more code.

- ✔ **In ScriptMaker:** When you use ScriptMaker to create a script, FileMaker saves that script under the name you give it. You can then reuse the calculation whenever you need it by assigning the script to a button or an event (such as creating a new record) or calling the script from another script.

If you're a programmer who is comfortable with other programming languages, such as C++, Java, or BASIC, you might feel a little lost when it comes to programming in FileMaker. The big difference is that you're used to just typing code in an editor, but with FileMaker, you do most of the programming via point and click. FileMaker assembles a lot of the programming syntax for you. So, the best approach to FileMaker for programmers skilled in other languages is to think of the ScriptMaker as your code-generator environment, and think of the Calculation Editor as a function and calculation wizard. Together, these two features generate the necessary programming code as you select the functions and calculations that you want FileMaker to perform.

Embedding calculations in your database

Why would you want to embed a calculation in your database? Take, for example, an employee database. You can create fields for an employee's salary, taxes, and insurance. The fields for taxes and insurance can have embedded calculations for determining how much to withdraw, based on the employee's gross pay. That's just one of many examples.

To insert a calculation in the database, here's an overview of the steps you need to follow:

1. **With your database open in Layout mode, click the Define Database tool on the FileMaker toolbar.**

   The Define Database dialog box appears.

2. **Create the field that will hold the calculation, if you haven't already done so.**

3. **Click the Options button.**

   The Options dialog box appears.

4. **Click the Calculated Value check box.**

   The Calculation Editor appears. The calculation you create in the edit box becomes the value for the field.

5. **Make sure that the table containing the field is selected from the Table drop-down list (pop-up menu on a Mac) in the upper left, and make sure that the field where you want to place the calculation is selected in the field list box (also in the upper left).**

6. **Use the operators and function list to create your calculation, which appears in the edit box at the bottom.**

7. **Click OK when you're done. Then click OK in the Options dialog box, and click OK in the Define Database dialog box to return to your layout.**

To help you understand how easy adding a calculation to your database is, complete the following task by using a sample database you can download from this book's Web site. (See the Introduction for details.) In this example, you're adding a randomly generated number to a field in the database.

1. **Download and open the `Dicey.fp7` database.**

   This database has a single table and a blank layout — all ready for you to add some calculations.

2. **Put the layout in Layout mode, and click the Define Database tool on the FileMaker toolbar.**

   You see that the Dicey database currently contains three fields — Result, MaxVal, and MinVal. You use these fields later for writing a dice-rolling simulator. However, for now, you're adding a new field with a calculated value.

3. **Create a new field, name it** Generated, **and assign the Number type. Then click the Create button.**

   This is the field for holding the calculated value. (Refer to Chapter 2 or the FileMaker Help if you've forgotten how to create a new field.)

4. **Click the Options button.**

   The Options For Field Generated dialog box appears.

5. **Click the Calculated Value check box.**

   The Calculation Editor appears. The calculation you place in the edit box becomes the value for the Generated field. You can tell that this is the correct field because the field name appears right above the edit box.

6. **In the function list, scroll down until you see the Round function. Double-click it to add it to the edit box.**

   You see the following calculation code in the edit box:

   ```
   Round ( number ; precision )
   ```

   This function is for rounding a number.

7. **Highlight `precision` and replace it with** 0 **(zero).**

   This tells FileMaker that you want to round to the nearest whole number (that is, no digits after the decimal point).

8. **Highlight `number`. In the function list, scroll until you see the Random function. Double-click it.**

   This places the Random function within the Round function. Basically, you're telling FileMaker that you want to generate a random number and round it to the nearest whole number. Now, you need to tell FileMaker what range of numbers you want to generate.

9. **Change the calculation to look like the following code:**

   ```
   Round (Random *(9)+1;0)
   ```

   This tells FileMaker that you want it to generate a random number between 1 and 10, rounded to the nearest whole number (0 decimal places). `Random` returns a number between 0 and 1, so you multiply it by 9 to get a number between 0 and 9 and then add 1 to that to get a number between 1 and 10. The calculation code is now complete and ready for testing.

10. **Click the next three OK buttons to save, and close the dialog boxes back to the layout.**

    FileMaker should have automatically added the new field to the layout (as shown in Figure 3-2). If it didn't, go ahead and add the Generated field to the layout.

11. **Switch the layout to Browse mode, and click the New Record button on the FileMaker toolbar.**

    Notice that as soon as you create a new record, FileMaker inserts a value in the Generated field. This is the result of the calculation that you embedded in the Generated field. Feel free to create multiple records to see the random number values for the field.

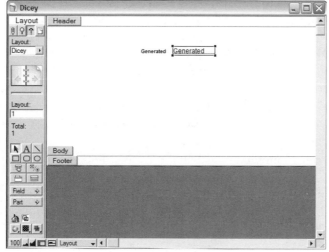

Figure 3-2:
The
Generated
field has an
embedded
calculation.

Building calculations and scripts in ScriptMaker

The more you get into FileMaker programming, the more you'll like the Calculation Editor and ScriptMaker. The two just go hand in hand — kind of like peanut butter and jelly, chocolate and ice cream, geeks and video games, and.... Well, you get the point. The reason is that the more often you work with your data, the more often you'll want to generate combined or calculated results or reformat the data. You also use the Calculation Editor to apply formatting based upon a value, such as displaying negative values in red and non-negative values in black.

Taking a look at the basic steps

The process of creating a script is different from putting a calculation in a database field. The following steps are an overview of how you access ScriptMaker, save a script, and then return to your layout:

1. **Open the database that you want to hold your script, and make sure it's in Layout mode.**

2. **Click the Define Database tool on the FileMaker toolbar.**

   The Define Database dialog box appears.

3. **Choose Scripts⊅ScriptMaker, or press Ctrl+Shift+S (⌘+Shift+S on the Mac).**

4. **Click the New button.**

   The Edit Script dialog box appears.

5. **Give your script a name in the Script Name text box.**

6. **Add any function to your script by double-clicking its name in the pane on the left.**

7. **If you need to set a target field, check the Specify Target Field check box, and then click the Specify button next to the check box to set that field.**

8. **If you need to include a calculation, click the Specify button next to Calculated Result. When you're done creating the calculation in the Calculation Editor that appears, click OK to return to ScriptMaker.**

   If needed, you can use the following buttons to work with your script in the Edit Script dialog box:

   - **Clear:** Remove a script.

   - **Duplicate:** Make a copy of a script.

   - **Disable:** Keep the script, but make it unavailable.

   - **Copy:** Place a copy of the script onto the clipboard, possibly for placing into another database.

   - **Paste:** Place a script which is on the clipboard into the database.

9. **When you're done creating your script in ScriptMaker, click OK to close and save your script.**

   The script is now available to add to a button or invoke via the Scripts menu.

Trying out the functions and features

To demonstrate the use of the Calculation Editor in ScriptMaker, I'm going to have you make some more changes to the Dicey database. (This example picks up where the earlier example leaves off, in the "Embedding calculations in your database" section.) After following these steps, you'll have a nifty dice-roller application:

1. **Load the `Dicey.fp7` file in FileMaker, and click Layout mode.**

   If you don't have the Dicey database, you can download it from the Web site mentioned in the Introduction.

2. **Click the Define Database icon on the FileMaker toolbar.**

   First, you need to make a minor addition to the Dicey database.

3. **From the Fields tab of the Define Database dialog box, create a new field, name it** Result2, **and set the field type to Number. Click OK to save the changes.**

   You now have two fields in the database for the dice-roller results — Result and Result2. The layout shows the Generated field and the newly added Result2 field.

   It's okay to use a number as part of a field name, as long as the field name doesn't start with the number.

4. **Delete the Generated label and field from the layout. Then delete the Result2 label from the layout.**

   All you need for this example is the Result and Result2 fields on the layout.

5. **Select the Field tool on the FileMaker Tool palette, and add the Result field to the layout. Position and resize both the Result and the Result2 fields on the layout, as shown in Figure 3-3. (When adding the Result field, be sure to turn off the Create Label check box.)**

   If you've forgotten how to move or resize a field, you can either drag it into place and drag the corners or use the Size palette (View⇨Object Size).

   You have two fields on the layout for holding the results of the dice rolls. However, the dice look a little strange with such a tiny font in the top-left corner of each box.

Figure 3-3:
The Result
and Result2
fields will
display the
results of
the dice
rolls.

6. **Select both of the fields on the layout (by dragging a box around them). Select the Center alignment icon and the Bold icon on the FileMaker toolbar. Then set the font size to 72.**

   Now you see two giant Rs on your layout. Now repeat after me, "Rrrr matie!" There, you are now a computer pirate!

7. **Select the Button tool from the FileMaker Tool palette, and place a button below and centered between the two fields. When the Button Setup dialog box appears, set it to Do Nothing, and click OK. Set the button text to Roll Dice.**

   You have the necessary objects on the layout for the dice roller. The next steps are to create the script code and calculations for generating the dice numbers.

8. **Choose Scripts⇨ScriptMaker, or press Ctrl+Shift+S (⌘+Shift+S on the Mac). Click the New button.**

   You're ready to enter new script code.

9. **Set the Script Name to RollDice. In the function list, double-click the Go to Record/Request/Page function.**

   The first script step in the script forces FileMaker to use the very first record of the database (just in case there is more than one record in the database). Because the default is to go to the very first record, you don't need to make any other changes to this script step.

10. **Double-click the Set Field function.**

    The first thing to do is set the initial values for the random number generator. Because the dice represent the standard 1 through 6 values, the MinVal and MaxVal fields need to be set to represent these values.

11. **Click the first Specify button. Double-click the MinVal field. Click the second Specify button. Enter the value of 1 in the edit field, and click OK.**

    Nothing too complicated here. You're telling FileMaker to store the value 1 in the MinVal field. Now, set the value for the max number.

12. **Double-click the Set Field function. Using the tasks in Step 11, set the MaxVal field to a value of 6.**

    The code in the Script looks like this:

    ```
    Go to Record/Request/Page [First]
        Set Field [Dicev::MinVal: 1]
        Set Field [Dicey::MaxVal; 6]
    ```

13. **Double-click the Set Field function, click the first Specify button, and then select the Result field. Click OK.**

    You're ready to generate the calculation for the first dice Result.

14. **Click the second Specify button to go into the Calculation Editor. Enter the following code in the edit box:**

```
Round(Random*(  )+(  );0)
```

You can also use the function list and the operators to enter this calculation if you want. Notice that you currently have no values in the parentheses. This is where you will place the values from the MinVal and MaxVal fields.

15. **Place your cursor in the first set of parentheses. In the field selection box, double-click the MaxVal field.**

This places `Dicey::MaxVal` in the calculation. Now, for the purpose of keeping the right values for the dice roll, you need to subtract from that value.

16. **After the MaxVal field, enter -1.**

Your calculation looks like this:

```
Round(Random*(Dicey::MaxVal-1)+();0)
```

17. **Place the cursor in the second set of parentheses. In the field selection box, double-click the MinVal field.**

The calculation looks like this:

```
Round(Random*(Dicey::MaxVal-1)+(Dicey::MinVal);0)
```

With this calculation, you're telling FileMaker to generate a number between MaxVal and MinVal and round the number to the nearest whole number (no decimals).

18. **Click OK to save this calculation.**

In the script window you see the Set Field function with your embedded calculation. You now need to do the same for the Result2 field. But I'll show you a quicker way to do it.

19. **Highlight the script step that begins with `SetField [Dicey::Result;` (if it isn't already highlighted), and click the Duplicate button.**

This tells FileMaker to make a duplicate copy of the script step. Now you need to change the field that is being updated.

20. **Click the first Specify button. Then double-click the Result2 field.**

Now wasn't that easy? You now have script steps that generate a random number for each of the result fields.

21. **As a nice little audible indicator, scroll the function list all the way to the bottom, and double-click the Beep function.**

This adds a script step for playing a beep at the end of the script. Your script code looks like Figure 3-4.

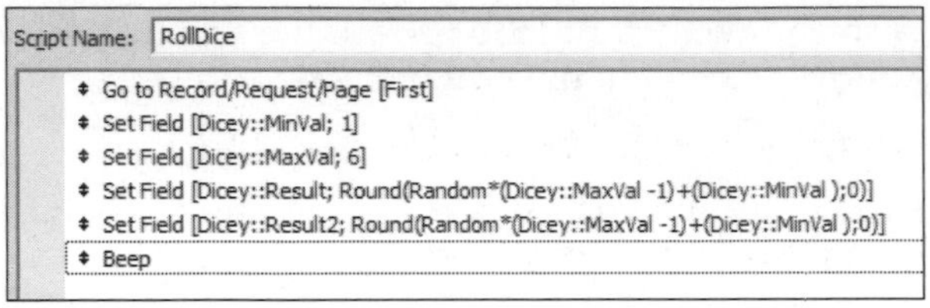

Figure 3-4:
The RollDice
script.

Script Name: | RollDice

```
◆ Go to Record/Request/Page [First]
◆ Set Field [Dicey::MinVal; 1]
◆ Set Field [Dicey::MaxVal; 6]
◆ Set Field [Dicey::Result; Round(Random*(Dicey::MaxVal -1)+(Dicey::MinVal );0)]
◆ Set Field [Dicey::Result2; Round(Random*(Dicey::MaxVal -1)+(Dicey::MinVal );0)]
◆ Beep
```

22. Click OK to close and save your script. Then click the next OK button to close the Scripts list.

You're ready to assign this script to your Roll Dice button.

23. Right-click the Roll Dice button (on the Mac, Option+click with a one button mouse), and select the Button Setup item. Select the Perform Script function. Click the Specify button, and then select the RollDice script.

This assigns your new script code to the Roll Dice button.

24. Click OK, and then click the next OK button. Select Browse mode, and test your Roll Dice script by clicking the Roll Dice button.

Feel free to click the Roll Dice button as much as you want — or as long as you can tolerate the constant beeping noise.

Getting Crazy with the Calculation Functions

Ah, now that you've had a taste of script programming and calculations, you want to get crazy, right? I mean, random numbers and dice rollers are fun and everything. But now you're ready for something a little more challenging.

Well, how about adding a nice information dialog box to a database application. Not only do you get to see how to use the Custom Dialog function, but you also get to play with more of the functions in the Calculation Editor.

Adding a database status dialog box

Sometimes we all need a little more information to make us feel better — information like the number of records in the database, today's date, the name of the current database that we're using, the size of the database file, and Steve Job's personal cell phone number. To provide this information (except for Steve's phone number), you can use many of the functions within the Calculation Editor.

The following steps show how to put together a script that displays some key information about the current database and some FileMaker information.

1. **Open the Hey, Look at Me! database application.**

   You can download the `HeyLookAtMe-Chap3-Start.fp7` file from the Web site mentioned in the Introduction.

2. **Choose FileMaker➪Scripts➪ScriptMaker, or press Ctrl+Shift++ (the plus key). (Or press ⌘+Shift+the plus key on the Mac.) Then click the New button.**

   You're going to create a new script for showing the System Information.

3. **Set the Script Name to SystemInfo. Then double-click the Set Variable function in the function list.**

   One of the coolest new features of FileMaker Pro 8 is the ability to define local and global variables within the script code. This also makes it handy for storing all the gathered information.

4. **Double-click the Set Variable script step (or click the Specify button).**

   This opens the Set Variable Options dialog box. As described in the top of the dialog box, variables prefixed with $ are local and usable only within the current script, and $$ makes the variable a global, which is available to the entire database application and all the scripts. For the System Information display, you need to use only a local variable because other scripts don't need the variable's value.

5. **Name the variable $SysInfo, and click the Specify button.**

   This is where you enter all the Calculation functions for gathering the system information.

6. **As shown in Figure 3-5, enter the following calculation functions in the edit box:**

   ```
   "Today is: " &Get(Current Date) & ¶ &
   "Current Databases: " &DatabaseNames & ¶ &
   "Current Layout: " &Get(LayoutName) & ¶ &
   "Total Records: " &Get(TotalRecordCount) & ¶ &
   "Current Record: " &Get(RecordNumber) & ¶ &
   "FileMaker Path: " &Get(FileMakerPath) & ¶ &
   "FileMaker Version: " &Get(ApplicationVersion) & ¶ &
   "Database Path: " &Get(FilePath) & ¶ &
   "Database Size: " &Get(FileSize) & ¶ &
   ```

   Basically, each calculation line in the edit box is a text label followed by the calculation function, which generates the requested information. The structure of each line is:

   ```
   "Text label" & Function & Carriage Return &
   ```

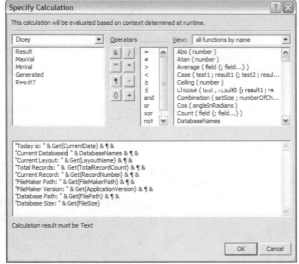

Figure 3-5:
Add
calculations
to create a
status
dialog box.

Even though the calculation is shown as multiple lines, it's actually just one continuous line of code. Via the use of the & symbol, the text, functions, and carriage returns are appended together. The carriage returns are added to make sure that the information is displayed correctly in the dialog box. Table 3-2 describes each of the functions used in this calculation.

7. Click OK to close the Calculation Editor, and click the next OK button to close the Set Variable Options dialog box.

Now that you have the calculation for gathering all the system information, you need to add the dialog box for displaying the information.

8. Scroll the function list to the bottom, double-click the Show Custom Dialog function, and click the Specify button.

The Show Custom Dialog Options dialog box appears. This is where you define what is to appear in the dialog box.

9. Enter System Information as the Title. In the Message text box, enter $SysInfo.

This tells FileMaker that you want to show the contents of the $SysInfo local variable when the dialog box is displayed.

10. Clear the Cancel text from the Button 2 box, and click OK.

Because the dialog is for showing system information only, there is no need for a Cancel button on the dialog.

11. **Click OK, and click the next OK button.**

    Now you're ready to add the button for the System Information to the layout.

12. **Click Layout mode, and click the Button tool on the FileMaker Tool palette. Place the button just to the left of the X button.**

    This button is used for calling the SystemInfo script.

13. **In the Button Setup dialog box, select the Perform Script function, click the Specify button, and double-click the SystemInfo script. Click OK to close the Button Setup dialog box.**

    This assigns the SystemInfo script to the button.

14. **For the button label, enter** i. **Click anywhere on the layout to deselect the i button. Select the i button again, and click the Bold icon on the FileMaker toolbar. Resize and position the button to match the layout in Figure 3-6.**

Info button

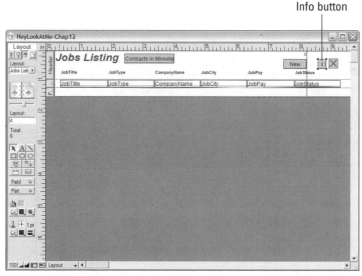

Figure 3-6:
The i button
runs the
SysInfo
script.

Now that you've assigned the script and placed the button, it's time to test it out.

15. **Select Browse mode, and click the i button.**

    The System Information dialog box appears. You can resize the dialog box to an appropriate size for viewing all the information, as shown in Figure 3-7.

Figure 3-7:
The System
Information
dialog
box gives
you the
information
you need.

Table 3-2	Calculation Functions in $SysInfo
Function	*Description*
Get(CurrentDate)	Shows the current date.
DatabaseNames	Grabs a list of the currently active databases in FileMaker.
Get(LayoutName)	Shows the currently active Layout name.
Get(TotalRecordCount)	Shows the number of records in the currently active table.
Get(RecordNumber)	Shows the currently active record number.
Get(FileMakerPath)	Gets the FileMaker Pro installation path and folder.
Get(ApplicationVersion)	Shows the version of FileMaker Pro.
Get(FilePath)	Shows the path and folder for the currently active database file.
Get(FileSize)	Gets the total byte size of the currently active database file.

Formatting a phone number by calculation

Now that you've seen some of the basic approaches to using the Calculation Editor, it's time to add a little sophistication. One of the most popular uses of the Calculation Editor is for the automatic formatting of the information in a field. To demonstrate this, I have you create a Calculation for formatting a phone number.

1. **Download and open the FormattingStart.fp7 database application.**

   You can find this database on the Web site mentioned in the Introduction. This is just a single-table database with a single field named PhoneNumber. If you don't want to download the database, you can just create a new database with a single table and a single field.

2. **Make sure that you're in Layout mode. Click the Define Database icon on the FileMaker toolbar. Then make sure that you're on the Fields tab in the Define Database dialog box.**

   You see a single field called PhoneNumber.

3. **Highlight the PhoneNumber field, and click the Options button.**

   The Options dialog box for the PhoneNumber field appears.

4. **Click the Calculated Value check box.**

   As soon as you do this, the Calculation Editor appears.

5. **In the edit box, enter the calculation code, as shown in Figure 3-8.**

```
In(Length(PhoneNumber)    7;Left(PhoneNumber;3) & "-" &
        Right(PhoneNumber:4) &
Tn(Length(PhoneNumber) > 7; "(" & Left(PhoneNumber;3)
        & ")" & Middle(PhoneNumber;4;3) & "-" &
        Right(PhoneNumber;4))
```

   I explain the functions used here and how they work together to format the number in the following sections.

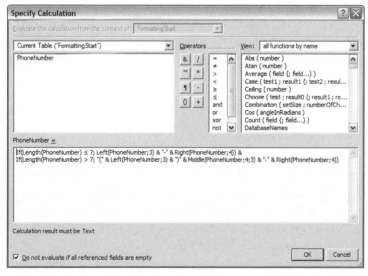

Figure 3-8: Getting started on the Phone-Number formatting calculation.

6. **Click OK to save the calculation code.**

   The calculation is saved and ready for use. But, next, you need to tell FileMaker that it is okay to replace the original value of the field with this newly calculated value.

7. **Uncheck the Do Not Replace Existing Value For Field (If Any) check box.**

   This tells FileMaker that it's okay to replace the original field value.

8. **Click OK, and click the next OK button.**

   Now you're ready to test.

9. **Switch the layout to Browse mode. Click to the right of the PhoneNumber label and enter a seven- or ten-digit number. Press the Tab key to tell FileMaker to accept the value.**

   Notice that the phone number is automatically formatted to the correct structure. Pretty nifty, eh? Keep in mind that the calculation can become even more complex by adding functions to make sure that the phone number is of the correct length. But at least you can now see how useful the Calculation Editor can be for your FileMaker databases.

Checking out the functions

The code you entered might seem like Greek (or, rather Geek!) to you right now. However, I explain each function to help you see what is going on here. First, I explain the functions that you're using.

- ✔ If   Similar to the If statement in the ScriptMaker environment, this If statement is structured (syntax) like this:

  ```
  If ( condition; do this; else do this)
  ```

  The first parameter is the condition to be met. If the condition is met, the *do this* code is performed. Otherwise, the *else do this* code is executed.

- ✔ Left   This function grabs a designated number of characters from the left side of the text. The syntax is:

  ```
  Left(text; #)
  ```

  text represents the text that you grab the characters from, and # represents the number of characters you want to grab.

- ✔ Right   The Right function works just like the Left function, except it grabs characters from the right side of the text. The syntax is:

  ```
  Right(text; #)
  ```

- ✔ Middle   The Middle function is similar to the Left and Right functions. However, because you're getting characters from the middle of the text, you need to identify where to begin and how many characters to grab. The syntax is:

  ```
  Middle(text, start#, chars#)
  ```

> ✔ *text* represents the text that you're examining, *start#* represents the position that you want to start grabbing characters from, and *chars#* represents the number of characters that you want to grab.

Understanding how the functions work together

To see how the telephone number formatting calculation works, imagine that a value has been placed in the PhoneNumber field. Perhaps, 1235551212. Now here's an explanation of the calculation, function by function:

```
If(Length(PhoneNumber)    7;
```

The preceding line tests whether the length of the PhoneNumber field is less than or equal to seven digits.

```
Left(PhoneNumber;3)
```

This line grabs the left three digits of the phone number. Because your imagined phone number is 1235551212, this part of the calculation is not executed because the length of the phone number is greater than seven digits.

```
& "-" &
```

This adds the – (dash) symbol after the first three digits of the phone number. Keep in mind that this happens only if the phone number is less than eight characters.

```
Right(PhoneNumber;4)
```

The preceding line grabs the right four digits of the phone number. Again, because the phone number is greater than seven digits, this function isn't executed.

The) & marks the end of the If statement. In this example, you do not use the second parameter of the If statement syntax. The & symbol is a connector that tells FileMaker that you want to continue execution of the calculation with the next function.

```
If(Length(PhoneNumber) > 7;
```

Again, the code is testing the length of the PhoneNumber field. Because the imagined phone number is 1235551212, this condition is met, and the next function is executed.

```
"(" &
```

This states that the first character of the PhoneNumber field is now a " (".

```
Left(PhoneNumber;3)
```

The first three digits of the entered phone number is appended to the new first character. Thus the new value so far is `"(123"`.

```
& ")" &
```

Another ")" is appended to the new value. Now the new value for PhoneNumber is `"(123)"`.

```
Middle(PhoneNumber;4;3)
```

The next three characters of the entered PhoneNumber field, beginning with the fourth character, are now appended to the new value. The new value for the PhoneNumber is now `"(123)555"`. Are you starting to see the pattern now?

```
& "-" &
```

This appends a – (dash) to the new PhoneNumber value, which is now `"(123)555-"`.

```
Right(PhoneNumber;4))
```

You're now at the end of the calculation code. The last four digits of the entered PhoneNumber field is appended to the new PhoneNumber value, which is now `"(123)555-1212"`. This is the format that the PhoneNumber field now uses.

Part II
Building the
Perfect Beast

In this part . . .

This part puts the fun in design fundamentals. It begins with Chapter 4 and the basics of creating a database application. I walk you through all the questions you need to ask, pictures you need to draw, and requirements you need to write in order to create an (ahem) fully functional application. But that's just getting you started.

Chapter 5 focuses on designing a looker of a layout, with neatly arranged fields, well-organized data, pictures, and more. In Chapter 6, I offer tips and tricks for enabling your users to search and sort data through your layouts. Chapter 7 is all about whiz-bang features you can add, such as buttons that run scripts, drop-down lists, and custom menus.

Chapter 4

Designing a Good FileMaker Application

*I*magine that you have just hired someone to build you a nice house. Then on the day that the work is to start, the builder shows up, grabs some lumber, and just starts nailing boards together. No blueprints, no foundation, and not even a chalk mark to show where the walls go. I bet it wouldn't take long for you to fire the builder and go find another one. That's because you understand that there are things that have to happen in order for the house to be built properly. With a house, you need to know what the purpose of the house is (single couple, family, large family, and so on). Then you pick or design a set of blueprints. Next comes the ordering of all the materials and resources. The ground is prepared, the foundation is built, and then the house is built. (A very simplified description.)

Well, software development and database application design have things in common with building a house. This chapter helps you understand the questions you need to consider before you actually begin developing the database. But, don't worry — database design is a lot easier than designing and building a house.

Analysis Isn't Just for Doctors

Don't you just love going in to see your doctor? You get poked, prodded, stretched, examined, and sometimes even x-rayed. Then you might not hear anything for days after the visit. Well, the doctor is analyzing the results to determine what is wrong and how to prescribe a remedy.

When doing software design, you are basically the doctor. Software comes about because there is a problem that needs to be resolved. Sometimes that problem can be as simple as not being able to find a phone number or as complex as needing to determine the necessary velocity to launch a 20-ton spacecraft off the surface of Mars — in the middle of a dust storm, on the dark side of the planet, when one of the booster rockets is broken. So, when trying to determine how to design the software, or in your case, the database application — you need to do some analysis.

Asking the initial questions

The first step in this analysis process is to ask yourself some questions about the problem. Working through the following list of questions, in order, can help you get started; I also offer a rationale for asking the questions that help keep your answers focused.

1. **What is the problem that I want this FileMaker database to solve?**

   Because you're thinking about using FileMaker, this implies that you've already identified something that you want to do with it — such as keeping track of your appointments, customers, business finances, and so on.

2. **What information do you want to keep?**

   Information is data, and FileMaker is a database — a storage base for your information. Answer this key question before you begin your database design. The more specifically you can answer this question, the better, because planning for something from the beginning is always easier than retrofitting the design to accommodate overlooked needs. Knowing the reports and other results you're going to want to produce lets you recognize the data you'll need to collect and maintain.

3. **Are you duplicating a paper-based process?**

   This is a very important question. For example, if you want to create a FileMaker database for a school which currently uses paper forms and filing cabinets, you need to consider how moving to an electronic system will be accepted by the school. The layouts in FileMaker should match or closely resemble the forms the school uses.

4. What processes will you be performing?

A *process* is a set of actions that has to be performed as part of the data gathering or data management activity. For example, if you're designing a FileMaker application for a real estate agency, you want to make sure that your application provides the entry of information about the property owner before you allow entry of information about the property itself.

5. Are you replacing an older software system?

You'd be amazed at how many people are still using DOS-based applications for keeping their data. If you are designing a FileMaker application to replace an older software application, you want to think about questions 2 and 4, and then determine if there are any additional processes or information that needs to be added.

6. Is your database for use on a single computer, multiple computers at one location, multiple computers at multiple locations, or should it be Web enabled?

Another very important question. The answer to this question affects how you design the database application. For example, if multiple users are entering information about a specific customer, you'll want to know which user entered specific information. So you'll need to include a field for keeping track of the current user.

7. What security issues should you consider?

If your database will contain private information, such as employees' salaries, the confidential phone numbers of celebrities, or customer credit card information, you need to make sure that you design the database to be secure. Such information should be displayed only to individuals with proper authorization.

8. How should the application look?

User interface is a very touchy subject. Everyone has their own ideas about what the screens should look like. The overall goal when answering this question is to come up with an interface that is easy to use and provides the desired functionality.

9. What printed output is needed?

I once heard an MIS director state that the software was only as good as the information he could get out of it. Basically, he was referring to printed reports that he could look at that would help him make good business decisions. Not only do you want to think about the type of reports that you want, but also give some thought to how those reports should be designed. A printed report is not any good if the user can't read it.

10. **How much pizza and Red Bull do you have to supply to the programmers to get the application completed?**

   This one is a total mystery. One can never predict how much food and caffeine a developer will go through while designing and developing a database application. My only advice here is — don't run out!

These questions are just enough to cover the basic requirements for designing a database application. If the application you want to design is complex, you might need to ask a more-extensive list of questions. For example, I once worked on an application that kept track of trucks, truck drivers, products, routes, customers, and incidents that happened to delivered products (broken, chipped, wrong color, and so on). To determine what was needed for that application, we had a group of people (developers, business reps, and an analyst) spend five days in a conference room asking lots of questions and reviewing how their business worked. Then it took another nine months to actually design and develop the application. If you find yourself in this situation, consider calling in a systems analyst to help.

Turning your answers into requirements

The set of things that you need to think about usually depend on the type of problem you're trying to solve. Even though FileMaker can be used for very complex and extensive database applications, for the purpose of this book, I present a simpler problem to resolve.

Calling in a systems analyst

Systems analysis: This is the process of analyzing information and processes to determine a good design for a particular system. A person who performs this activity is usually called a *systems analyst.* A *system* can be a piece of hardware, or it can be a software application. It is the job of the systems analyst to come up with a list of requirements for the design and development of the system. The analyst creates a document called a *specifications document.* The programmers or engineers then use this document to help them develop the desired system.

Here's the scenario: A school has a library where students can check out books, music CDs, DVDs, and media equipment. In the past, the school has always used paper-based cards in a filing cabinet for keeping track of items checked out. Now, the school wants to use a computer-based database for keeping track. So, using the same questions from the preceding section, here's an example of how to apply those questions:

1. **What is the problem?** The school needs a database to track items checked out to students.

2. **What information do you want to keep?** Assets (books, music CDs, DVDs, media equipment), students, and a history of student and asset activity.

3. **Are you duplicating a paper-based process?** Yes.

4. **What processes will you be duplicating?** Asset tracking, student tracking, check out of asset, check in of asset, reminder e-mail to student before asset is due and when asset is overdue.

5. **Are you replacing an older software system?** No.

6. **Is this for use on a single computer, multiple computers at one location, multiple computers at multiple locations, or should it be Web enabled?** Just two computers in the school library.

7. **What security issues should you consider?** None needed at this time.

8. **How should the application look?** Easy to use. Have assets and student records easily accessible.

9. **What printed output is needed?** Asset details, student details, asset list, student list, status report, items on loan report.

10. **How much pizza and Red Bull do you have to supply to the programmers to get the application completed?** Cafeteria is just down the hall.

From your answers, you create a list of requirements, which you'll use to figure out what you need to include in your application and how you need to design it. As you design your application, return to check that it meets all the requirements laid out in this phase of the planning process. For example, based on questions 2 and 4, you know you have the following requirements:

✔ The application must track library assets, including books, CDs, DVDs, and media equipment.

✔ The application must track students, including their first and last names, student ID numbers, and e-mail addresses.

✔ The application must track which assets are checked in and out, who has an asset checked out, and when that asset is due.

✔ The application must include a policy enforcement system that e-mails students reminders before books are due and e-mails students when books are overdue.

With your complete list of requirements in hand, the only thing missing is the name of the application. However, you do need to design the database.

Data In: Creating a Well-Designed Database

What is good database design? Now that is the forty-two dollar question! There are volumes of books about good database design. And if you had a chance to ask ten different database administrators the question, "What is good database design?" you would get ten different answers. Basically, it boils down to a few key concepts. Initially, you want a database to be a place to store information. But how you organize that information within the database can have a big impact on being able to retrieve the data and upon the performance of the database. In the following sections, I introduce how you can account for all these factors.

Identifying the fields

Starting with the basics, a FileMaker database uses tables for storing the data. As shown in Figure 4-1, each table contains individual records. And each record breaks the stored data into individual fields.

Columns (Fields)

Asset	Condition	CreatedBy	AddDate	Make
Camera	New	jcool	05/05/2005	Nikon
Television	Used	jcool	05/04/2005	Sony
Digital Camera	New	jcool	05/04/2005	Kodak
Wireless Phone	New	jcool	05/05/2005	Motorola
Laptop Computer	Used	jcool	05/03/2005	Sony
Lava Lamp	Used	jcool	05/05/2005	Spencer
Receiver	New	jcool	05/04/2005	Sony
CD Player	New	jcool	05/04/2005	Sony

Rows (Records)

Figure 4-1: This database contains data in all fields I'm tracking.

The answer to question 2, "What information do you want to keep?" is a key factor in identifying all the necessary fields for the database, and what type of data (text, numbers, dates, and so on) the field should hold. To continue with the School Library Database example, here is an analysis of the school library database requirements for field specifications (Table 4-1):

Table 4-1		Required Data Fields
Field	*Type*	*Description*
Description	Text	Description of the asset item
Condition	Text	Amount of wear/use on the item
CreatedBy	Text	User who enters the information
DateBought	Date	Date the asset was purchased
Manufacturer	Text	Who made the item
Model	Text	Model name
Serial	Text	Serial number of the item
Type	Text	Type of item
Price	Number	Cost of the item
UPC/ISBN	Text	Bar code number of an object or ISBN of a book
FirstName	Text	First name of the student
LastName	Text	Last name of the student
Email	Text	E-mail address of student
Phone	Text	Phone number of student
Address	Text	Address of student
City	Text	Address city
State	Text	Address state
Zip	Text	Address zip code
Notes	Text	Notes about the student
CheckoutDate	Date	Date the item checked out
CheckinDate	Date	Date the item checked in
DueDate	Date	Date the item due back in

The required data fields have now been identified. You could put all these fields into a single table. However, doing so makes the database inefficient and takes up a lot more storage space than is really necessary. No one likes a FAT database (more commonly known as a *flatfile* database). Because a new record would have to be created for the same asset every time it is checked out, this would result in a lot of duplication of the asset information and the student information. What you need is a nonfat database (more commonly called a *relational* database).

Organizing fields into tables for efficiency

The process of designing the database tables for efficiency is called *normalization.* A computer scientist by the name of Edgar F. Codd came up with a set of rules for defining a *relational model* for database design. If you're feeling geeky and would like to find out more, I recommend you do a search on the Internet for "Edgar F. Codd" and "normalization."

Yep, what you currently have is abnormal data! (Not to be confused with abnormal software developers. Those are quite acceptable!) So, how do you make your data normal? Well, because the data structure in Table 4-1 is fat and inefficient, you need to *normalize* the database. You can do this by breaking the table into three different tables — one for Assets, one for Students, and another for the Activity. The tables would then look like Figure 4-2.

In general, the process of normalization means identifying the discrete data entities, around which you organize your tables. In the library database example, those are Assets, Students, and Activity tickets.

Assets	Students	Activity
Description	FirstName	CheckoutDate
Condition	LastName	CheckinDate
CreatedBy	Address	DueDate
CreatedDate	City	Status
DateBought	State	
Manufacturer	Zip	
Model	Phone	
Serial	Email	
Type	Notes	
Price		
UPCISBN		

Figure 4-2: An efficient table design.

Building good relationships (between tables)

Sorry, but I can't help you with finding a great relationship with another person. Now, table relationships — *that,* I can help you with! After you design the tables to be more efficient, you need to perform still another step. Currently, the database is not yet normalized. Take a look at the Activity table in Figure 4-2 and ask yourself, "How can I associate the Activity with the Assets and the Students?" Currently, there's no way to associate the data. What you need is a way to define relationships among all three tables — and you can do this by adding Key fields to each table.

A *primary key* is a unique identifier field — usually a number. This not only makes the record unique, but it also gives you a way to link tables together. Notice in Figure 4-3 how the AssetID and StudentID are used as primary keys to define a relationship between the tables.

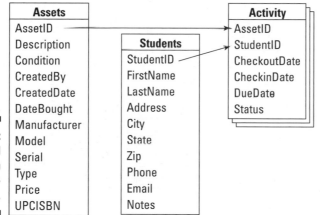

Figure 4-3: Normalized tables with relationships.

Assets	Students	Activity
AssetID		AssetID
Description	StudentID	StudentID
Condition	FirstName	CheckoutDate
CreatedBy	LastName	CheckinDate
CreatedDate	Address	DueDate
DateBought	City	Status
Manufacturer	State	
Model	Zip	
Serial	Phone	
Type	Email	
Price	Notes	
UPCISBN		

Now our example database matches the intended real-world use of the database application. There is one record per Asset, which reflects what is physically in the library. There is one record per Student — at least until cloning becomes the norm. And there are multiple Activity records per each Asset and/or Student. With the database designed this way, there is no unnecessary duplication of the Asset or Student information. Performance of the database will be better because searches and the display of the data will have less information to dig through.

Data Out: Designing an Effective Layout

Carlos Santana once said about his music, "If it isn't pretty then the girls won't come." Not exactly word for word, but you get the point. Apply that same thinking to the design of layouts and reports — if it isn't appealing, no one is going to want to use it! Many software applications have been designed and delivered by developers who thought they had the greatest applications since the invention of the spreadsheet — only to discover that their programs were shelved because the clients didn't want to use them.

A screen layout can make or break the acceptance of your database application. As an example, take a look at these two screens (Figures 4-4 and 4-5) and decide which one you would prefer to use.

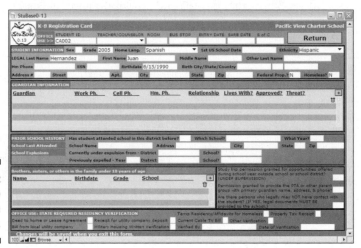

Figure 4-4:
A possible application layout.

In Figure 4-4, the layout is functional, and it actually duplicates a real-world, paper-based form. But it's also a very busy screen. If the client was not comfortable with the use of the paper-based form, he won't have a clue about using the layout.

In Figure 4-5, this layout is also functional. Notice how the fields are all symmetrically aligned, data is grouped by type (Contact Info, Company Info, Locations, and so on), and it's easier to figure out what to do without having prior knowledge of the application.

Figure 4-5:
An
alternative
layout.

So, what are some things to keep in mind when designing a layout for the screen or for reports? Here's a list of things to consider when thinking about the design of a layout:

✔ **Use a metaphor that relates to *real-world* concepts.**

Notice in Figure 4-5 the use of folder tabs. Folder tabs are easy for the user to relate to, and they're a good way to group data and functional areas of the layout. Especially, when you design icons for buttons, use pictures that relate to the functionality of the buttons. For example, use a house icon on a button that takes the user to the home layout.

✔ **Who is going to use the application?**

If engineers will use the database application, it's pretty acceptable to use terminology, field names, and graphics that they're comfortable with. But if the user is someone who doesn't have extensive computer skills, make sure that the layout is easy to understand and use. For example, an application designed to be used by a law enforcement officer needs to be clear, specific, and easy to use. The officer isn't trained to be a computer geek. The officer uses the computer as just another tool to aid in crime fighting.

✔ **Be consistent!**

When you select a specific design and format for your layout, be sure to apply that same theme for the rest of the application. This promotes comfort and ease of use. For example, if you're going to use graphic icons on buttons on one layout, don't confuse the user by using text-only buttons on a different layout. And placement of the buttons, controls, and fields should be consistent as well.

✔ **Focus on what is important!**

The layout should have the most important information in the most prominent area of the layout. For example, in Figure 4-5, the most important information is the Contact Info and the Company Info. The Phone and Email, Locations, Co-workers, and Invoices fields are secondary. When the user goes to this layout, he or she will want to see the Contact Info first. At least, in Western societies, we tend to read from the top and left, so that is usually where you want to place the most significant information. (You might place it at the top right in a database geared toward users who are native speakers of Arabic or Hebrew.) Another way to make certain fields stand out is to display them in a different color from the rest or against a background that makes the grouping stand out — but this method involves aesthetic choices (some folks might find the chosen colors garish or distracting).

✔ **Always provide help.**

You can't always expect the user to be comfortable with all features of your application. There are just too many distractions in life — like football, Calvin and Hobbes comics, computer games, Chinese food, good beer, and . . . oh, yeah, back to the topic. So, it's important to always provide some form of online help information about the currently displayed layout. Give users a nice big question mark icon to click when they need it, and then be sure that the helpful information is clear and easy to understand.

Here's another example (Figure 4-6) of a nice, clean layout — based on the example School Library Database I use in this chapter:

Figure 4-6:
This Lending Library database should be easy for just about anyone to use.

Do you think you could use this layout without any specific training? Hopefully, you answered affirmatively. This layout is very easy to understand and use. But just in case, the Help button is available in the top-right corner.

Additionally, if you're using FileMaker Pro 8 Advanced to create your database for others, you can add helpful tips that appear when the user lets the mouse hover over a layout object. See Chapter 5 for details.

For each layout you want to create, FileMaker offers an abundance of options. In the sections that follow, I walk you through the main options so you'll be ready to create layouts for your own custom applications with ease.

Adding a layout to a database

Adding a layout to a database is the first step in creating a layout. Here are the steps you need to follow:

1. **With your database open in Layout mode, choose Layouts⇨New Layout/Report. Or just click the New Layout/Report icon on the FileMaker toolbar.**

   The New Layout/Report Wizard appears, as shown in Figure 4-7. This is where you select the type of layout that you want to create and specify the name that you want to give it.

Figure 4-7: The New Layout/Report Wizard helps you get started with creating a layout.

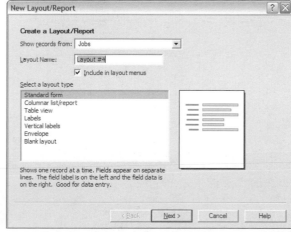

2. **In the Show Records From drop-down list (pop-up menu on the Mac), select the table on which you want to base your layout.**

To create a layout for the Hey, Look at Me! database, I start with the Jobs table.

One option in the Show Records From drop-down list (pop-up menu on the Mac) is Define Database. If you need to create a new layout *and* a new table, you choose this option. Once selected, the standard Define Database dialog box appears, which allows you to create a new table, make changes to existing tables, and manage the table relationships. When you're done, you return to the New Layout/Report Wizard.

3. **In the Layout Name box, type the name for your layout.**

If you select the Include In Layout Menus box, anyone who uses this layout selects it by this name, so choosing a name that describes what the layout does is helpful. For the example database, I'm creating a layout to display the details about a job prospect, so I name my layout **Job Details**.

4. **Select or deselect the Include In Layout Menus check box.**

5. **Select a Blank Layout as your layout type in order to build a custom layout, and click Finish.**

When you're done, FileMaker returns you to Layout mode, with your newly created layout ready for editing, as shown in Figure 4-8. This is typically a good point to set options for the layout, which I explain in the next section.

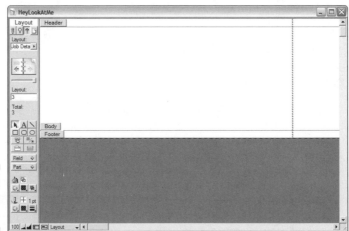

Figure 4-8:
A new,
blank layout.

When you use one of the templates, the wizard lets you select a theme. This allows you to select from FileMaker-provided color schemes that you might want to use for your layout, which makes creating a consistent look a little easier. If you want to create a custom layout that looks similar to a template, go ahead and select the template. Templates can be the foundation for custom layouts because FileMaker enables you to tweak them after you set the template options. Be aware that the *only* time you can specify a layout theme is when you're using the wizard to create the layout — after the layout exists, there is no option to apply a theme to it.

Setting options for a layout

Even though you established many of the layout settings when you used the New Layout/Report Wizard, you can still configure some settings that determine how the layout functions. To access these options, make sure your layout appears in Layout mode, and then choose Layouts➪Layout Setup. The Layout Setup dialog box appears, as shown in Figure 4-9, with tabs for general, viewing, and printing options.

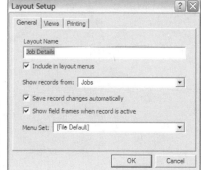

Figure 4-9:
Setting up
your layout.

The following sections give you a tour of the Layout Setup dialog box by tab.

General options

The following options are contained in the General tab of the Layout setup:

- ✔ **Layout Name:** This is the name assigned to the layout.

- ✔ **Include In Layout Menus:** If selected, the name of the layout appears on the layout selection menus. Sometimes, you want to turn this off. For example, if you use a layout for showing a warning message, you wouldn't want a user to be able to select the layout.

- ✔ **Show Records From:** This is where you select which table you want to have associated with the layout.

- ✔ **Save Record Changes Automatically:** When selected, any changes to the data shown on the layout are automatically saved in the database table. Otherwise, you need to create a manual process (via a function or script) to save the data.

- ✔ **Show Field Frames When Record Is Active:** When selected, the currently active field on the layout has a frame border around it. This helps the user see which field is going to receive the keyboard input.

- ✔ **Menu Set:** You can select which menus you want to be available when this layout is active. This is handy when you have your own custom menus just for the layout. (See Chapter 7 for details about creating custom menus.)

Views options

On the Views tab, shown in Figure 4-10, you see three views you can make available under the Browse and Find modes:

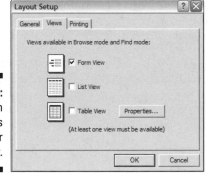

Figure 4-10:
Establish what users see on your layout.

- ✔ **Form View:** Form views are most frequently used to emulate (surprise!) data entry forms.

  For the purpose of the Job Details layout in my example Hey, Look at Me! database, only the Form view is needed.

- ✔ **List View:** List views are most commonly used to provide a scrolling presentation of data, such as when creating a report. Unlike with table views, described next, you can include summary and sub-summary parts to appear on a printed list view report.

✔ **Table View:** Select this view if your users need to see a table of rows and columns that simply reflect the contents of a database table. The column titles contain the names of the database table fields, and each row of the visible table shows a record from the database table. If you click the Properties button next to Table view, you see the options shown in Figure 4-11. The following list describes each option.

- **Grids, Horizontal & Vertical:** If selected, displays the horizontal and/or vertical *grids* (separation lines) in the table.

- **Grid Style:** Lets you choose the color and pattern for displaying the grid.

- **Include Header Part:** If selected, the layout shows the header part.

- **Include Footer Part:** If selected, the layout shows the footer part.

- **Include Column Headers:** When selected, includes the field names in the top row of the table.

- **Resizable Columns:** When selected, allows the user to change the width of the columns.

- **Reorderable Columns:** When selected, allows the user to change the order of the columns.

- **Sort Data When Selecting Column:** When selected, allows the user to change the sort order of the table. When the user clicks the column header, the table is sorted by that column. Pretty cool!

- **Rows, Use Custom Height:** If selected, allows you to set the default height of the rows in pixels, centimeters, or inches.

Figure 4-11:
Change the look and functionality of tables.

Printing options

On the Printing tab, shown in Figure 4-12, you can select some settings for how the layout will print. The following list describes the available options:

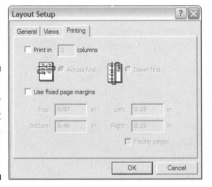

Figure 4-12:
Decide how
your layout
looks on the
printed
page.

✔ **Print In *n* Columns:** When selected, prints the layout in columns — very useful for designing labels.

✔ **Across First / Down First:** Determines the order of printing when using multiple columns.

✔ **Use Fixed Page Margins:** If selected, the values in the Top, Bottom, Left, and Right fields override the default printer settings — useful for printing on labels with tight margins.

✔ **Facing Pages:** When selected, forces the left and right margins to alternate between printed pages — useful for printing for a book format.

Organizing Data within FileMaker's Layout Parts

In FileMaker, each part within the layout handles how the database fields are displayed, and that gives you the ability to control how FileMaker shows the data. In the following sections, I introduce you to the parts you have at your disposal and how they work. I also explain how you size them so that you can fit all the elements you want to include in your layout.

Checking out the available parts

The following list shows the various parts and how they affect the display of data on the layout:

- ✔ **Title header:** This part shows a title at the top of the first page of the layout. It's useful for creating a report that needs a title on the very first page. If the layout includes a header part, this replaces it on the first page of the layout. You can use only one title header on a layout.

- ✔ **Header:** This part displays objects on the layout that need to be displayed at the top of each page (or screen). It's great for placing column titles at the top of each page of a report. Any fields in this part show the first record for that page.

- ✔ **Body:** Just like the body of a letter, this part holds the primary contents of the layout. The body part is repeated for each record displayed. You can have only one body part per layout.

- ✔ **Sub-summary:** If you need to generate subtotals on your layout or reports, use a sub-summary part on your layout. This requires you to use summary fields in the part, a subset of sorted records, and a *break* field that identifies what the sub-summary is for. An example is a SubTotal field on an Invoice layout and the break field is the name of the customer that the invoice is for.

- ✔ **Grand summary:** Similar to the sub-summary part, this part displays summary calculations for all the records (or all the records in a found set, if it's in a search). An example is the grand total at the bottom of an invoice layout or the total number of parts in a inventory layout. See Chapter 5 for more details on working with summaries.

- ✔ **Footer:** This part works just like the header part, except it's at the bottom of the layout. It displays objects on the bottom of every page of the layout. A good example is a layout that shows the page numbers. Any fields in this part show the last record for that page.

- ✔ **Title footer:** The title footer works like the title header, except it's applied to the bottom of the layout — but only on the first page of the layout. It overrides the footer part for the first page only. Any fields in this part show the data in the last record of the first page.

Figure 4-13 shows an example of a layout in Layout mode with four parts and then in Preview mode. Notice how the parts affect the display of the data.

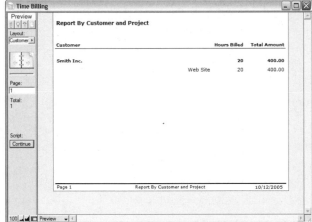

Figure 4-13:
Four parts in
Layout
mode (Top)
and Preview
mode
(Bottom).

Sizing, showing, and hiding parts

You may think that, for an area where you're supposed to create a nice-looking layout, a part is sure small! Well, you're right. And before you can increase the size of an object within a part, you need to change the size of the part itself. Also, you may not need every type of part in every layout you create. Here's how to do a few basic, but essential, moves with the layout parts:

✔ **To size a part:** Click and drag the edge of the part to the desired size.

FileMaker provides some guides for measurement so that you can get a good idea of how to resize the layout. If you choose View➪Graphic Rules, you see a set of rulers for helping you gauge where to place objects on the layout and the size of the layout. Also, notice that as you move the mouse pointer around on the layout, guide lines move along the rulers.

✔ **To hide the part labels:** Click the Part Label Control on the bottom toolbar.

Adding basic objects to a layout

It's time to get out your paintbrush! The blank layout form is your canvas, and you're about to paint a masterpiece! Well, at least this is how I like to think of the process of creating a new layout form. The correct placement of the form objects onto the layout can make the difference between an unreadable, confusing layout, and a pleasant, intuitive layout. In the sections that follow, I explain basic layout maneuvers including setting a layout's size, adding text, moving and resizing objects, adding fields, and more.

If you make a mistake with moving an object, resizing, mistyping some text, or performing just about any action in FileMaker, you can take it back by pressing Ctrl+Z.

Typing text

Usually, the first object that I like to dip my figurative brush into is the Text tool. Using the Text tool can help you get a feel for how the layout is going to be . . . well, laid out. The following steps explain how to utilize this tool.

1. **Select the Text tool from the Tool panel.**

   The cursor changes to a vertical bar that looks like a steel girder when viewed from the end.

2. **Click the cursor where you want to place your text.**

3. **Type your text, and then click the mouse anywhere else on the layout.**

   You now have a text object. The little black squares at each corner of the text object show which object is currently active, and they give you something to grab onto when you want to resize the object.

   By default, the Text tool is a single-use tool. If you need to create several text objects, double-click the Text tool and it locks for multiple objects.

4. **To change attributes of the Text object, right-click (Control+click on a Mac with a one-button mouse) the text object, and choose Text Format from the context menu that appears.**

   You can open a similar context menu for other objects as well. You see this menu a lot as you construct the layout for your database.

5. **In the Text Format For Selected Objects dialog box, shown in Figure 4-14, select the Font, Size, Color, and Style options you want to apply.**

   I tend to like Comic Sans MS as a font for titles. I think maybe it's because of the word *Comic*. But, you can continue to use Arial if you want. With these settings, the title now looks like a real title!

Figure 4-14: Personalize layout text in this dialog box.

6. **When you're done, click OK in the Text Format dialog box to return to your layout.**

   You can edit a text object anytime. Simply double-click it, make your changes, and then click somewhere else on the layout to save the change.

Moving and resizing an object

It's easy to not get the object into the correct spot the first time around. Especially if you drink as much coffee as I do. But that's okay. Just follow this step to move the object to wherever you want it.

1. **Click the object once to select it.**

   You can tell that the object is selected when the little black corner markers surround the object.

2. **Click and drag the object to where you want it, and release the mouse button.**

   Notice that while you drag the object around on the screen, the original image of the object remains in its current location. A border around the dragged object will appear to help you line up the object on the layout.

Changing the size of an object on the layout is just as easy as moving it around. Just click the object once to select it and make the black corner squares appear. Then drag a corner in or out until you reach the desired size. Now, if I could just figure out how to increase the size of my paycheck this way. . . .

If you want to move or resize multiple objects, you can select them in one swoop by clicking just outside the objects and then dragging a selection box around the elements you want. If you want to select all the objects on the layout, simply press Ctrl+A.

Adding fields to the layout

Adding database fields you want to present on the layout is quick and easy. Just follow these steps to put fields from your selected table into the layout:

1. **Click the Field control in the toolbar on the left, and hold down the mouse button while dragging the field box that appears on the layout.**

2. **Release the mouse button when the box is in the correct position.**

   When the field is placed, the Specify Field dialog box appears.

   For the Job Details dialog box, I place the field box at the 1-inch position horizontally and vertically, as shown in Figure 4-15. Remember that if you make a mistake, just press Ctrl+Z to go back and try again.

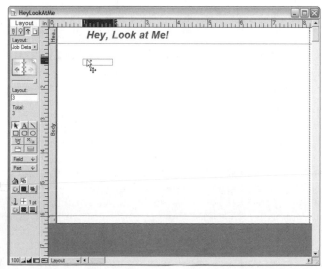

Figure 4-15: Placing a field on the layout.

3. **In the Specify Field dialog box, shown in Figure 4-16, make sure that the table you want is selected at the top.**

4. **Select or deselect the Create Label check box.**

Figure 4-16: Choose a table and create a label.

By leaving the Create Label option selected, the field name is automatically added to the layout as the field label. If you don't like to use the field name as the label on the layout, you can always go back and change it later.

5. **Double-click the field that you want to add to the layout.**

Double-clicking selects the field, closes the Specify Field dialog box, and places the field on the layout — without you clicking OK.

Figure 4-17 shows my Job Details layout after I added all the necessary fields to it.

What a nice stack of fields! Although, they do need a little polishing up, I made some fields bigger, and I still need to shorten the labels for some fields so they don't overlap with the field itself. You can click and drag the corner squares to resize field objects, just as you do with text objects.

Or if you're inclined to size and place objects with mathematical precision, select the object and then choose View⇨Object Size to open the Size palette. Here, you can enter the exact dimensions in inches (or whatever measure you select in your preferences) for the left, top, right, and bottom of the object, as well as the horizontal and vertical placement of the object on the layout as a whole.

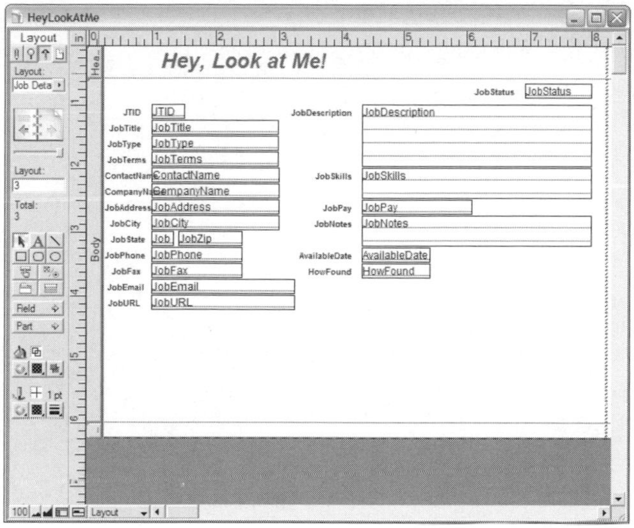

Figure 4-17:
All the fields
on the Job
Details
layout.

Saving and Previewing a Layout

After you create a layout for your database application, I bet you want to see how good it looks. In FileMaker, previewing and saving layouts go hand in hand. Here's how it works:

1. **Select Browse mode from the Tool panel (or choose View⊅Browse Mode).**

   FileMaker displays a dialog box asking if you want to save your changes.

2. **Click Save.**

   You now see how your layout looks when being browsed. Pretty blank eh? That's because you don't have any data in the database yet.

3. **Click the mouse just to the right of the Title label.**

   This puts the database in Edit mode. At least in this mode, you can get a good idea of where the fields are and how the layout looks.

Chapter 5

Whipping the Layout into Shape

In This Chapter

▶ Getting the layout objects to line up

▶ Putting the Format Painter to work

▶ Using graphics to make the layout pretty

▶ Turning a picture into a button

▶ Managing field behavior

▶ Adding subtables to the layout

*A*ll right, you objects! I want you all to snap to attention! Get into proper alignment, and show me your best behavior! You think they listen to me? Of course they do! Because I have the power of FileMaker! Muhahahaha!

You've got the power too. FileMaker has an extensive set of tools and features for making those layouts look nice and orderly. Just take a look at the current view of the Job Details layout in the Hey, Look at Me! database, as shown in Figure 5-1. At first glance, this might look like a nice layout. However, the labels are slightly out of alignment; the font type and style of the labels is too close to the style used for the fields; the black on white is nice for printing, but for a pleasant look on the monitor, it's a little plain. So, what to do? Well, I guess it's time to whip this layout into shape!

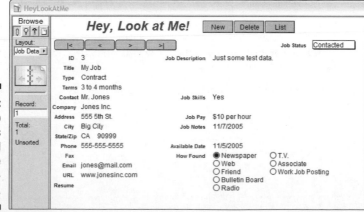

Figure 5-1:
The Job Details layout could use some improvement.

Aligning Objects the Easy Way

Ever see a crooked row of growing corn? If you have, the farmer has been planting while drunk. In a typical cornfield, the rows of plants are nice and straight. Having nice and straight alignment on a FileMaker layout form is appealing as well. Luckily, getting layout elements to line up is easy, as the next steps demonstrate:

1. **In your database, display the layout that needs alignment adjustment in Layout mode.**

   Because this chapter uses the Hey, Look at Me! database for demonstrating functionality, you can use the `HeyLookAtMe-Ch5.fp7` file available at the Web site listed in the Introduction.

   I load the Hey, Look at Me! database and open the Job Details layout — might as well start on the primary form for the application. Notice that the labels on the left are out of alignment.

2. **Select all the objects you want to align by holding down the Shift key and clicking each one. Or you can try dragging a selection box around all of them.**

   I select the labels on the left.

   When selecting multiple objects by dragging a selection box around them, remember that the objects have to be completely within the selection box in order to be selected.

3. **Select an alignment option (Left Edges, Centers, Right Edges, Top Edges) in any of the following ways:**

   Click an alignment tool on the FileMaker toolbar. In my example, I click the Align Right Edges tool. See how easy that is? Notice that the objects align with the farthest right object edge.

   • *Use the pop-up menu.* Right-click (Control+click on a Mac with a one-button mouse) any object in your selection, and choose Arrange➪Align➪Right Edges, as shown in Figure 5-2.

   • *Press the keyboard shortcut.* Press Ctrl+Alt (or ⌘+Option on the Mac), and press the arrow key for the edge you want to align (Left, Right, Top, Bottom). Center and Middle alignment don't have keyboard shortcuts, though.

   The labels are all aligned, nice and straight, and the layout looks a lot better.

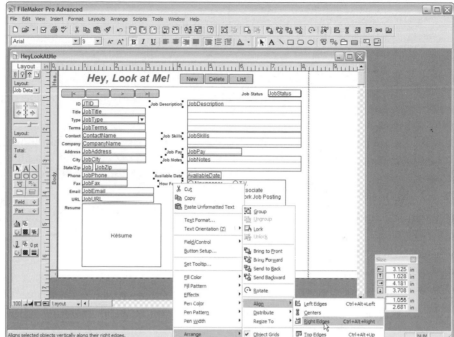

Figure 5-2:
Setting
alignment
via the
menus.

Inserting the Current Date on the Layout

This is not the "How To Put a Picture of Your Date on the Layout" section. Though, with what you know about adding pictures to the layout, you easily could. However, the following step is actually for showing the current calendar date on your layout. (This is so easy, you can do it in one step!)

While in Layout mode, choose Insert⇨Current Date. The current date appears on your layout. You can then change the size, font, and style as needed.

Simplifying Life with the Format Painter

Let's say that after spending an hour on it, you finally find the right font, size, color, and style for your labels. Now that you know what you want, you realize that you have 21 different labels on the layout that you have to change.

Let's see, now . . . that's 21 times 4 selections plus 21 clicks to select the object — that comes to over 105 mouse clicks to make the necessary changes. Better cancel that afternoon online gaming session!

Fortunately, FileMaker has a tool just for this purpose — the Format Painter. You can make all the changes to one label, and then apply those changes to all the other labels on the layout. To show how easy it is to use, just follow the next steps:

1. **Right-click (Control+click on a Mac with a one-button mouse) the label, and select Text Format. In the Text Format dialog box, shown in Figure 5-3, select the options you want the Format Painter to apply. Click OK when you're done.**

   I set options that allow the labels to fit with a little extra spacing.

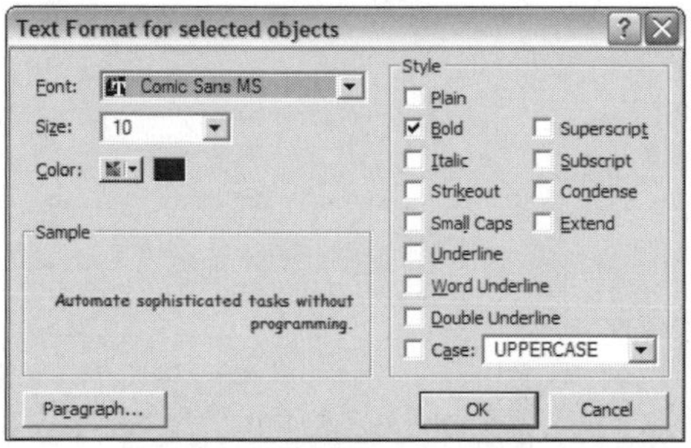

Figure 5-3:
Using Text
Format to
standardize
style.

2. **Double-click the Format Painter tool (it looks, depending upon your perspective, like either a paintbrush or an umpire's whisk broom) on the FileMaker toolbar.**

   By double-clicking the tool, you're telling FileMaker to apply the formatting changes to multiple objects on the layout.

3. **Click each object on the layout that you want to apply the changes to.**

4. **Press the Esc key when you're done.**

   The Esc key toggles off the Format Painter tool.

Adding Pretty Pictures to the Layout

Some color and graphics give your layouts a little pizzazz. Just a simple background picture can help a lot! Also, you can use images as buttons, instead of the boring square buttons.

Inserting a background image

Originally, I wanted to put a picture of my favorite scene from Star Trek on Hey, Look at Me! — but then there's the whole copyright issue, registered trademarks, expensive lawyers, and so on. So, I settled for a little graphic that I put together in my favorite drawing program.

Just use these steps to add a background to your layout:

1. **Put your layout in Layout mode, and choose Insert⇨Picture.**

2. **In the dialog box that appears, select the picture file that you want to insert, and click Open.**

   If you want to experiment with these steps, you can find the graphic file that I use at the Web site mentioned in the Introduction. The filename is `HLMBackground.tif`.

   The picture is added to the layout, but there is a slight problem. The picture is covering up the rest of the objects on the layout. Don't panic! This is easy to fix.

3. **Move the picture so that it covers the entire layout.**

4. **Right-click (Control+click on a Mac with a one-button mouse) the picture, and choose Arrange⇨Send to Back.**

   Isn't that pretty now? All the other layout objects are in front of the picture, as shown in Figure 5-4. Just one last step left for the picture.

5. **With the picture object still selected, click the Lock tool on the FileMaker toolbar.**

   This locks the picture to prevent it from being accidentally moved or deleted.

Using pictures for buttons

Are you tired of the plain gray buttons? If so, there is relief. You can use pictures and graphics for your buttons in FileMaker. The following steps walk you through it:

1. **With your layout in Layout mode, choose Insert⇨Picture.**

2. **Select the image file you want to use as a button in the dialog box that appears.**

   This inserts the picture file on the layout.

3. **Move the picture where you want the button to appear.**

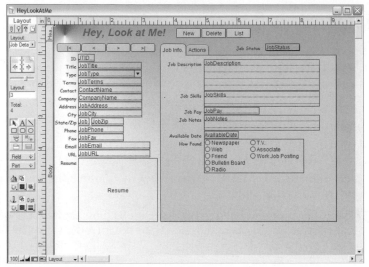

Figure 5-4:
Adding a
background
picture to a
layout.

4. **Right-click (Control+click on a Mac with a one-button mouse) the picture object, and select Button Setup.**

   You now see the Button Setup dialog box with the list of available functions on the left.

5. **Choose the function or script you want to assign to the button, and click OK.**

   That's all there is to it. Feel free to go into Browse mode, and try out your new button.

Adding a border to a button

When you use an image as a button, you might notice that the picture doesn't have the nice black border like the rest of the buttons. To add a border, follow these steps:

1. **Right-click (Control+click on a Mac with a one-button mouse) the picture object, and select Pen Color.**

2. **Select the color for your border — probably black.**

3. **Right-click (Control+click on a Mac with a one-button mouse) the picture object, and select Pen Width. Then select the width you like, such as 1pt.**

   The picture object has a nice border and is in position, just like a regular button.

Make Those Fields Behave

You don't want your layout to just look great; you want it to have brains, too. You want it to anticipate what users will want to do.

Although you can't quite build a database that's as smart as an android (then you wouldn't need to work at all), FileMaker does help you fine-tune the way the fields work. In the sections that follow, you take a tour of the Field Behaviors dialog box, and I explain how you set the tab order so that users can enter data in ways that make sense — and make life easier.

Setting field options

Some folks like pickles on their hot dogs, and some don't. Some folks like their data fields to be completely highlighted when selected, and some don't. That's where the FileMaker Field Behavior options come in. These options allow you to define just how you want the data fields to behave.

You open the Field Behavior dialog box, shown in Figure 5-5, by right-clicking (Control+clicking on a Mac with a one-button mouse) a field and choosing Field/Control➪Behavior. Just what can you do with the Field Behavior options? I thought you'd never ask!

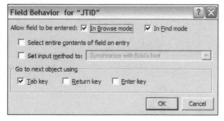

Figure 5-5:
Field
Behavior
dialog box.

✔ **Allow Field To Be Entered:** Using these check boxes, you can tell FileMaker in which modes you want to be able to edit the contents of this field.

For example, in Hey, Look at Me!, the JTID field is a unique identifier that is automatically generated, so there is no need to edit it. The In Browse Mode option and the In Find Mode option can both be deselected.

However, I think the only field in the Jobs table that you don't need to search would be the Resume field because it's a Container field, so you can turn off allowing entry to the Jobs field in Find mode.

✔ **Select Entire Contents Of Field On Entry:** This option tells FileMaker to highlight an entire field when the user selects it. This makes it easier for the user to replace the contents of the field by just typing over the already highlighted data. However, the drawback is that if you accidentally press a key while the field is highlighted, you replace the content of that field by that one keystroke.

✔ **Set Input Method To:** This is for computers that use special input methods for foreign languages. For example, if your OS has an input method configured for entry of Japanese, you would set this field to the appropriate input method for that language.

✔ **Go To Next Object Using:** You can designate the Tab, Return, or Enter key for advancing to the next field. In most cases, the Tab key is used by default.

You might be wondering, if I have 30 fields on the layout, am I going to have to set the Field Behavior for each one individually? That's a good question because it does present a lot of potential steps to go through. Fortunately, FileMaker allows you to select a group of fields and set the Field Behavior, and then the options apply to all the currently selected fields.

Setting the tab order for layout fields

I'm a touch typist. Some folks say that I'm just touched! But, that's another story. As a touch typist, I love software applications that let me type in information as quickly as possible. However, one of the biggest things that I get peeved about is when the application doesn't go to the next field that I think it should go to. For example, if you're typing in a group of addresses, the normal order of data entry would be contact, address, city, state, and zip code. If the entry order was contact, address, zip, city, and state — it wouldn't seem natural.

When designing a layout in FileMaker, consider the proper order of the fields for doing data entry. This is called the *tab order*.

If you've tried doing any data entry in the Hey, Look at Me! database application, you might have noticed that the field order for entering the data was a bit out of whack. Fortunately, FileMaker lets you reset the order of entry for the fields, as the following steps demonstrate:

1. **Open your layout in Layout mode.**

2. **Choose Layouts⇨Set Tab Order.**

   You see the Set Tab Order dialog box and a bunch of arrows on the Job Details layout, as shown in Figure 5-6. Each arrow points to an object on the layout. An arrow that has a number in it indicates the current tab order for that object. As you can see, the tab order on this layout is not exactly the best for doing data entry. Arrows that don't have numbers cannot be tabbed into.

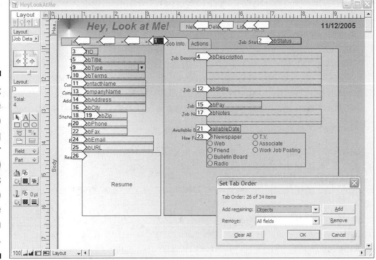

Figure 5-6:
Opening the
Set Tab
Order dialog
box (lower
right)
prompts
FileMaker to
show the
tab order on
the layout.

3. **Click the Clear All button in the Set Tab Order dialog box.**

   This clears all the numbers from the tab order arrows. Now you can set
   the correct tab order for the layout.

4. **Choose an option from the Add Remaining drop-down list/pop-up
   menu (or the Remove drop-down list/pop-up menu if you want to
   limit the tab order to a certain type of object).**

   Your options are Objects (that's anything on the layout), Fields, and
   Buttons. For Remove, you can choose either All Fields or All Buttons.

   For example, notice that no tab order is assigned to the buttons. This
   helps prevent the selection of a button by accident.

5. **On your layout, click the tab order arrows in the order you want the
   tab order to be.**

6. **Click OK on the Set Tab Order dialog box.**

   This saves your tab order changes. You can try it out by switching to
   Browse mode and entering some data. If you need some test data to
   practice with, you can just grab some job ads out of your local newspaper or visit one of the many job-posting sites on the Internet.

I Need a Tooltip!

Sometimes a user can get confused about what type of data to put in a field
or what a specific button does. To cut down on this confusion, FileMaker provides a new feature in FileMaker Pro 8 Advanced called *tooltips*. A *tooltip* is
that cute little box that pops up when you place the mouse cursor over the

top of the object, and it tells you what that object is for. Personally, I think whoever invented the first tooltip should be given a free, two-week, paid vacation to anywhere in the world.

To see how easy these are to add, just step through the following tasks:

1. **In Layout mode, right-click (Control+click on a Mac with a one-button mouse) the object you want to add a tooltip to, and choose Set Tooltip.**

   The Set Tooltip dialog box appears.

2. **In the Tooltip box, enter the text for your tip, and click OK.**

   That's all there is to it! You can check out the result by switching over to Browse mode and hovering the mouse cursor over the New button.

The Set Tooltip dialog box also has a button called Specify. This brings up the Calculation Editor, which can be used for creating a tooltip with a calculated response. (I cover the Calculation Editor in Chapter 3.)

While FileMaker lets you add a *lot* of text to the tooltip, I recommend that you be brief. Especially because the tooltip remains visible for only around five seconds. For example, the following short and sweet tooltips appear on the Hey, Look at Me! layout:

- ✔ **Delete the current record** pops up for the Delete button.
- ✔ **Show the job details** appears for the Job Info tab.
- ✔ **Go to the last record** is the tooltip for the >| button.

Before assigning a tooltip to a Tab Control, you need to select the tab that you want to assign the tooltip to. Then you can right-click the tab text (Control+click on a Mac with a one-button mouse) and assign a tooltip. We talk more about Tab Controls (and tabs) in the next section.

Organizing the Layout into Tabs

File folders are great for keeping pages of information separate. It seems that the folks at FileMaker think so, too, because they decided to add a new Tab Control feature to FileMaker Pro version 8. Tab Control is a great way to present a group of related information on the same layout.

Just follow these steps to place and use Tab Control:

1. **With your layout in Layout mode, click the Tab Control tool on the FileMaker Tool palette.**

2. **Use the mouse to drag a bounding rectangle where you want the tab to appear.**

When you release the mouse, the Tab Control appears on the layout, and the Tab Control Setup dialog box appears, as shown in Figure 5-7. This is where you enter the settings for creating the tabs on the control.

Figure 5-7:
The Tab Control Setup dialog box.

3. **In the Tab Name text box, enter the name you want to appear on the tab, choose a justification and appearance, and click the Create button. Click OK when you're done.**

Each tab you create appears in the Tabs list (upper-left area of the dialog box). Use the Tab Justification drop-down list/pop-up menu to specify whether the tabs appear from left-to-right (Left), from the middle out (Center), from right-to-left (Right) or are sized to fit the width of the Tab Control (Full). The Appearance drop-down list lets you specify whether the tabs have squared or rounded corners.

4. **On the layout, move and resize the tab as needed, as shown in Figure 5-8.**

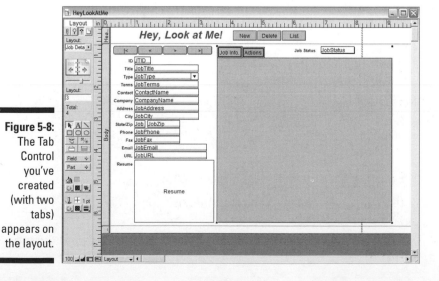

Figure 5-8:
The Tab Control you've created (with two tabs) appears on the layout.

5. When the control is in the correct position, lock its position and size by clicking the Lock tool on the FileMaker toolbar.

This is a very important step. By locking the object, you prevent any accidental movement or selection of the object when you place other objects on top of it — which you're about to do.

For Hey, Look at Me!, I wanted to move the job details to this layout, as shown in Figure 5-9, so I selected them all before I added the Tab Control. Then I right-clicked (Control+clicked on a Mac with a one-button mouse) the Tab Control object and selected Paste Layout Object(s). All those objects that I cut from the layout earlier now reappear on the Tab Control object. Most likely, they are not in the correct position. In Figure 5-9, you can also see that I added rounded corners to the Tab Control.

You can also add objects to your tab by using any of the methods you'd use for a layout.

Figure 5-9:
Adding
objects to
the Tab
Control.

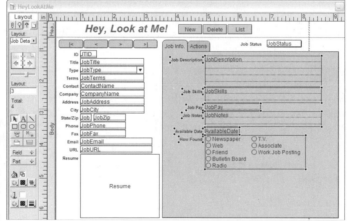

Feel free to try out the Tab Control on the layout — go into Browse mode, first.

While checking it out, you might wonder what the Actions tab is for. Remember that the idea of tabbed layout is that you can group different categories of information on one handy layout. I added this tab as well for displaying another group of information, which I add as a subtable, explained in the next section.

FileMaker developers in the past thought that tabbed layouts were such a good idea that they designed their database applications to look like they had Tab Controls by adding invisible buttons and using script programming to switch to another layout. Chapter 3 introduces scripts.

It's Mini-Me! — Adding Subtables

If Austin Powers were a programmer, he would use FileMaker — just because it's so easy to create mini-tables to place on the layout. The ability to show multiple, related tables on the same layout is a very powerful feature of FileMaker. I recently watched a friend of mine try to do this with the C# programming language and a SQL database. He spent a good four hours, interspersed with colorful metaphors, getting it to work the way he wanted. I came close to telling him that I could do it in FileMaker with around 30 minutes of work, but I felt safer just keeping quiet.

Using a subtable on the layout requires that a relationship is established between the *parent table* (the table associated with the layout), and the *child table* (the table you want to have in the subtable). See Chapter 2 for details on setting table relationships.

To add a subtable (which you view through a portal) to the layout, follow these steps:

1. **With your layout in Layout mode, click the Portal tool on the FileMaker Tool palette.**

2. **Drag a control box on your layout.**

   I add mine to the Actions Tab Control. When you release the mouse, the Portal Setup dialog box appears, as shown in Figure 5-10.

3. **From the Show Related Records From drop-down list/pop-up menu, select the Actions table.**

   This is a child table with a relationship to the Jobs table. The purpose of this table is to show any actions associated with the currently displayed job opportunity.

Figure 5-10:
Adding a subtable to the layout.

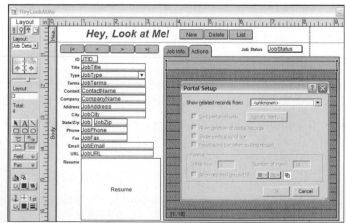

4. **Click the Sort Portal Records check box.**

   The Sort Records dialog box appears. In my example, because these are Action items associated with the current Job opportunity, it makes sense to set the sort on the date of the action.

5. **Select the field you want to use for sorting, and then click the Move button. Highlight the field in the Sort Order list box, and then select the Ascending Order or Descending Order radio button. Click OK.**

   I choose Descending Order because with dates, you usually want to have the most current date at the top of the table and the older dates at the bottom.

6. **If you like, click the Allow Deletion Of Portal Records check box.**

   I select this box because I want to allow the user to delete records directly from the table.

7. **If you like, select the Show Vertical Scroll Bar check box.**

   I select the box because there can be more than 18 actions associated with a single Job opportunity (unlikely, but possible), and I want to be able to scroll through the records in the table.

8. **Click the Reset Scroll Bar When Exiting Record check box if you want FileMaker to reset the scroll bar back to the first record in the portal when you are done editing a record.**

9. **Set the Initial Row and Number Of Rows in the text boxes near the bottom of the dialog box.**

   Keeping the Initial Row at 1 means that you want only the first row of the table to show in the portal by default. The setting 18 in Number Of Rows indicates that I want the portal to always show 18 rows.

10. **If you want to set the color, click the Alternate Background Fill check box. Then click the color control box. Select a color that you like.**

    When selected, this places the colored background behind every other row in the portal. This makes it easier to see the individual records in the portal table. You can always come back and change the color later if you don't like the one you selected.

    The control next to the color control box is for selecting a texture for the background. I usually go with the default, but you can play around with it and see what you like. (Warning: I once spent an entire hour trying to decide what color and texture I wanted for my portal rows background.)

11. **Click OK in the Portal Setup dialog box when you're done.**

    Now the Add Fields To Portal dialog box appears, as shown in Figure 5-11.

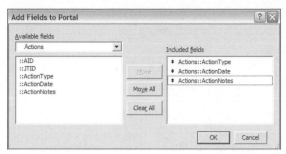

Figure 5-11:
Add Fields
To Portal
dialog box.

12. Select the fields you want to have appear in the portal. Click OK when you're done.

In our example, we select the ActionType, ActionDate, and ActionNotes fields from the Actions table.

Congrats! You've just added a subtable to the Job Details layout. However, you might notice that the fields on the portal could use a little adjusting.

13. Select all three of the fields at the top of the Tab Control, and then drag them down into the first row of the portal.

The fields should fit evenly between the top and bottom border of the first row in the portal.

Now that you have the portal on the layout, you might want to make some adjustments to the fields. First of all, you'll want to add some column titles at the top of the table. Then adjust the widths of the fields to appropriate sizes. So, what-cha waiting on? Get started with these steps:

✔ **To move the subtable:** Click it once to select it, and use the arrow keys to move it.

✔ **To size a field:** Click it once to select it, and use the Size Control to set the width. (If you don't have the Size Control showing, choose View➪ Object Size.)

✔ **To add labels:** Use the Label tool from the FileMaker Tool palette, as shown in Figure 5-12.

You can switch over to Browse mode to see how it looks.

When working with the Tab Control, the tab that is currently active during a save is the default tab to be viewed when switching to Browse mode. Usually, you want the first tab in the control to be the default. So, just remember to click the first tab, and save your database.

Figure 5-12:
Labels at
the top of
the portal.

Adding a Grand Summary

You can put data on tabs, and you can show data in tables. But, can you summarize data on your layout? Of course you can! You do this by using the grand summary layout part. *Layout parts,* which I introduce in Chapter 2, are basically special areas of the layout.

As you can see in the following steps, the grand summary part is a good tool for generating totals (or averages) for your data:

1. **Open the layout in which you want to add a grand summary. Make sure it's in Layout mode.**

   If you'd like to follow along with my example, load the `Products.fp7` database (which is available from the Web site mentioned in the Introduction), and open the Product List layout. This database contains one table named Products, which holds some sample data of exotic food products. It even has a record for escargot! Yum! Figure 5-13 shows the Products table in Layout mode. There are currently two layout parts on this layout — the header and the body.

2. **Click and hold the mouse button on the Part tool from the Tool palette, and drag the mouse onto the layout below the current layout parts.**

   The Part Definition dialog box appears.

3. **Select the Trailing Grand Summary option, and click OK.**

   This tells FileMaker that you want to use the grand summaries part that you just added to the bottom of the layout.

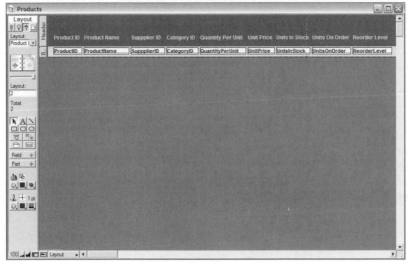

Figure 5-13:
Products
List.

4. **Size the grand summary layout part by dragging the bottom edge up until the part is big enough to hold the fields you want to include in your summary.**

   Now, in order to add summary fields to this part, you need to create the necessary summary fields in the table.

5. **Click the Define Database button on the FileMaker toolbar.**

   The Define Database dialog box opens. In my example, the required Summary fields need to be added to the Products table.

6. **In the Field Name box, enter a name that describes what you want to see in the grand summary. In the Type drop-down list/pop-up menu, select Summary. Then click the Create button.**

   In my example, I want to show the total units in stock, so I name the field **TotalUnits**.

   After you click Create, your new Summary field is added to your table, and the Options For Summary Field dialog box appears, as shown in Figure 5-14. This is where you indicate what type of summary you want to generate.

7. **On the left side of the Options For Summary Field dialog box, select one of the following options:**

   • *Total Of:* Computes a total of the values in the field specified. This is the default and the one I select for my example TotalUnits summary, because I want to see the total number of units added together.

   • *Average Of:* Computes the arithmetic mean (average) of the values in the specified field.

Figure 5-14:
Options For
Summary
Field.

- *Count Of:* Computes the number of records having a value in the specified field.

- *Minimum:* Returns the smallest value in the specified field.

- *Maximum:* Returns the largest value in the specified field.

- *Standard Deviation Of:* Computes the standard deviation (how much values vary from one another) for the values in the specified field. If you want to know all the nitty-gritty about standard deviation, check a statistics text.

- *Fraction Of Total Of:* Computes the quotient of the specified field's value divided by the total of all the fields' values.

8. **On the right side of the dialog box, select the field that you want FileMaker to summarize.**

   I select the UnitsInStock field, which holds the number of units I have for each product.

9. **Select from the other options, if you need them.**

- *Running Total:* Total of the field's values for records up to (and including) the current record.

- *Restart Summary For Each Sorted Group:* Restart the computation each time the sorted value changes for the specified sorted field. This is useful when computing sub-summary data.

- *All Together:* This tells FileMaker to compute a single summary value for all repetitions in a repeating field.

- *Individually:* This tells FileMaker to compute separate summary values for each repetition in a repeating field.

10. Click OK to return to the Define Database dialog box.

11. Repeat Steps 6 through 10 if you want to add any other summaries to the grand summary layout part.

If you're following my example, repeat the steps to add a field for Total of UnitsOnOrder. Choose Total Of for the summary option, and select the UnitsOnOrder field as the field to summarize.

You can see the added Summary fields in the Define Database dialog box shown in Figure 5-15.

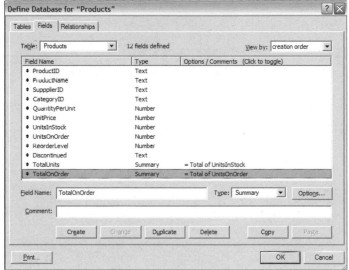

12. Click OK to close the Define Database dialog box.

You now have the necessary table fields for adding to the trailing grand summary layout part. FileMaker thinks that you want to add them to your layout in the body layout part, which can be seen on the current Products List layout. Normally, this is true. However, in this case, you want them in the summary part. Unfortunately, FileMaker just doesn't have the I-know-exactly-what-you-want-to-do module yet.

13. Move the newly added fields and labels to the summary layout part, as shown in Figure 5-16. Then resize the body layout part if needed.

Now you can test it out.

Figure 5-16:
Reposition-
ed fields.

14. **Switch to Browse mode. Scroll to the bottom of the list.**

You'll now see your Summary fields at the bottom of the list with the grand totals for Units in Stock (TotalUnits), and Units on Order (TotalOnOrder), as shown in Figure 5-17.

Product ID	Product Name	Supplier ID	Category ID	Quantity Per Unit	Unit Price	Units In Stock	Units On Order	Reorder Level
61	Sirop d'erable	29	2	24 - 500 ml bottles	28.5	113	0	25
62	Tarte au sucre	29	3	48 pies	49.3	17	0	0
63	Vegie-spread	7	2	15 - 625 g jars	43.9	24	0	5
64	Wimmers gute	12	5	20 bags x 4 pieces	33.25	22	80	30
65	Louisiana Fiery	2	2	32 - 8 oz bottles	21.05	76	0	0
66	Louisiana Hot	2	2	24 - 8 oz jars	17	4	100	20
67	Laughing	16	1	24 - 12 oz bottles	14	52	0	10
68	Scottish	8	3	?	12.5	6	10	15
69	Gudbrandsdalsost	15	4	10 kg pkg.	36	26	0	15
7	Uncle Bob's	3	7	12 - 1 lb pkgs.	30	15	0	10
70	Outback Lager	7	1	24 - 355 ml bottles	15	15	10	30
71	Fløtemysost	15	4	10 - 500 g pkgs.	21.5	26	0	0
72	Mozzarella di	14	4	24 - 200 g pkgs.	34.8	14	0	0
73	Röd Kaviar	17	8	24 - 150 g jars	15	101	0	5
74	Longlife Tofu	4	7	5 kg pkg.	10	4	20	5
75	Rhönbräu	12	1	24 - 0.5 l bottles	7.75	125	0	25
76	Lakkalikööri	23	1	500 ml	18	57	0	20
77	Original	12	2	12 boxes	13	32	0	15
8	Northwoods	3	2	12 - 12 oz jars	40	6	0	0
9	Mishi Kobe Niku	4	6	18 - 500 g pkgs.	97	29	0	0

TotalUnits 3119   TotalOnOrder 780

Figure 5-17:
Products
List with
Summary
fields.

Chapter 6

Finding and Sorting Your Data

* * *

* * *

*I*f you have ever moved from one house to another, you know what a nightmare it is! Especially if you have a bunch of unmarked boxes. What I really like, though, is when I help my friends move. I throw in a box that I packed with junk from my own place. Then I wait for the stories later about how they found a strange box full of stuff they never saw before. (Snicker.)

When moving a bunch of boxes from one location to another, if they're not sorted or marked, it becomes a major pain in the seat. You feel the same pain if you can't find the data that you want. FileMaker shines in avoiding that pain. Not only does FileMaker have a very sophisticated search function, but it also provides functions for easily sorting your data.

If you need a FileMaker database to work with to try your hand at the searching and sorting tasks covered in this chapter, you can download the Hey, Look at Me! database file for this chapter from the Web site mentioned in the Introduction. This file has some additional data for searching and sorting, and I've included some code for supporting the addition of Actions records, which are records providing an audit trail of the actions you've performed.

Searching for Data

Searching for data in FileMaker is actually very easy. You can almost do it blindfolded. But then, it would be hard to see the results. Anyway, the following sections walk you through all the basic searching tricks you need to know. I start with a simple search and then explain a few tricks for fine-tuning your search results — a must when you're sifting through tons of data. And for those searches you do all the time, I explain how to pack all those steps into one little button — so you can make FileMaker do most of the work for you while you grab a cup of coffee.

Doing a simple search

As the following steps show, searching is as easy as clicking a button and entering some text:

1. **Launch the database that you want to search.**

   The Hey, Look at Me! database opens in the Jobs Listing layout view, which lists specifics about job titles, job types, company names, cities, and so on under the respective column (or field) names.

2. **Select Find mode by clicking the Find mode tool on the Tool palette.**

   Notice that the layout is now showing just the core field names of the Jobs table, as shown in Figure 6-1.

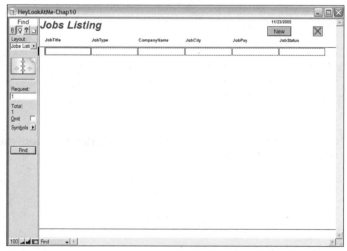

Figure 6-1:
A database
in Find mode
can look
something
like this.

3. **Type your search term in the text box for the field that contains the data you want to find. Then click the Find button on the Tool palette.**

   For example, in the Hey, Look at Me! database, I type **PC** in the JobTitle field.

After you click Find, FileMaker shows the records that match the entered search criteria (or the record, if there's only one match). Notice that the Tool palette shows that there is 1 matching record out of 14 total records. (See Figure 6-2.)

Figure 6-2:
A search result shows the record of the matching item(s).

Returning to view all the records is just a single click away. Just click the Show All Records tool on the FileMaker toolbar, and they reappear, sending FileMaker into Browse mode.

Narrowing a search criteria

Every now and then, you might want to be very specific about what you want. Just like when ordering coffee at the latest trendy coffee house: "Yes, I'd like a double, nonfat, vanilla latte with extended pulls." At least with FileMaker, you can progressively filter down your search criteria to find just what you want. The following steps show how you can do this:

1. **Open your database in the layout that shows the data you want to search. Click the Find mode tool.**

   In the Hey, Look at Me! sample database, I start in the Jobs Listing layout. This time my search is focused on the JobStatus field.

2. **Type your search term in the text box for the field you want to search. Then click the Find button on the Tool palette.**

   I type **sent** in the JobStatus field, click Find, and see three records that match the Sent Resume criteria in the JobStatus field. However, I'm interested in seeing only the Full Time job positions, and that information is listed in the JobType field.

3. **Choose Records⇨Modify Last Find (or press Ctrl+R on a PC, press ⌘+R on a Mac).**

   This shows the last search criteria that you entered.

4. **Type a second search term in the text box for another field, and then click the Find button.**

   I use the Tab key to move to the JobType field and type **full**. Now the list displays the jobs that meet the Full Time and Sent Resume criteria.

Omitting a record from the search

Sometimes you get a little more than what you want. For example, you might want to remove duplicate records from a database. When you perform your Find operation, you will get all the matching records — both the one copy of each you want to retain and the duplicate entries. Before you can remove the duplicates, you need to omit the originals from the set of found records. In those cases where your search result has given you too much information, you might want to omit some data. Here are some easy steps for doing just that:

1. **Open your database, and click the Find mode button.**

2. **Type your search term in the text box for the field you want to search. Then click the Find button (or just press Enter/Return).**

   I Tab over to the JobType field and type **contract**. After clicking Find, a list of only the Contract jobs appears. Notice that there are a total of five records showing.

3. **Click a record, such as My Job at the top of the list, to select it.**

   This takes you to the Job Details layout for this specific record. Because this job pays only $10 per hour and the others in the list look better, you decide to omit this specific record from your search.

 4. **Click the Omit Record button on the FileMaker toolbar (or press Ctrl+T, or ⌘+T on a Mac) to make the result disappear.**

   In the case of my example, the omitted job is no longer a part of the search results. The next available record that matches the search criteria is now being shown. Click the List button to return to the Jobs Listing layout.

   Notice that there are now only four records showing. However, what do you do if you want to see the records that have been omitted?

Viewing omitted records

If you've omitted a number of records from your search results, then you might realize that you want to bring one of the records back into the results.

The next steps assume that you are continuing from the previous set of steps:

1. **After doing a search (and with your results displayed), click the Show Omitted button on the FileMaker toolbar.**

   You see a list of all the records in the table which do not match the previous search criteria that you entered.

2. **Click the record that you previously omitted (see the preceding section) and want to add back to your search results.**

3. **Click the Omit Record button (or press Ctrl + T, or ⌘+T on a Mac).**

   Basically, you're omitting the record from the omitted records. But this doesn't mean that the record disappears.

4. **Click the List button.**

   Your omitted record reappears with the search results. Click the Show All button on the FileMaker toolbar to return to the standard Browse mode with no search results.

Creating a button to do your search automatically

Computer users are inherently lazy. If they can do something with a single click, they avoid anything with multiple steps, especially when it comes to repetitive tasks. Fortunately, FileMaker provides the ability to create a custom search, which you can assign to a button or script. This is a great feature if there's a search you find yourself doing over and over.

Just look at the following steps to see how easy it is:

1. **Start by opening your database in the layout that contains the data you want to search.**

2. **Click the Layout mode button.**

   For the purpose of showing how this is done, I'll have you use a button for the custom search function.

   If you're not the database owner and you can't get into Layout mode, you don't have permission to create the button. See Chapter 11 for details about permission. But if you don't have it, you need to ask whomever owns the database if you can get permission to create search buttons.

3. **Click the Button tool on the Tool palette. When the button appears on your layout, drag it to the desired position.**

   As shown in Figure 6-3, after the button is positioned, the Button Setup dialog box appears.

New button object

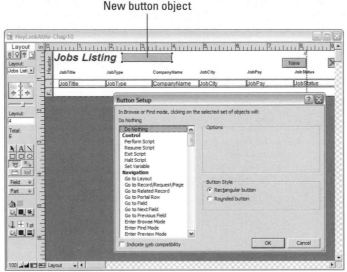

Figure 6-3:
Custom
search
button
placement.

4. **In the function list on the left side of the dialog box, scroll down to the Found Sets section and select the Perform Find function. Then click the Specify button that appears.**

The Specify Find Requests dialog box appears. This is where you define any custom searches that you want to use in FileMaker. After a Find Request is defined, it's always available in this dialog box for use by buttons or scripts. But first, you need to create the Find Request.

5. **In the Specify Find Requests dialog box, click New.**

The Edit Find Request dialog box appears. This is where you build the Find Request.

In my example, I want to search for all JobTypes of Contract and in the city of Miniville.

6. **Because you're performing a search, keep the Action set at Find Records selection. In the Find Records When drop-down list (pop-up menu on a Mac), make sure the correct table is selected.**

If you opened your database to the layout you want to use in Step 1, these options should be okay.

7. **Select the field you want to search in the Find Records When list box.**

8. **Click once in the Criteria box to the right, and enter the term you want to search for. Then click the Add button. Repeat this step and further refine your search by adding search terms for additional fields.**

The Edit Find Request dialog box should look like Figure 6-4. In my example, I added a criteria for *contract* and then added a second criteria for the city of *Miniville*, which you see in Figure 6-5.

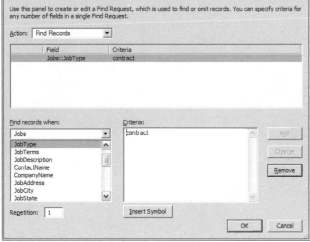

Figure 6-4:
Define your search in the Edit Find Request dialog box.

9. **Click the OK button.**

The Specify Find Requests dialog box now has an entry in it for the new search criteria. (See Figure 6-5.)

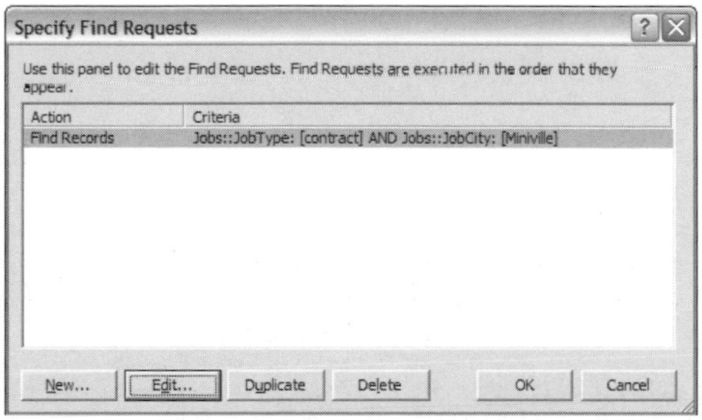

Figure 6-5:
New search criteria appear in the Specify Find Requests dialog box.

10. **Click the OK button in the Specify Find Requests dialog box. Click OK to close the Button Setup dialog box.**

You now have a button that runs your custom search criteria.

11. **Click the Text tool on the Tools palette, and double-click your button to add text to your button.**

    In our example, I name the button Contract Jobs Miniville.

12. **Click the Browse button to switch to Browse mode. Then click your new custom search button.**

    As shown in Figure 6-6, the list has been filtered based on the search criteria used when the button is clicked.

Figure 6-6:
Custom
search
results.

Putting Your Jobs in Order (By Sorting)

It's amazing how much paper shuffling still goes on in this high-technology world. Especially in government offices! If you want to see how upset a government file clerk can get, just try reorganizing the sort order of his file cabinet. If you don't get shot or severely beaten, I'm sure you'll experience some colorful metaphors that would make a sailor blush. Sorting seems to be a very personal thing. Even on computer desktops, users have their own preference for sorting their files, icons, and folders.

Just to keep everyone happy, FileMaker provides an easy-to-use process for sorting your data. Here, I show you how to do basic sort. Then you find out how to take your sorting up a notch — sorting by multiple columns or even deciding on your own sort order.

Sorting A to Z and 1, 2, 3

The following tasks take you through sorting your data:

1. **Open the layout with the data you want to sort in Browse mode.**

   Using the Hey, Look at Me! database, I load the Jobs Listing layout, which shows the list of jobs in the Jobs table.

2. **Click the Sort tool on the FileMaker toolbar.**

   As shown in Figure 6-7, the Sort Records dialog box appears. This is where you define how you want the Jobs table sorted. The top-left selection list is for selecting which layout or table the sort order will be applied to. For my example, I use the default Jobs Listing layout for defining the sort.

Figure 6-7:
Define a
sort in the
Sort
Records
dialog box.

3. **In the field list on the left, select the field on which you want to base your sort. Then click the Move button (or just double-click the field name) to move it to the Sort Order box on the right.**

   For this example, I base my sort on the CompanyName field. You can add as many fields as you like. The first field in the list is the primary sort, the second field in the list is sorted next, and so on.

   Notice that on the Sort Records dialog box, little up and down arrows appear just to the left of the fields in the Sort Order box. These let you drag the fields up or down to change precedence of the fields for the sort order. You just click and drag an arrow, and the associated field moves to where you place it.

4. **Choose a sort order for Ascending, Descending, or Custom.**

   For details on how to set up a custom sort order, see the next section.

5. **Click the Sort button.**

   The Jobs Listing layout is now sorted by the CompanyName field, as shown in Figure 6-8.

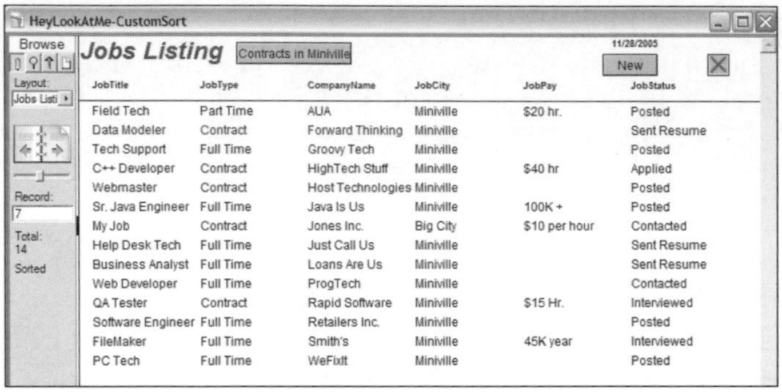

Figure 6-8:
Records are
sorted by
Company
Name in
ascending
(A-to-Z)
order.

6. **To cancel the sort, just click the Sort button on the FileMaker toolbar, and then click the Unsort button in the Sort Records dialog box.**

This cancels any sorts that are currently employed. Now, what about sorting on multiple fields?

Setting up a custom sort order

There are times when you just want to step outside of the ordinary. There are times when the structure of the alphabet or the increment of numbers is just not going to work. In those situations, FileMaker provides a Custom sort order. Think of it as a way to define your own alphabet. For example, in our example database, we have a JobType field that can contain only certain values, and neither an alphabetic nor numeric sort reflects the priority of the various job classifications. To see how defining a custom sort order works, just follow these steps to sort the records based upon the possible job category priority:

1. **Follow Steps 1–3 in the preceding section to move a field into the Sort Order box in the Sort Records dialog box.**

2. **Double-click the JobType field to select it for the sort. Highlight the JobType field in the right Sort Order box.**

When the field is selected, the various Sort Order options become available, via the radio buttons, as shown in Figure 6-9.

3. **Select the Custom Order Based On Value List option, and in the drop-down list (pop-up menu on a Mac), select the Job Type List.**

Notice that the icon next to the JobType field in the Sort Order box has changed to show that the sort order is now a custom sort. The Job Type List is a list that was defined for use when doing data entry of new job postings. However, it can also be used for defining the order that you want to sort the records in the Jobs Listing layout. Now the sort order is:

1. Full Time
2. Part Time
3. Contract
4. Temporary
5. Commission

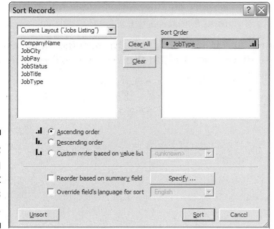

Figure 6-9: Exploring other Sort Records options.

4. **Click the Sort button.**

   Now the sort order of the Jobs Listing is the same order as in the Job Type List, as shown in Figure 6-10.

JobTitle	JobType	CompanyName	JobCity	JobPay	JobStatus
FileMaker	Full Time	Smith's	Miniville	45K year	Interviewed
Sr. Java Engineer	Full Time	Java Is Us	Miniville	100K +	Posted
Software Engineer	Full Time	Retailers Inc.	Miniville		Posted
PC Tech	Full Time	WeFixIt	Miniville		Posted
Help Desk Tech	Full Time	Just Call Us	Miniville		Sent Resume
Business Analyst	Full Time	Loans Are Us	Miniville		Sent Resume
Tech Support	Full Time	Groovy Tech	Miniville		Posted
Web Developer	Full Time	ProgTech	Miniville		Contacted
Field Tech	Part Time	AUA	Miniville	$20 hr.	Posted
My Job	Contract	Jones Inc.	Big City	$10 per hour	Contacted
QA Tester	Contract	Rapid Software	Miniville	$15 Hr.	Interviewed
Data Modeler	Contract	Forward Thinking	Miniville		Sent Resume
C++ Developer	Contract	HighTech Stuff	Miniville	$40 hr	Applied
Webmaster	Contract	Host Technologies	Miniville		Posted

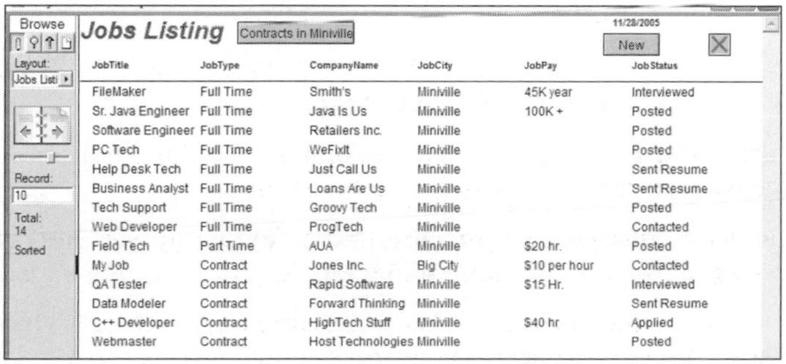

Figure 6-10: This custom sort shows records of Full Time JobTypes first.

Adding a button to sort columns

I know you've been wanting to know how to do this! It's a cool feature that has become so common that many computer users just automatically expect it to be there. I'm talking about the ability to click a column header to sort the table by that column. Can it be done in FileMaker? You bet it can! Here's how:

1. **Open the layout, and switch to Layout mode, where you want to make clicking the column headers initiate a sort.**

   Starting with the first column, you will be adding a function to the column title for performing a sort on the data.

2. **Right-click (Control+click if you're using a one-button mouse) the text label for the column and select Button Setup from the context menu that appears. (See Figure 6-11.)**

   Figure 6-11 shows how I selected the text of the JobTitle column header.

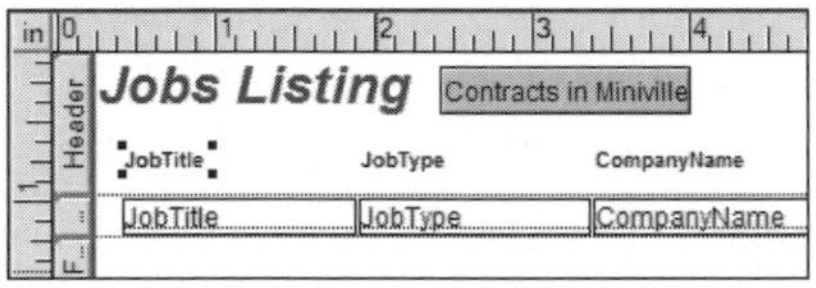

Figure 6-11:
JobTitle
column text
selected.

3. **In the function list, scroll down to the Found Sets section, select the Sort Records function, and then click the Specify button.**

4. **Double-click the name of the field whose header you selected in Step 2.**

   I double-click the JobTitle field so it moves to the SortOrder box with the default sort order of Ascending. *Note:* You can clear any fields that might be in the Sort Order box by clicking the Clear All button.

5. **Click OK to close the Sort Records dialog box.**

6. **In the Button Setup dialog box, select the Perform Without Dialog check box.**

   This performs the function without displaying the Sort Records dialog box, when the JobTitle text is clicked.

7. Click OK, and you're done setting up the button.

You just assigned a Sort function to the JobTitle text, which makes it act just like a clickable button. However, you might want to increase the size of the text to the same size as the column. This makes it easier for the user to click for doing a sort. You can do this by choosing View⇨Object Size and entering a value for the button size in the Size palette. You can repeat these steps to add a button for each column.

To use your column sort button, make sure you're in Browse mode and then simply click it. You'll notice that the cursor changes to a hand over the text to show that this is a clickable object.

Chapter 7

Making FileMaker Do Tricks

I have a smart dog. She knows how to shake hands, sit up, roll over, speak on signal, sit, lay down, walk next to me, and even how to balance a piece of cheese on her nose. Yes, she has taught me well. Every time she does tricks, I've been taught to give her a treat.

FileMaker is good at doing tricks too, and you don't need to feed it. By tricks, I'm talking about functionality. The number of things that FileMaker is capable of doing is amazing. It's just a matter of showing the owner how to use these functions. In this chapter, you find out how to add buttons and assign functions to them and add drop-down lists, pop-up menus, check boxes, radio buttons, and custom menus to your layouts. FileMaker makes creating these features easy, and they can make your layouts much easier to use.

Buttoning Up the Layout

Buttons are a handy way to add functionality to a layout. For example, in Figure 7-1, the layout on the top is perfectly functional with the built-in features of FileMaker. However, compare it to the layout on the bottom, which has more functionality built into the layout itself. The buttons reflect common tasks that users will want to do — navigating records, adding and deleting records, and switching to a list of records — and thus make the layout easier to use.

Figure 7-1:
Adding
buttons
makes a
layout
easier to
use.

Okay, are you sitting down? Oh, yeah — that's right — you're at your computer. I just didn't want you to fall over when you see how easy it is to add functional buttons to the layout. Follow these steps to add functional buttons to your layout:

1. **With the layout open in the Layout mode, click the Button tool on the FileMaker Tool palette.**

   The mouse pointer turns into a plus sign (+).

   If you want to experiment with these steps by using the Hey, Look at Me! database application, download `HeyLookAtMe-Ch7.fp7` from the sites listed in the Introduction.

2. **Where you want the button to appear, click and drag to create a rectangle box, as shown in Figure 7-2.**

   After you place the button, the Button Setup dialog box appears (shown in Figure 7-3).

   Don't worry if you get it in a weird spot. You can always move and resize it later.

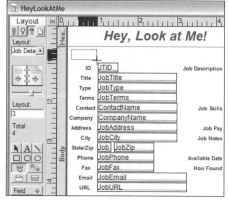

Figure 7-2:
Positioning
a button on
the layout.

3. **On the left of the Button Setup dialog box, select the function you want the button to perform.**

   For example, for my first navigation button, I selected the Go to Record/Request/Page function (in the Navigation section).

   If you're unsure which function to select, the appendix in this book explains each FileMaker function in detail.

   If you're creating a layout for the Web, check the Indicate Web Compatibility check box. When selected, only the functions that support Web functionality are available. (Chapter 12 has the details on putting a database on the Web.)

4. **In the Options area, select any options for the function you selected.**

Figure 7-3:
The Button
Setup dialog
box.

These options are specific to the function that you selected in Step 3. Here are a few examples from the various buttons I added to my example layout:

- For my navigation button, the only option is the Specify drop-down list, which enables the user to select the record to be displayed. I left it at First, the default, because I want this button to take the user to the first record in the found set.

- When I created the Delete button, I selected the Delete Record/Request function and got an option for Perform Without Dialog box. I made sure this option was deselected, because I wanted a dialog box to appear so that the user can confirm that yes, the record should be deleted and clicking the button wasn't a mistake.

- When I created the List button, I selected the Go to Layout function, which displays the records in a list. In this case, the Options area lets me choose which layout to show when a user clicks the List button.

5. **Choose a button style — either rectangular or rounded.**

6. **Select the Change to Hand Cursor Over Button check box, if you prefer.**

   When selected, a hand cursor appears when the user moves the mouse over the button. This option shows users that they can click the button to perform a function. You may be thinking, "Isn't it obvious that it's a button?" Well, FileMaker allows you to use graphic pictures as buttons. So, users may not realize that they can click the graphic. For details about how to add pictures as either backgrounds or buttons, see Chapter 5.

7. **Click OK in the Button Setup dialog box to return to your layout.**

   You now see a blank button with a blinking text cursor in the middle of it.

8. **Type a name for your button (I added |<). Then click the mouse somewhere else on the layout.**

   Congrats! You just created a button on the layout. My navigation button goes to the first record in the database when it is clicked.

9. **If the button's position and size are off, use the settings in the Object Size palette, as shown in Figure 7-4.**

   Of course, you could reposition and resize by dragging, but unless you have incredible eyesight and manual mouse control, you won't be as precise or consistent as you will be by entering exact coordinates and sizes.

As you do more work with objects on the layout, the Object Size palette is handy to have open off to the side of the layout form. If you don't have it open, choose View➪Object Size.

Figure 7-4:
The Object
Size palette.

Size		
←	0.333	in
↑	0.653	in
→	1.097	in
↓	0.917	in
↔	0.764	in
↕	0.264	in

If you're creating a set of buttons that all need to look the same, such as the navigation bar in my example, select your button and press Ctrl+D (⌘+D on the Mac) to duplicate it. Then just move your new button to the desired location. Press Ctrl+D (⌘+D) for as many buttons as you need, all spaced consistently with the first button. Then just repeat Steps 3–9, substituting the unique options for each one.

Putting a Data Field to Work

One of the really cool features in FileMaker is the ability to assign functions to just about any object on a layout form. One way to use this feature is for loading a new layout when the user clicks a field. For example, after adding a list button that jumps from an individual record to a list of all the records, I added a function to all the fields in the list layout. With a click, users are magically back on the layout.

Follow these steps to add a function to an object on your form:

1. **Open your layout in Layout mode.**

   In my example, I loaded the Jobs Listing layout, which has a single row of fields. When in Browse mode, a list of the records in the Hey, Look at Me! database shows.

2. **Select the fields to which you want to add a function. If you're selecting multiple fields, hold Shift while clicking to select all the fields at once.**

   I selected all six fields, because I want to assign the exact same function to all of them.

   Selecting all the fields enables you to assign the same options to all at once.

3. **Right-click (Control+click if you're using a one-button mouse) a selected field and choose Button Setup from the context menu that appears.**

   The Button Setup dialog box appears (refer to Figure 7-3).

4. **Select a function from the list on the left, and then select any options for that function in the Options area.**

   I selected Go to Layout from the function list and then selected Job Details from the Specify list. Now, when a user clicks any of the fields, FileMaker loads and displays the Job Details layout.

5. **Click the Browse mode tool.**

   Now that you've added functionality to the fields, it's a good time to test it.

6. **Click the record.**

   And suddenly, you're back on the Job Details layout. Feel free to jump back and forth as much as you want by clicking on the List button and then on the record. (This answers the question, "How do you keep a computer geek busy?")

Using Those Wonderful Drop-Down Lists

Drop-down lists are great when you want users to select from a list of choices instead of guessing what needs to be entered. For example, if you want users to select a status of a job or categorize by type, giving them a list of options is the way to go. Otherwise, you end up with inconsistent categories, such as Résumé Sent and Mailed Résumé for a status, or Contract and Temporary for a type.

Drop-down lists are an excellent way to easily add data to your database — especially when you put a finite set of data in the field. The most common type of drop-down list selection is the use of a Yes/No list, but FileMaker makes adding whatever options you want to include easy.

Just follow these steps:

1. **Open your layout in Layout mode.**

   In my example, the JobType, JobStatus, and HowFound fields are all good candidates for a drop-down list.

2. **Right-click (Control+click if you're using a one-button mouse) the field that you want to set as a drop-down list and choose Field/Control⇨ Setup from the context menu that appears.**

   The Field/Control Setup dialog box appears, as shown in Figure 7-5.

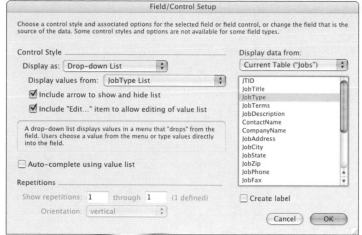

Figure 7-5:
The Field/
Control
Setup dialog
box.

3. **Select Drop-Down List from the Display As drop-down list (pop-up menu on the Mac).**

4. **Select Define Value Lists from the Display Values From drop-down list (pop-up menu on the Mac).**

   The Define Value Lists dialog box appears.

5. **Click the New button.**

   The Edit Value List dialog box appears (see Figure 7-6), which is for creating and editing value lists.

6. **To create a custom list, give your list a name at the top, select the Use Custom Values radio button, and enter the values that you want users to select from.**

   You can also opt to have FileMaker generate the list of possible values from the contents of a field in one of your tables (Use Values From Field) or use a value list you've defined in another file (Use Value List From Another File).

7. **Click OK in the Edit Value List dialog box, and then click OK in the Define Value Lists dialog box.**

   You return to the Field/Control Setup dialog box.

8. **Select the Include Arrow To Show And Hide List option.**

   This option displays a drop-down arrow to the right of the field. It's a good clue to give users to let them know that the field is a drop-down list.

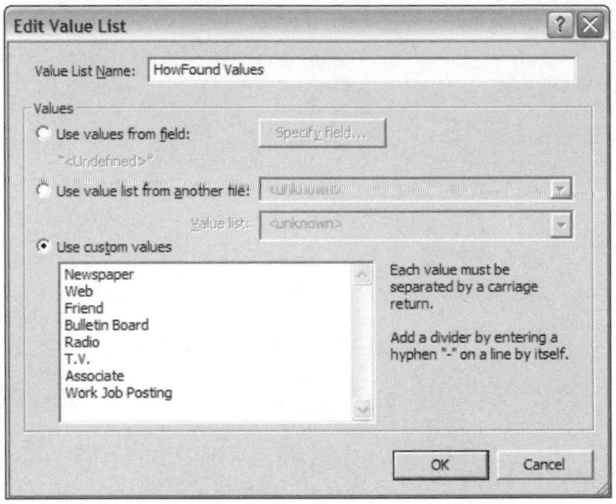

Figure 7-6:
Edit Value
List dialog
box.

9. **If you want to allow users to add new values to the list, select the Include Edit check box.**

   Select the Include Edit check box if you want to give users the most likely choices to save typing, but still allow them to add new choices.

10. **Click OK.**

You can now test your drop-down list by going into Browse mode and clicking the field.

Popping Up Menus

Pop-up menus are a cool feature to add to a data field. They show a pop-up menu list of available values for the field. Pop-up menus are very similar to drop-down lists, but are far more commonly used (particularly on Macs) to present a constrained list of choices without an associated edit box.

Follow these steps to add a pop-up menu to your layout:

1. **Load your database in Layout mode.**

2. **Right-click (Control+click if you're using a one-button mouse) the field to which you want to add a pop-up menu and choose Field/Control⇨ Setup.**

   The Field/Control Setup dialog box appears.

3. **Select Pop-up Menu from the Display As drop-down list.**

   This step tells FileMaker that you want the field to show a pop-up menu of items when the field is selected.

4. **Select Define Value Lists from the Display Values drop-down list.**

   The Define Value Lists dialog box appears.

5. **Click the New button.**

   The Edit Value List dialog box appears (refer to Figure 7-6).

6. **Enter the values that you want to include in your pop-up menu.**

7. **Click OK in the Edit Value List dialog box, and then click OK in the Define Value Lists dialog box.**

   You return to the Field/Control Setup dialog box.

8. **To give users the ability to add their own unique values, select the Include Edit check box to allow editing of value list.**

   Users can now select Edit from the list and add or edit any of the items in the list.

9. **Click OK.**

   Go ahead and give it a try by switching to Browse mode and then make changes to some test data.

Presenting Choices with Check Boxes and Radio Buttons

Check boxes and radio buttons are other ways of giving users a limited list of options to choose from. Unlike drop-down lists, all the options appear front and center on your layout. The advantage is that the user can see all the available values for the field. The drawback is that it requires more space on the layout form. Also, remember that check boxes enable users to select more than one item, whereas radio buttons are like filling in those SAT answer sheets from my school days (whew, that was a *long* time ago!) — the user can choose (or fill in) only one radio button.

Usually, the use of check boxes or radio buttons are limited to selections of less than 4 or 5 items. If you had a value list of 20 items, your layout would be cumbersome for the user of your application. In that situation, a drop-down list would make more sense.

Again, via the use of the Field/Control Setup dialog box, it's a simple task to set a field to use the radio buttons or check boxes. Follow these steps:

1. **Put your layout in Layout mode.**

2. **Right-click (Control+click if you're using a one-button mouse) the field you want to turn into a set of check boxes or radio buttons, and from the context menu that appears, choose Field/Control⇨Setup.**

   The Field/Control Setup dialog box appears.

3. **Select Checkbox Set from the Display As drop-down list (pop-up menu on a Mac).**

4. **Make sure that Display Values From is still set to HowFound Values.**

   A check box is created for each item in the HowFound Values list.

5. **Click OK.**

   If only one check box is showing on your layout, then the size of the field is too small to contain all the check boxes for the list of values.

6. **If needed, select the field and drag a corner to increase its size so that all the check boxes appear, as shown in Figure 7-7.**

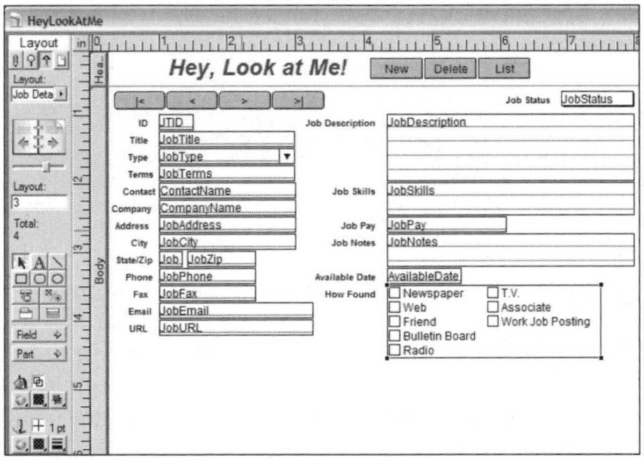

Figure 7-7: Check boxes for the How Found field.

7. **Switch to Browse mode.**

   Notice that you can select multiple values for the field. All the selected values will be placed into that field.

So, what about radio buttons? They basically work the same way, except for one big difference — the user can select only one value. Just follow the previous steps, except in Step 3, select Radio Button Set. Figure 7-8 shows how they look in Browse mode.

Figure 7-8:
Radio
buttons for
the How
Found field.

Screenshot showing a FileMaker database form titled "Hey, Look at Me!" with fields including ID, Title, Type, Terms, Contact, Company, Address, City, State/Zip, Phone, Fax, Email, URL, Job Description, Job Skills, Job Pay, Job Notes, Available Date, and How Found radio buttons (Newspaper, Web, Friend, Bulletin Board, Radio, T.V., Associate, Work Job Posting).

Storing Pictures, Documents, Sounds, and More in a Container Field

The Container field is a very powerful feature of FileMaker. It can give you flexibility to allow users to add things such as documents and pictures that just isn't possible with drop-down lists and check boxes. First you need to create the field. Then I show you how to add stuff to it.

Creating a Container field

To create a Container field, follow these steps:

1. **Put your layout in Layout mode.**

2. **Click the Define Database tool on the FileMaker toolbar.**

   The Define Database dialog box appears with the currently selected table fields.

3. **Enter a new field name in the Field Name box. Set the type to Container, and click the Create button. Then click OK.**

   You've just added a Container field and FileMaker adds this field along with a label to your document. Figure 7-9 shows the Container field I added — the Résumé field, which allows users to add a document.

4. **Move and resize the field and label as you need.**

   You can use either the mouse or the Object Size palette for positioning the field and label. Now your Container field is ready to hold files.

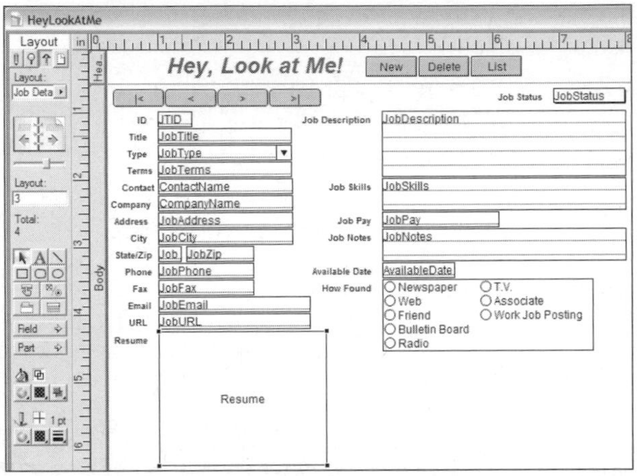

Figure 7-9:
The Job
Details
layout with
the new
Résumé
field.

Adding stuff to the Container field

After you add a Container field to your layout, you can add most anything you like (as long as its binary) to it. First switch to Browse mode, and then right-click (Control+click if you're using a one-button mouse) the field to see all your options.

Table 7-1 breaks down the different options for the Container field and what they do.

Table 7-1	**Container Field Options**
Option	*Description*
Cut	Cuts the contents of the field to the Clipboard.
Copy	Copies the contents of the field to the Clipboard.
Paste Picture	Pastes a picture from the Clipboard.
Insert Picture	Allows you to select a picture file from your computer and insert it into the field.
Insert QuickTime	Inserts any QuickTime object (movie, sound, and so on) into the field. Very cool!
Insert Sound	Records and stores the sound into the field (if you have a microphone or other sound input device). Great for dictating a message and adding it to the field.

Option	Description
Insert File	Stores any type of file into the field. An image of the appropriate file icon appears in the field. You can then access the contents by choosing the Export Field Contents option.
Insert Object	Inserts any Windows object that supports OLE object into the field. The user can double-click the object in the field to either launch the appropriate Windows application or edit that file in the field itself.
Export Field Contents	Exports that file back out to your computer in the original file format.

Customizing the Menus

Sometimes a limited pop-up menu or even a Container field doesn't quite do the job you need. Maybe you're designing a custom application and you want the users to have access to only the menu items that you want them to have. In this situation, you can customize your own menu. Here are the steps to follow:

1. **Load the layout in Layout mode.**

2. **Choose Tools⇨Custom Menus⇨Define Custom Menus.**

   The Define Custom Menus dialog box opens with a long list of custom menus already provided (see Figure 7-10). Notice the two tabs at the top of the dialog box: Custom Menus and Menu Sets. The Custom Menus are the individual menus that you can build for your application. After you create the menus, you can add them to existing or new Menu Sets.

3. **Click the Create button.**

   The Create Custom Menu dialog box appears. At the top you can select Start with an Empty Menu or Start with a Standard FileMaker Menu.

   Generally, you select Start with a Standard FileMaker Menu when you want to customize an existing menu to add one or more of your own menu items or remove one or more that you don't want to offer the user. You typically start with an empty menu when you are creating a totally new menu of custom actions.

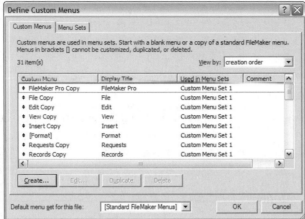

Figure 7-10:
Define
Custom
Menus
dialog box.

4. Click the Start with an Empty Menu radio button. Click OK.

The Edit Custom Menu dialog box appears (see Figure 7-11).

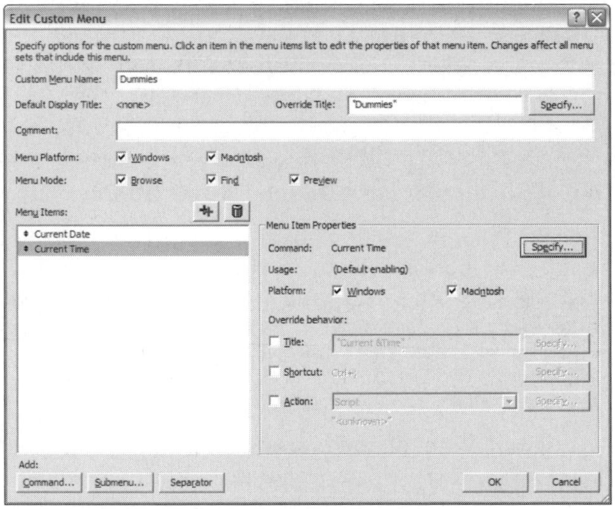

Figure 7-11:
The Edit
Custom
Menu dialog
box.

5. Enter a name in the Custom Menu Name box, and enter the same name in the Override Title area.

This menu title appears in the main menu bar at the top of FileMaker.

6. **Select the menu platforms you want to work with and the modes where you want the custom menu to appear.**

   This gives you the ability to select which OS platform the menu is available for. And the menu mode enables you to select the modes in which the menu will be active.

7. **Click the Command button.**

8. **Add commands for the functions you want to appear on your custom menu.**

   The purpose of the custom menu for the Hey, Look at Me! database is to make it easier to add the current date and time to any of the fields during data entry. So, I added the CurrentDate function, which is a built-in FileMaker function.

   As you add these commands to the menu, the right side of the Edit Custom Menu dialog box shows a series of properties available for the selected command. These properties provide a way to use your own custom scripts, shortcut keys, titles, and define which OS platforms you want the commands to be available on.

   Good user interface design for menus is to group related menu items (such as Print and Page Setup), separated from other related groups in the same menu (such as Open and Open Recent) by a thin line called a Separator. Click the Separator button to add such a line to your menu. Similarly, if your menu has a lot of choices, so many that the menu would fill or overflow the screen height if opened, you should group related items into a submenu that branches off a single choice, such as FileMaker's View menu's Toolbars choice. Create a submenu entry by pressing the Submenu button and fill in the options presented.

9. **Click OK.**

   Now that you have a custom menu created, you can add it to one of the existing FileMaker menu sets.

10. **Click the Menu Sets tab at the top of the Define Custom Menus dialog box.**

    Two menu sets appear: The Standard FileMaker Menus (the [ ] show that it can't be edited) and the Custom Menu Set 1.

11. **Select the Custom Menu Set 1, and then click the Edit button.**

    The Edit Menu Set dialog box appears. On the left is a list of available custom menus, and on the right is a list of the menus installed in the current menu set.

12. **Scroll down the list of available custom menus until you see the name of your custom menu. Select it, and then click the Move button in the middle of the dialog box.**

   The menu is placed into the Custom Menu Set 1.

13. **Click OK twice.**

   About this time you're probably thinking, "I created this menu, but it's not showing up at the top. This book is wrong, and the author is coocoo." Well, actually the latter might be true, but you still have a few more steps to go through to get the menu to appear.

14. **Choose Layouts⇨Layout Setup.**

15. **Select Custom Menu Set 1 from the Menu Set drop-down list (pop-up menu on a Mac), and click OK.**

   Now you can see your custom menu. Go into Browse mode and you see it appear at the top. To try it out, just select one of the fields and then one of the items in the menu. Ooooh, such power. I sense the force of FileMaker programming growing inside you!

To help as you design databases, you can also use this feature to group all your favorite features — items that you use the most — into a single menu.

Part III
Taking Control with FileMaker Programming

The 5th Wave   By Rich Tennant

I told Russell he should data model before we go any further.

Miss Claudia Schiffer, please.

In this part . . .

The real power of FileMaker lies in adding calculations to scripts, and in Part III, you find out more about the scripting side of FileMaker. Chapter 8 introduces timesaving ways you can put FileMaker scripts to work, explains the basics of writing scripts, and walks you through example scripts to help you get a feel for this awesome feature. In Chapter 9, I share a few programming tricks that I use to help you streamline your script writing and keep your scripts in order.

Chapter 8

It's All in the Script!

*L*ights! Cameras! Action! (I always wanted to say that.) Except for reality shows, just about every other show, movie, or play requires a script so that the actors have something to follow and know what to do. In a way, a movie script is a top-down program. You start at the top and work your way down 'til it's done. When you use FileMaker's script editor to create such a script, FileMaker is like your very own actor, and you can tell it to perform certain actions for you.

However, there is a significant difference between movie scripts and FileMaker scripts! With scripting in FileMaker, you can perform specific actions based on the results of prior actions, or the state of data.

During the script-writing process, the writer basically has to have the entire story in mind, or at least on some type of outline or storyboard. Writing scripts for FileMaker is very similar. You have to first know what it is that you want FileMaker to do. Then you write the script telling FileMaker to do it. A review of Chapter 4 is a good refresher for any new projects that you want to take on.

In this chapter, you can discover the magic of script programming in FileMaker. I walk you through several examples that illustrate how you can write your own scripts from start to finish. Although the topic of programming itself can be overwhelming, I'm sure you'll find that programming scripts with FileMaker is actually quite easy and enjoyable. After you give FileMaker scripting a try, you might come up with all kinds of ideas for scripts that you want to write for your FileMaker applications.

Saving Time with FileMaker Scripts

"Why should I use scripts in FileMaker? After all, isn't FileMaker designed to make it easy to design databases, forms, and reports, without having to know how to program? Besides, I'm not a programmer. I'm lousy at math! I even have problems with programming the recording of my favorite TV programs!"

Does this sound like you? The FileMaker scripting environment is designed to make it easy for folks like you. But why should you even have to write scripts in FileMaker? If you've been adding buttons to your FileMaker layouts and assigning functions to those buttons, then in a sense, you're already writing scripts — just really small ones! Basically, a *script* is just a list of FileMaker functions put together. Say for example, that you perform the following steps on a regular basis:

1. You open your customer database.

2. You search for all the customers that you're supposed to deliver products to tomorrow.

3. You open up another layout that shows all your products on hand.

4. You check to see if you have enough product on hand to fulfill the deliveries for tomorrow.

5. You discover that you're short on some of the products, so you do a database search for the vendor who supplies those products.

6. You print out an order form for the missing products and fax it to the vendor.

7. Finally, you print out a list of customers and their addresses for tomorrow's delivery route.

Even with FileMaker, doing these few steps could actually take several hours of your time, depending on how many customers and products you have. What if you had a script program to do the work for you? Here's how it could work:

1. You start up FileMaker, and it automatically launches your customer fulfillment script.

2. While you're getting your morning coffee, FileMaker matches the customers with their product orders for the next day.

3. FileMaker discovers that you're short on some of the products, so it automatically locates the vendors for those products, determines how much product you need, and then faxes or e-mails the product orders to the vendors.

4. Based on stock on hand, FileMaker prints out a list of customers and their addresses for tomorrow's deliveries.

5. You get back with your cup of coffee and notice that FileMaker is displaying a list of customers that you need to call, to let them know that their deliveries will be late.

6. You check your printer and see copies of the orders that were placed with your vendors and a list of deliveries for tomorrow.

Overall, the script program did several hours of manual work in a matter of minutes. This is the power of FileMaker scripting!

Checking Out the Parts in a Script

Unless, like Spock, you have pointy ears and strange-looking eyebrows, you might find the whole topic of programming logic to be a bit daunting. But like most movie scripts, a FileMaker script has several parts. It's just that FileMaker reads each one so that it can execute the task that you ask it to do. This section breaks the script logic into its key parts so you can better understand how it works.

Each line in a FileMaker script is called a *step*. There are four *parts* that can comprise a script step. They are:

- **Function:** A function tells FileMaker what action to perform. For example, `Go to Layout`, `Set Field`, and `Go to Next Field` are all FileMaker functions. (These are the same functions that you use when assigning a function to a button on a layout, as I explain in Chapter 7.)

- **Statement:** A statement directs FileMaker to make a decision based on the contents of data or the result of a previous function. Statements in FileMaker include `If`, `End If`, `Loop`, `Exit Loop If`. For example, a statement might direct FileMaker to display a dialog if a field containing the stock on hand falls below a set threshold.

- **Operators:** This is where a lot of the logic of script programming takes place. Operators are also used for making comparisons between data elements. These include `AND`, `OR`, `=`, `<`, `>`.

- **Data Elements:** Data is what it's all about! Data elements in a script step can be a database field or a variable.

Variable is a symbolic name for a value. For example, you could initially assign the value of `0` to the variable name `MyCount`. Then you could use the following programming logic:

```
If MyCount = 5 then
MyCount = MyCount - 1
Else
MyCount = MyCount + 1
End If
```

The above logic says that if `MyCount` contains the value of 5, subtract 1 from `MyCount`, making `MyCount` now hold the value of 4. But if `MyCount` does not equal 5, add 1 to the current value of `MyCount`. In brief, in a looping situation, this increments the `MyCount` variable until it reaches the value 5 and then alternates it between the values of 4 and 5.

Creating a Script in ScriptMaker

After you take your great ideas for creating scripts and determine which steps belong in the script and their order of execution in the script, you're ready to actually make your ideas happen. In this section, I show you how to get started. First, you start by creating a simple script. Then find out how to add `If` statements and other conditional logic to a script. Also, I show you how to assign a script to a button on one of your layouts so that all you have to do is click — and FileMaker takes care of the rest!

Creating a script

A good way to begin your adventures in scripting is by creating a simple script. Almost every "how-to" book or article about programming has you create a *Hello World* program for the very first example, but I don't get it! Why would you want to say hello to the entire world? Wouldn't that create a huge amount of e-mail? I think a *Hey Neighbor* program is more appropriate. At least you know who your neighbor is!

So the following steps show you how to create a simple Hey Neighbor script. With a few modifications, you can use the basic steps here to create the foundation for just about any script you want to create. Ready to dive in? Here goes:

1. **Download and open the `HeyNeighbor.fp7` database.**

   You can download this database from the Web site mentioned in the Introduction. This database has a single table with a single field and a layout with a button on it — all ready for you to add some script code.

2. Choose Scripts⇨ScriptMaker.

You now see the Define Scripts dialog box. If this is your first time using ScriptMaker, no scripts are listed.

3. Click the New button.

This is where all the script-editing work is done. As shown in Figure 8-1, the available script functions and statements are listed on the left.

4. In the Script Name field, type ChangeText **and press the Tab key.**

This sets the name of the script that you're creating. Now it's time to enter a script step.

5. Scroll the list on the left until you see the Fields category. Double-click the Set Field script step.

The selected script step is added to the edit window on the right. The Set Field script step is for changing the value of a field within a database table. Below the edit window, you see the Script Step Options for the selected script step. This is where you modify options for the current script step. For example, if you want FileMaker to change text, this is where you indicate which text FileMaker needs to change.

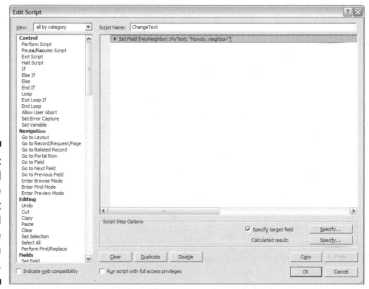

Figure 8-1:
Scroll through the list of script steps and select the ones you want.

6. **Click the Specify button next to the Specify Target Field check box.**

   This is where you tell FileMaker for which field you want to set a new value. Because the `HeyNeighbor Start.fp7` example has one table with one field, the MyText field is the only option you have.

7. **Highlight the MyText field, and click OK.**

   The Repetitions option at the bottom is for telling FileMaker how many repetitions you want to create for the selected field. In most situations, you'll need only one.

8. **Now click the Specify button next to Calculated Result.**

   The Specify Calculation dialog box appears. This is where you tell FileMaker what value you want to put in the selected field.

   Don't get overwhelmed by all the features shown in this dialog box. (Especially those mathematical functions in the top-right list box. Just ignore those for now — I dig into more general calculations in Chapter 10. Move along — nothing to see here.) The only box that you're concerned with for now is the big one at the bottom of the dialog box.

9. **In the big blank box, type "Howdy, neighbor!" (including the quotes because FileMaker wants text — they're also called *string* — arguments enclosed in quotes). Click OK to save your script, and then click the next OK button to close the Define Scripts dialog box.**

   Congrats! You created your first script step. You see the following in the Edit Script dialog box:

   ```
   SetField[HeyNeighbor::MyText; "Howdy, neighbor!"]
   ```

   `SetField` is the function. `HeyNeighbor::MyText` is the table and field that you're setting a new value for, and `"Howdy, neighbor!"` is the value that you're putting in the field.

Click OK to dismiss the Edit Script dialog box, and you see your ChangeText script listed in the Define Scripts dialog box. Click OK to dismiss the Define Scripts dialog box. Later in this chapter, I show you how to attach your script to an object on the layout.

As you worked through this example, you likely noticed several other options in the Edit Script dialog box — especially the long list of functions. To help you sift through all these functions, I've included a handy Scripting Reference in the appendix of this book. The Scripting Reference is a brief overview of the script functions and statements, with some examples on how to use them.

Table 8-1 outlines how those options work in more detail.

Table 8-1	Features of the Edit Scripts Dialog Box	
Feature	*What It Does*	*Tips for Using It*
View drop-down list	This sets how you want to view the list of functions and statements.	The default is All By Category, which makes it easy to see which script step you want to use.
Script Name text box	This is the name of the currently displayed script.	If you want to rename a script, this is where you would do so.
Indicate Web Compatibility check box	When selected, this prompts FileMaker to display which script steps are compatible with use on a Web-enabled layout.	Check when creating a script for a Web layout. Chapter 12 has more details about publishing databases on the Web.
Run Script With Full Access Privileges check box	When selected, this script executes with full access rights. (You can find information in Chapter 11.)	You can use this when you want a script to run to completion even if the current user doesn't have sufficient access privileges to perform the operations manually.
Clear button	This clears all the script steps in the main edit window.	Use this button when you want to restart the script definition from scratch.
Duplicate button	This duplicates the currently highlighted script steps.	Frequently, you'll find that you need more than one script that varies only slightly from one to the other. Duplicating one and making the minor changes necessary is faster and easier than creating each script from scratch.
Disable/Enable button	This is a toggle that disables or enables the currently selected script steps.	One use of this button is to enable and disable debugging steps you've inserted when trying to determine why a script isn't doing quite what you expected.

(continued)

Table 8-1 *(continued)*

Feature	What It Does	Tips for Using It
Copy button	Copies the currently selected script steps to memory.	Use this button to copy the selected steps to the Clipboard so that you might paste them into another script.
Paste button	Pastes the script steps currently in memory into the edit window.	(See Copy button.)

Defining and editing scripts

Although the first piece of the ScriptMaker environment that you see is the Define Scripts dialog box, as shown in Figure 8-2, you can't do much with it until you create a script. When you open Define Scripts, by either choosing Scripts➪ScriptMaker or pressing Ctrl+Shift+S (⌘+Shift+S on a Mac), you see a list of the scripts that you have built. You also see the features described in Table 8-2.

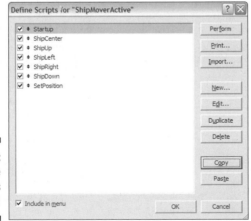

Figure 8-2: I built these scripts myself!

Table 8-2	Features of the Define Scripts Dialog Box	
Feature	*What It Does*	*Tips for Using It*
Script check box(es)	(On the left side of the script list) When selected, the script name appears in the FileMaker Scripts menu.	If you don't want the user to have direct access to a script (maybe it should only be available to other scripts), uncheck the box.
Movement arrows	(Between the check box and the script name) This allows you to move the script up or down within the list.	It's faster and easier to find and choose scripts near the top of a list, so you can move the scripts you expect to be most often used toward the top.
Include In Menu check box	When selected, this shows the currently highlighted script in the FileMaker Scripts menu.	This checks the script check box described above.
Perform button	This runs the currently selected script.	The Scripts menu isn't accessible when the dialog box is open, so this gives you a way to perform the script.
Print button	Prints the currently selected script.	Like a backup, documenting what you do is a good thing.
Import button	This allows you to import script code from other FileMaker databases.	You might have created scripts in another database that are useful in this project.
New button	Creates a new script.	I think you can figure this one out on your own.
Edit button	Opens up the script editor with the currently selected script.	. . . and this one.
Duplicate button	This makes a full copy of the currently selected script and appends *Copy* to the script name.	. . . and this one.

(continued)

Table 8-2 *(continued)*

Feature	What It Does	Tips for Using It
Delete button	Deletes the currently selected script.	. . . and this one.
Copy button	Copies the currently selected script to memory.	This is useful for copying script code from one FileMaker database to another FileMaker database. Note that this *does not* copy the script to the OS Clipboard. So you can't paste a script into a different software editor. Personally, I would love to be able to do this! (Hi, FileMaker Inc.? You taking notes?)
Paste button	This pastes a script from memory to the currently active Define Scripts dialog box.	Paste is very handy, in conjunction with the Copy button, for copying a script from one database to another.

Adding conditionals and other logic to a script

This section dives into the meat and bones of programming — decision logic. One of the biggest advantages of having a script for your database is the ability to let FileMaker make decisions based on data or calculated results. Because we humans are prone to making wrong decisions, having a program make good decisions for us is a great help. But then, the programmed decisions are only as good as the human programmer who put them in. But, I think you see my point.

To demonstrate this, say you want a script that displays different messages based upon the value in a data field. I'll have you make more modifications to the Hey Neighbor database and add some decision logic to the script. This first step is to create a global variable. Then you're ready to add the logical decision-making.

Creating a global variable

A *global variable* is a variable that is available to all scripts and layout objects within your FileMaker database. A *local variable* is a variable that is available only within the script in which it is defined. If other scripts might need access to the value, or if the value might be referenced in subsequent executions of a single script, a global variable is called for; otherwise, a local variable will suffice.

1. **Open the Hey Neighbor database (if you haven't already done so), and switch to Layout mode.**

   You can download this database (HeyNeighbor.fp7) at the Web site mentioned in the Introduction to this book.

 2. **Click the Define Database icon on the FileMaker toolbar.**

   Global variables in FileMaker are actually defined as field names within a table. My personal preference is to have a table dedicated to just global variables. Guess what I call that table? *Globals!*

3. **Click the Tables tab. In the Table Name text box, type** Globals. **Then click the Create button.**

   This creates a new table named Globals.

4. **Click the Fields tab. In the Field Name text box, type** TextItem, **set the Type to Number, and then click the Create button.**

   This creates a field in the Globals table named TextItem. However, to truly make this a global variable, you need to set some special options for this field. We're going to use the number stored in this variable to determine which text string to display (that is, which item in a list of text strings).

5. **Click the Options button, and click the Storage tab.**

   This displays the global storage options for the TextItem field, as shown in Figure 8-3.

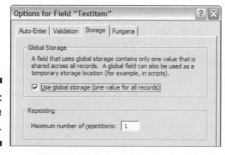

Figure 8-3:
Storage
Options.

6. **Click the check box for Use Global Storage, click OK, and click the next OK button to close the Define Database dialog box.**

   You've set the TextItem field as a global variable. This field is now available for lookup or editing from any table, layout object, or script in the FileMaker database.

Adding the decision logic

Now you're ready for some logical reasoning in your script file.

1. **Continuing with the Hey Neighbor database, choose Scripts⇨ ScriptMaker.**

   You see the only script currently in the database — the ChangeText script from the previous "Creating a script" section of this chapter.

2. **Select the ChangeText script, and click the Edit button.**

   The current ChangeText script has just one script step.

3. **Double-click the If statement under the Control category.**

   This adds two statements to your script: If and End If. Your script code should now look like this:

   ```
   Set Field[HeyNeighbor::MyText; "Howdy, neighbor!"]
   If[]
   End If
   ```

4. **Highlight the If [] statement, and then click the Specify button.**

   Or, you can just double-click the If [] statement.

   Either way, the Specify Calculation dialog box appears. This is where you add the decision criteria for your If statement.

   In this decision branch, you want to test the new TextItem global variable to see if it contains any values and, if so, which text string to display.

5. **From the Table list box at the top left, select the Globals table, and then double-click the TextItem field just below the Table list.**

   This places Globals::TextItem in the Calculation code window. This tells FileMaker that you want to perform some type of calculation on the TextItem field from the Globals table.

6. **In the center Operators list, double-click the < (less than) symbol.**

   This adds < to your calculation.

7. **In the Calculation code window, type a space and the number 1 after the < symbol.**

   Your code in the Calculation code window should look like this:

   ```
   Globals::TextItem < 1
   ```

Thus, you are telling FileMaker to check to see if the `TextItem` field holds a value that is less than `1`.

8. **Click OK.**

You'll see that your script code has a decision branch that says:

```
If [Globals::TextItem < 1]
```

If the `TextItem` field matches this criteria, any script code under the `If` statement and before the `End If` statement executes. So, now you need to tell FileMaker what you want it to do when this criteria is met.

9. **Using the mouse, grab the arrows icon next to the `Set Field` function at the top of your script and drag it down under the `If` statement, but before the `End If` statement.**

Your script code looks like this:

```
If [Globals::TextItem < 1]
    Set Field [HeyNeighbor::MyText; "Howdy, neighbor!"]
End If
```

So, basically, you're telling FileMaker that if the `TextItem` field value is less than 1, put the value `"Howdy, neighbor!"` in the `MyText` field of the Hey Neighbor table. You just created your first decision branch! Now you need to add another statement to the script to show that you've used the `Howdy` text already.

Did you notice that when the script step was moved within the `If-End If` code, it became indented? This is called *nested code*. The `Set Field` statement is nested within the `If-End If` code. This is basically a visual aid to help you see where the `If` statement begins, what code is a part of the `If` decision branch, and where the `If` code ends.

10. **Double-click the Set Field statement in the list of functions, and then double-click the new `Set Field` statement in your script code.**

The Specify Field dialog box appears, where you can select which table and field you want to set.

11. **Select the Globals table from the drop-down list, and then select the TextItem field. Click OK to close the dialog box.**

To show that the `"Howdy, neighbor!"` text has already been used, you're going to use the TextItem global field as a counter. You're going to tell FileMaker to increment the value in that field.

12. **Click the Calculated Result Specify button.**

Again, the Specify Calculation dialog box appears. This time, instead of just setting a fixed value for the global variable field, you're going to perform a calculation.

13. **In the Table list on the top left, select the Globals table, and then double-click the TextItem field.**

This places the `Globals::TextItem` field in the Calculation code window.

14. **Double-click the + (plus) Operator.**

   You're now telling FileMaker that you want to add a value to the field.

15. **In the Calculation code window, type a space and the number** 1.

   Your Calculation code looks like this:

   ```
   Globals::TextItem + 1
   ```

16. **Click OK to close the Specify Calculation dialog box.**

   With the addition of your new `Set Field` statement, the script code looks like this:

   ```
   If [Globals::TextItem < 1]
       Set Field [HeyNeighbor::MyText; "Howdy, neighbor!"]
       Set Field [Globals::TextItem; Globals::TextItem + 1]
   End If
   ```

   The script code now sets the `MyText` to a new message and then adds 1 to the current value of `TextItem`, for keeping track of which message was displayed.

17. **Now, from what you now know about the `If`, `End If`, and `Set Field` statements, add the following script code to your script (as shown in Figure 8-4).**

   ```
   IF [Globals::TextItem < 1]
       Set Field [HeyNeighbor::MyText; "Howdy, neighbor!"]
       Set Field [Globals::TextItem; Globals::TextItem +
           1]
       Exit Script []
   Else If [Globals::TextItem = 1]
       Set Field [HeyNeighbor::MyText; "We sure are having
           fun."]
       Set Field [Globals::TextItem; Globals::TextItem +
           1]
       Exit Script []
   Else If [Globals::TextItem = 2]
       Set Field [HeyNeighbor::MyText; "You must like
           clicking that button!"]
       Set Field [Globals::TextItem; Globals::TextItem +
           1]
       Exit Script []
   Else If [Globals::TextItem = 3]
       Set Field [HeyNeighbor::MyText; "Wow! This code
           really works!"]
       Set Field [Globals::TextItem; 0]
   End If
   ```

The purpose of this additional code is to allow you to click the Hello button and get a different message each time. After the four different messages have been displayed, it rolls back to the first message. Not only does this code demonstrate the use of `If`, `Else If`, and `End If` statements for decision branching, but you also get a small taste of writing calculations.

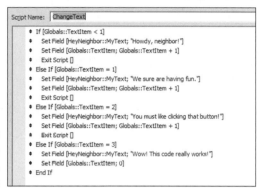

Figure 8-4:
Script code.

```
Script Name:  ChangeText

  If [Globals::TextItem < 1]
     Set Field [HeyNeighbor::MyText; "Howdy, neighbor!"]
     Set Field [Globals::TextItem; Globals::TextItem + 1]
     Exit Script []
  Else If [Globals::TextItem = 1]
     Set Field [HeyNeighbor::MyText; "We sure are having fun."]
     Set Field [Globals::TextItem; Globals::TextItem + 1]
     Exit Script []
  Else If [Globals::TextItem = 2]
     Set Field [HeyNeighbor::MyText; "You must like clicking that button!"]
     Set Field [Globals::TextItem; Globals::TextItem + 1]
     Exit Script []
  Else If [Globals::TextItem = 3]
     Set Field [HeyNeighbor::MyText; "Wow! This code really works!"]
     Set Field [Globals::TextItem; 0]
  End If
```

18. **After you've entered the code, click OK to close the Edit Script dialog box. Click the next OK button to close the Define Scripts dialog box.**

19. **Assign the script to a layout object, such as a button, by following the steps in the upcoming section, "Assigning a script to a layout object."**

20. **Test out your code by going into Browse mode and then clicking the button assigned to the script multiple times.**

    Notice that with each click of the Hello button, you get a different message. Then after four different messages, you go back to the first one. If you remembered about the Copy and Paste buttons at the bottom of the Edit Script dialog box, you might have even used those to copy lines of code, paste them, and then make minor changes to the pasted code.

Assigning a script to a layout object

After you create a script to use in your FileMaker database, it's time to add it to your layout. Assigning a script to an element on the layout is easy, as the following steps illustrate:

1. **Switch to layout mode.**

   While in layout mode, you can assign scripts to objects on the layout.

2. **Right-click (Control+click if you're using a Mac with a one-button mouse) the button, and select Button Setup from the context menu that appears.**

   This displays the Button Setup dialog box, which is where you select which function or script you want the button to perform. As a default, the Perform Script function should be highlighted.

3. **Click the Specify button, select the name of the script, click OK, and then click the next OK button to close the Button Setup dialog box.**

   You have added the script to the button on the layout.

4. **Switch to Browse mode and click the button.**

   Wow! It works! You just executed your script program with a single click.

If you edit a script but don't change its name, there is no need to change anything on the layout. The button in your layout still calls the same script. It just runs different code.

Find out more about programming

Now that you've had a taste of what it's like to be a script programmer, you're addicted! You just *have* to have more! You'll do whatever it takes to write more code! Where do you go? First, you have to buy a pocket pencil protector! Actually, the days of looking like a geeky programmer are gone. But, it is trendy to be high tech and geeky!

For starters, just study the script code from other applications. FileMaker comes with a lot of great examples for looking at script code. Here are a few steps to help you get started:

1. **Go to your FileMaker directory on your computer and look for the Extras folder. Go to the Templates folder, then the Home-General folder. Then load the Inventory database.**

   The Inventory sample database provided with FileMaker is a good place to start looking

at script code. It most closely resembles the type of database applications you might want to develop for yourself or your business.

2. **Switch to Layout mode.**

   While in Layout mode, you can select the various objects on the layout and find out which scripts they are using.

3. **Right-click (Control+click if you're using a one-button mouse) the Find icon, then select the Button Setup menu item.**

   In the Button Setup dialog box, as shown in the following figure, notice that the Perform Script function is highlighted. Just above the function list window, FileMaker shows which script code is being used when the Find icon is clicked. In this case, it's the Find script.

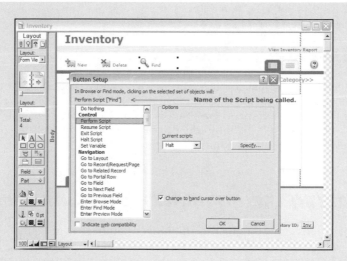

4. **Click OK to close the Button Setup dialog box. Select the Scripts menu, and then select the ScriptMaker menu item.**

   Now, you can look for the actual script code to see what is executed when you click the Find icon.

5. **Double-click the Find script.**

   You're looking at the script code for the Find script. The following figure is a screen shot of the code, along with my comments on what this script is doing. (All my comments start with / / and appear in a bolder type.)

6. **Repeat Steps 3–5 for any other scripts that you want to look at.**

   You can find out a lot by examining how other programmers have written their scripts. Use the many other FileMaker databases in the Extras folder to look at and learn from.

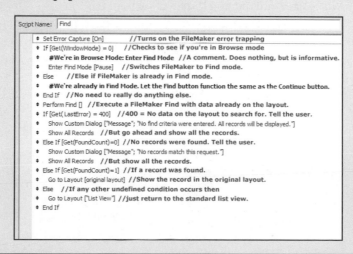

Playing with Animation: The ShipMover Database

Sometimes, you just want to sit down with FileMaker and try out some ideas. This is what happened with this sample database called ShipMover. I wanted to see if there was a way to graphically depict the movement of a spaceship by using FileMaker. (The ShipMover database file is available for download from the Web site mentioned in the Introduction.)

Laying the groundwork for ShipMover

The process for building the ShipMover database is actually quite simple.

1. I knew that I needed some type of grid on the screen for positioning the ship. Because FileMaker does not provide a way to actually move an object on a layout, I needed some other method for making it appear that the ship is being moved. I did this via the use of fields within the table.

   The Ship picture is stored in the ShipPic field, which is aContainer field. And the other nine fields are for setting the position of the ship on the layout. There is only one record needed.

2. The only other table needed is for the use of a global variable for keeping track of the current position of the Ship picture. I named the table Globals (of course) and named the field CurrentPosition.

3. The next step was to create a layout for the database, as shown in Figure 8-5. The first objects on the layout were the nine slot fields. Then I placed the five buttons for positioning and moving the ship. A nice little border box around the slots, some text at the top.

4. The only thing left was the script code for the movement, which I explain in more detail in the next section.

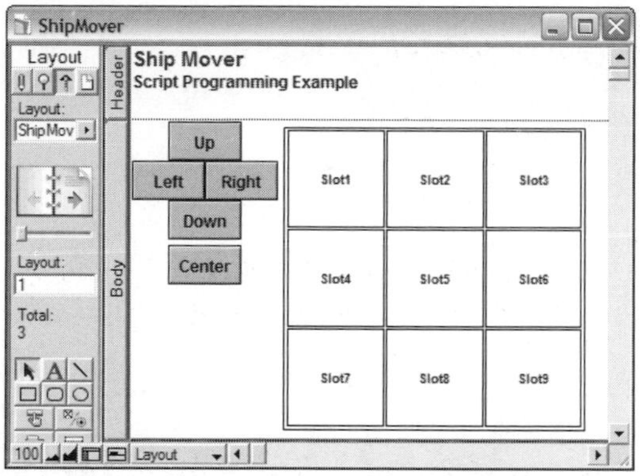

Figure 8-5:
ShipMover
table.

Managing a global variable with several scripts

To match up with the five buttons, I knew that I needed a script for each button. I also wanted to create a script for starting up the application and then a script that would actually manage the placement of the ship into the correct slot. As shown in Figure 8-6, I created the following scripts:

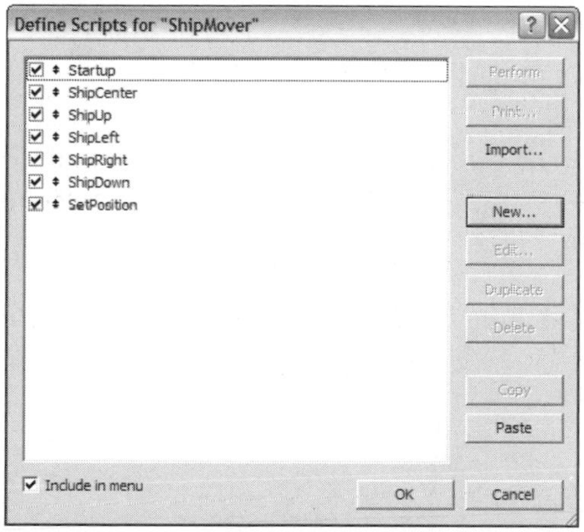

Figure 8-6:
The
ShipMover
layout.

✔ **Startup:** Sets the dimensions of the layout form, sets the initial value for the global variable, and sets the starting position for the ship. This executes when the database is loaded (by setting the File Options under the File menu).

✔ **ShipCenter:** Sets the global variable to position the ship in the center of the grid.

✔ **ShipUp:** Changes the global variable to move the ship up.

✔ **ShipLeft:** Changes the global variable to move the ship left.

✔ **ShipRight:** Changes the global variable to move the ship right.

✔ **ShipDown:** Changes the global variable to move the ship down.

✔ **SetPostion:** Determines the correct position of the ship based on the global variable, and then positions the ship.

From examining the scripts in this list, you might be wondering why I didn't just set the position of the ship in each of the ship movement scripts. I could have. But, in thinking about keeping the size of the individual scripts as small as possible, I knew that the code in the SetPosition script would be, basically, the same in every ship movement script. So, instead of duplicating that code in every single script, it is just as easy to put it in a separate script and call it from the other scripts.

Designing the ship-movement script

The following script code demonstrates the logic for moving the ship from one slot field to another (Figure 8-7):

```
Set Field [Globals::CurrentPosition;
          Globals::CurrentPosition + 1]
If [Globals::CurrentPosition > 9]
   Set Field [Globals::CurrentPosition; 7]
   Perform Script ["SetPosition"]
   Exit Script []
Else If [Globals::CurrentPosition = 4]
   Set Field [Globals::CurrentPosition; 1]
   Perform Script ["SetPosition"]
   Exit Script []
Else If [Globals::CurrentPosition = 7]
   Set Field [Globals::CurrentPosition; 4]
   Perform Script ["SetPosition"]
   Exit Script []
End If
Perform Script ["SetPosition"]
```

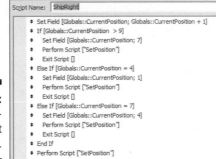

Figure 8-7:
Ship-
movement
script.

Notice that not only do I increment the global variable for the ship position, but I test (via If statements) to see if the ship has gone off the right side of the grid. If it has, I reset the global variable to point to the first slot on the left side of the grid — like a wraparound effect.

Then after the ship-movement script executes, it calls the SetPosition script. This script basically clears all the slot fields and repositions the ship picture into the correct slot.

Now, you might be thinking, "You just moved a picture of a ship around a layout. I just don't see the business applications." So why is the example of the ShipMover database application important enough for this book? Because it demonstrates that just about anything can be done with the FileMaker programming environment. With some creativity and some script coding, the ShipMover application could actually turn into quite a fun programming project. Plus, it demonstrates that you don't always have to confine yourself to the perceived limits of an application. If you had told another FileMaker programmer that you were going to move an object around on a FileMaker layout, the chances are that they would have told you that it was impossible because FileMaker doesn't have a function for moving objects. However, with some creative thinking, it can be done. That's what programming is all about — the ability to creatively come up with solutions via the use of the programming environment. And to never say, "It can't be done."

Chapter 9

Your Programming Toolbox

●●●

●●●

I remember an old TV show about a doctor who would visit his patients. He always had words of wisdom for helping to resolve the situation that the patient was facing. What impressed me the most was his little black bag. Regardless of what problem the patient was facing, the doctor always had some medicine or a special tool in his black bag. I'm sure that years of wisdom and experience helped the doctor to decide just what to put into that bag.

Being a software programmer is very similar. During the years of programming and writing software, programmers gradually develop what is generally referred to as their bag of tricks. It is in this bag of tricks that the programmers keep their best tools, tricks, and techniques for writing software applications. It isn't a literal bag that the programmer carries around; rather, it's usually just stored in the programmer's head. And for those who can't seem to hold everything in memory (this author included), the programmer keeps a library of files and programs that contain the routines that the programmer wants to keep at hand. Therefore, I present to you a sampling of some of the tricks and tips of FileMaker programming that I have created, copied, morphed, and gleaned during my years of programming.

Good Commenting Practices

Programmers hate to comment their code! Especially when the creative juices are flowing. But it's an important necessity. Why? Well, suppose that you spend three months writing a complex FileMaker application for one of your customers, and then you don't touch the code for over a year. The customer calls you back and wants you to do some modifications to the application. You've probably worked on lots of different FileMaker (and other) projects in the interim, and unless you have total recall, you aren't going to remember what some of the fields are for, what some of the layouts are for, what some of the scripts or script steps are meant to accomplish, and so on. And it's even worse for someone else who might have to maintain your code (think about how you'd feel if you had to make sense of someone else's database project and they hadn't left you any hints in the code). The bottom line: Embedding comments that describe what you've done and why you've done it makes picking up where you left off a lot easier.

If you make comments in your code, it's a lot easier to remember what the code is doing.

The following code (a snippet from a much longer script program) is an example of commented code:

```
Set Field [ Globals::Status; "Building Teacher Lookup
        table..." ]
Go to Record/Request/Page [ First ]
Loop
   Set Field [ gStudents::Teacher; tblStudents::Teacher ]
   # if teacher field has data
   If [ IsEmpty(gStudents::Teacher) <> 1 ]
   Go to Layout [ "TeachersImport" (tblLUTeachers) ]
   # look to see if teacher already in table
   Set Variable [ $TeachFound; Value:False ]
   Set Variable [ $tCurRec; Value:1 ]
   Go to Record/Request/Page [ First ]
   # loop through the teacher lookup table
   Loop
      If [ gStudents::Teacher = tblLUTeachers::TName ]
      # teacher found, set flag then exit loop
      Set Variable [ $TeachFound; Value:True ]
      Exit Loop If [ $TeachFound = True ]
      End If
      Set Variable [ $tCurRec; Value:$tCurRec + 1 ]
      # if at end of teacher lookup table, exit loop
      Exit Loop If [ $tCurRec   Get(TotalRecordCount) ]
      Go to Record/Request/Page [ Next ]
   End Loop
   # if teacher not found then create rec & add teacher
        name
```

```
   If [ $TeachFound = False ]
   New Record/Request
   Set Field [ tblLUTeachers::TName; gStudents::Teacher ]
   End If
   End If
   Go to Layout [ "StudentImport" (tblStudents) ]
   Exit Loop If [ tblStudents::SID =
         Globals::TotSourceRecs ]
   Go to Record/Request/Page [ Next ]
End Loop
```

Notice that the commented lines start with a # and the font is in bold. Look at the comments, and you see that this code is looping through a table to see if a teacher's name is in the table. If the teacher's name is not found, it's added to the table. Also in this example, you can see that my comments follow these overall guidelines:

- ✔ They tell you what condition is being evaluated.
- ✔ They tell you what steps will be taken as a result of the evaluation.

Adding a comment

As the following steps show, adding a comment to your script code is easy:

1. **With your target database loaded in FileMaker, choose Scripts⇨ ScriptMaker.**

2. **Open a script file from the Define Scripts list by double-clicking it.**

   You see the script code in the editor.

3. **Select a line of script code above the point where you want to insert a comment.**

   When you have existing script code and want to insert a script statement, it's inserted below the currently selected script step.

4. **Scroll the list of script steps to the very bottom, and double-click the Comment script statement.**

   This inserts a comment line — a blank line of code with a # at the beginning — into your script code.

5. **Double-click the script code line with the #.**

   A blank Specify box appears.

6. **Enter the text for the comment that you want to add to your code, and click OK.**

   I usually like to add a space at the beginning of the comment. Otherwise, the text starts immediately after the #.

Adding header comments

Another good idea for commenting your code is the use of a set of header comments at the start of each of your script code modules. Here's an example:

```
#Routine: EnroleDateClicked
#Description: Calls the DatePicker for allowing the
           selection of a date
#History:
# 060605, tlt, Created the routine
# 061105, tlt, Added Get (CurrentDate) to EnroleDate
```

These first few lines of comments provide the name of the routine, a description of what the routine does, and a history of changes to the script code. Multiple programmers working on the same project find this especially helpful because they can see who made what changes during the life of the project.

To facilitate adding header comments, I have a code template. Follow these steps for creating a reusable code template with the header comments:

1. **With your target database loaded in FileMaker, choose Scripts⇨ ScriptMaker.**

   The Define Scripts list appears.

2. **Click the New button.**

   This creates a new script module.

3. **Give your script module a name. I recommend naming it CodeTemplate.**

   You need to use a name that helps you identify this as your master code template.

4. **In the script code, enter the following comments:**

```
#Routine:
#Description:
#History:
#
```

   Use this template for creating any new script code modules.

5. **Click OK to save your script code.**

When you want to add a new script code module to your project, you can highlight the CodeTemplate script module and click the Duplicate button. I like to keep my CodeTemplate module at the top of my scripts list for easy access.

Keeping application notes

Another good practice for documenting your FileMaker database application is to keep an *application notes script*. Although you create this like you create a script, all it contains is an extensive list of comments for documenting the entire application. As shown in Figure 9-1, the first script in the project is named AppNotes. This script contains information about the application and a history of changes to the project.

Figure 9-1: Use periods and dashes in the names of scripts to help organize your scripts list.

The script looks like this (with some of the proprietary information changed):

```
#StuBase v1.015, Copyright (c) 2006, iTi
#All rights reserved
#FileMakerPro 7.0 v2 required
#
#Student Information Management System
#Name of development company
#Address of development company
#Web site of development company
```

```
#Primary developer: Timothy Trimble, email address
#
#APPLICATION HISTORY
# Date     By   Action
# 031805   tlt  Initial database design
# 032105   tlt  UI graphic elements designed
# 032305   tlt  App UI designed
# 032405   tlt  Main form, student list form
# 032505   tlt  Student detail form
# 032605   tlt  Table relationships, Notes subform added
```

This script goes on for another 40 plus lines. However, by taking a look at this script, a programmer or manager can get a quick review of the details about the application and its development history.

Structuring your script listing

When you start doing a lot of script programming, you soon discover that it can be a challenge trying to keep track of your script code modules — especially if you're trying to keep track of hundreds of scripts. As you add new scripts to a database, they pile up in the Define Scripts dialog box, where you pick and choose the scripts you want to assign to buttons and the like. In a particularly long list, finding a script you need can become time consuming.

One solution, through the use of creative names of scripts, is to create sections of scripts (refer to Figure 9-1). To do this, you create a blank script code module, such as Primary Form Functions — notice that I added dashes to the beginning and end of the script name to make it stand out in the list. The only purpose of Primary Form Functions is to act as a section separator for the scripts listed below it. After you create this separator, you group scripts into the section by dragging the double arrows to the left of the script names up or down the list to follow their header.

Another trick is to indent the name of a script with spaces, periods, or dashes, for showing that the script codes modules are related to the previous script. You can see this in the three scripts indented with periods "....." in Figure 9-1. The scripts with the "....." are actually used by the RecStudentFind script. These scripts actually contain code, but the names are indented to show the relationship.

Auto-Centering a Layout

One of the first routines that I created in my FileMaker bag of tricks was for auto-centering. It does a good job of auto-centering the currently displayed layout, regardless of the user's screen size. Here's how to create the routine:

1. **With your target database loaded in FileMaker, choose Scripts⇨ ScriptMaker.**

   The Define Scripts list appears.

2. **Click the New button, and name your script routine.**

   I named my script routine **CenterMe**, but you can give yours a different name if you want. Remember that if you are using the CodeTemplate method that I discuss in the earlier "Adding header comments" section, you would make a duplicate of your code template and then rename the duplicated script code module.

3. **Double-click the Move/Resize Window script statement.**

   This is the only script statement in this module. The Move/Resize Window Options dialog box appears.

4. **In the Window To Adjust frame, make sure that the Current Window radio button is selected.**

   You want any other script code modules to be able to reuse this routine. Therefore, you want it to affect the currently active window.

5. **Click the Specify button next to the Distance From Top option.**

   This opens the Calculation Editor.

   For defining the top position of the current layout, you need to know two things: the height of the current FileMaker desktop (the FileMaker application itself) and the height of the current window. If you divide the height of the FileMaker desktop by 2, you get the middle of the FileMaker application. Likewise, dividing the height of the current window by 2 tells you how much to shift the top of the window up from the middle of the FileMaker desktop. So, to calculate the position for the top of the current window, use this formula:

   ```
   (FileMaker Desktop Height/2) - (Window Height/2)
   ```

6. **In the Calculation Editor, enter the following calculation:**

   ```
   ((Get(WindowDesktopHeight)/2) - (Get(WindowHeight)/2))
   ```

The calculation tells FileMaker that you want the result of the middle of the FileMaker desktop window height minus the middle of the currently active window height. The result is where you want to put the top of your layout.

7. **Click OK to save your calculation.**

   You now have the calculation for the Distance From Top option for your layout.

8. **Click the Specify button next to the Distance From Left option.**

   You need to calculate the position for the left side of the current layout window. Find out the width of the FileMaker application desktop and the width of the current layout window. To calculate the correct left position for the layout, use this formula:

   ```
   (FileMaker Desktop Width/2) - (Window Width/2)
   ```

9. **In the Calculation Editor, enter the following calculation:**

   ```
   ((Get(WindowDesktopWidth)/2) - (Get(WindowWidth)/2)
   ```

   The calculation generates the result of the middle of the FileMaker desktop width minus the middle of the currently active window width. This is where you want to put the left position of your layout.

10. **Click the next three OK buttons to save the calculation, the script statement options, and the script.**

    You now have a script for automatically centering the current layout. Just call this script from any script that loads a layout.

Using External Scripts and Value Lists

 When you've built your black bag of programming tricks, keep all your reusable script routines in one location so that you don't have to copy code every time you want to use it. I have a file I named `MyLibrary` where I have script code modules and value lists (such as yes/no, the days of the week, and so on) that I reuse on a regular basis. Chapter 3 introduces ScriptMaker, and Chapter 5 covers value lists in more detail.

Linking to an external file

In order to take advantage of your bag of tricks, you need to link your library to the application that you're doing development on. Here's how:

1. **With your target database loaded in FileMaker, choose File⟹Define⟹ File References.**

   The Define File References dialog box appears.

2. **Click the New button.**

   The Edit File Reference dialog box appears.

3. **Click the Add File button, select the file that you want to link to, click the Open button, and then click OK to save your file link.**

   This creates a path reference to your file. The filename and the file path appear in the Define File References dialog box.

4. **Click OK to save your file reference.**

   Your application now has a link to your FileMaker file containing your library of scripts and value lists.

Using linked scripts

After you've added your library of scripts as a reference link, using the scripts in your file is easy. Here are the steps:

1. **With your active database loaded in FileMaker, choose Scripts⟹ ScriptMaker.**

   The Define Scripts list for your current database appears.

2. **Select (or create) the script that you want to use for calling the linked script.**

   The script editor appears.

3. **Select the point in your code where you want to call the linked script, and double-click the Perform Script step on the function list.**

   The Perform Script function is inserted in your script code.

4. **Double-click the Perform Script step to open the Specify Script Options dialog box.**

   This is where you select the linked file and script.

5. **Click the down arrow for the drop-down list box, and select the linked file from the list.**

   You now see a list of available scripts in the linked file.

6. **Select the script that you want to perform, and click OK.**

   As part of the Perform Script statement, you now see the name of the script that you're calling and the name of the file from which it is being called.

Be sure that when you're using a file reference link to another file, it will always be accessible by the database. If the referenced file resides on a file server or on a remote host, keep in mind that you might encounter performance issues because network access is never as quick as accessing local hard drives.

Using linked value lists

The approach for using a value list from a referenced file is just as easy as using the scripts. Here's how:

1. **With the target database loaded in FileMaker in Layout mode, click the Define Value Lists icon on the FileMaker toolbar.**

   The value lists for the currently active database appear. However, what you want to show is the value lists in the referenced file.

2. **Click the New button.**

   You see the Edit Value List dialog box.

3. **Select the Use Value List From Another File radio button, select the name of the referenced file from the associated drop-down list (pop-up menu on a Mac), and select the value list that you want from the Value List drop-down list (pop-up menu on a Mac).**

   Now you have a link established to the referenced file value list.

4. **Give your linked value list a name, and then click OK to save your selection.**

   You see the Define Value Lists with your newly linked value list. In the Source column, you can see that the list is from another file.

5. **You can now link to other value lists in the same referenced file or click OK to finish.**

   You're now able to use the linked value list like any of the other value lists in your database.

Calling Up an Address with Google Maps

One of the cool features of FileMaker is the ability to load the default web browser with a specific Web address. One example of this would be to click an address and have FileMaker load the user's web browser with a map (via MapQuest, Yahoo!, Google, or another service) showing that address. I show you that here.

The following script code shows how to build a Web URL address with physical address information and then launch a map for that address with Google Maps (`http://maps.google.com`). This code example is based on the database structure in the Contact Management sample database that comes with FileMaker. (Note that in the code listing that follows, some of the script code lines are wrapped to the next line due to length.) The comments walk you through how it works:

```
#Routine: MapIt
#Description: Builds a URL string for calling Google Maps
          with a street address
#History:
#021706 tlt Created for Dummies Guide
#
# Predefine the variables so we know what we're using
Set Variable [ $URL ]
Set Variable [ $Address ]
Set Variable [ $City ]
Set Variable [ $State ]
Set Variable [ $GooglePrefix;
          Value:"http://maps.google.com/maps?f=q&hl=en&q=
          " ]
# Check for valid address data. Warn user if not valid.
If [ IsEmpty(Contact Management::Street 1) = True ]
    Show Custom Dialog [ Title: "Warning"; Message: "Street
          Address is empty. Please enter a valid
          address."; Buttons: "OK" ]
    Exit Script [ ]
End If
If [ IsEmpty ( Contact Management::City 1 ) = True ]
    Show Custom Dialog [ Title: "Warning"; Message: "City
          is empty. Please enter a valid city."; Buttons:
          "OK" ]
    Exit Script [ ]
End If
```

```
If [ IsEmpty ( Contact Management::State Province 1 ) =
        True ]
   Show Custom Dialog [ Title: "Warning"; Message: "State
        is empty. Please enter a valid State.";
        Buttons: "OK" ]
   Exit Script [ ]
End If
# Replace spaces with "+" for Google formatting
Set Variable [ $Address; Value:Substitute( Contact
        Management::Street 1; " " ;"+" ) ]
Set Variable [ $City; Value:Substitute( Contact
        Management::City 1; " " ;"+" ) ]
Set Variable [ $State; Value:Substitute( Contact
        Management::State Province 1; " " ;"+" ) ]
# Build the Google URL string then call browser with url
Set Variable [ $URL; Value:$GooglePrefix & $Address & ","
        & $City & "," & $State ]
Open URL [ $URL ][ No dialog ]
```

Automated Error E-Mails

As a developer, the last kind of e-mail that I want to receive is from an irate user who is having difficulties with the application. (I prefer to receive e-mails praising my abilities as a master FileMaker developer. I'm still waiting for one of those.) So, one method I use for keeping up-to-date on how well an application is working is by letting the FileMaker application check itself for errors and then automatically e-mail me when an error occurs. Then by the time the user gets around to calling or e-mailing me, I already know about the problem and have usually started on determining how to fix it.

First of all, in order for this to work, you have to include a Set Error Capture [On] statement in your FileMaker application. This tells FileMaker that you want to capture any error messages that occur, instead of automatically displaying them to the user.

The next step is to write a script that performs an error check. The following script code is a sample of how you can do this:

```
#Routine: ErrorCheck
#Description: Checks to see if an error has occurred.
#History:
#021706 tlt Created for Dummies Guide
#
If [ Get (LastError) <> 0 ]
   Set Variable [ $User; Value:Get(UserName) ]
```

```
        Set Variable [ $Version; Value:Get(SystemVersion) ]
        Set Variable [ $Platform; Value:Get(SystemPlatform) ]
        Set Variable [ $CurScript; Value:Get(ScriptName) ]
        Set Variable [ $ErrorNum; Value:Get(LastError) ]
        Set Variable [ $Layout; Value:Get(LayoutName) ]
        Set Variable [ $File; Value:Get(FileName) ]
        Set Variable [ $Time; Value:Get(CurrentTimeStamp) ]
        Set Variable [ $ErrorMsg; Value:"FileMaker Error
            Occurred! " & ¶ &
    "Error #: " & $ErrorNum & ¶ &
    "User: " & $User & ¶ &
    "Version: " & $Version & ¶ &
    "Platform: " & $Platform & ¶ &
    "Script Name: " & $CurScript & ¶ &
    "Layout Name: " & $Layout & ¶ &
    "File Name: " & $File & ¶ &
    "TimeStamp: " & $Time & ¶ &
    "Automated Error Message sent by FileMaker. " ]   Send
            Mail [ To: $$Administrator; Subject: "Msg from
            FileMaker"; Message: $ErrorMsg ]
End If
```

If an error occurs, this script sets variables with information about the current state of the FileMaker application. After it sets the variables, the last `Set Variable` statement builds a text message with all the information. Then it uses the `Send Mail` statement to send the error message to the e-mail address contained in the `$$Administrator` variable — which you should define in a script that is run when the FileMaker application is started.

In FileMaker, a single $ prefix for the variable indicates that it is a local variable. A *local variable* is good for only the duration of the script that it is defined in. A $$ prefix indicates that the variable is *global* and, therefore, available throughout the entire FileMaker application, regardless of which layout, table, or script is active.

The last step in implementing this error-trapping process is to include a call to the ErrorCheck script in your other scripts, whenever you think it's necessary to check for the occurrence of an error. For example, you might want to include `Perform Script [ErrorCheck]` after the following: updates to any data, user login, complex calculations, sorts, or printing reports. Keep in mind that you want to do this only after you have determined that your application is stable — otherwise, you could be flooded with e-mails every time an error occurs.

Part IV

FileMaker Exposed! Sharing and Protecting Your Database

The 5th Wave   By Rich Tennant

"We're here to clean up the database."

In this part . . .

What good is an application if you can't share it with others? In this part, you find out all the details of sharing. Chapter 10 explains how you import data from other sources into FileMaker (and vice versa) and how you can set up FileMaker so users can work with your application across a network. When you're sharing data — especially confidential data — you also need to protect it, which is what Chapter 11 is all about. And Chapter 12 tells you what you need to know about designing applications for the Web and explains FileMaker's easy-to-use Web publishing features.

Chapter 10

Share (Data) and Share Alike

*E*ver notice how very little kids are so willing to share their food, even though you might not want what they have? (Soggy cookies come to mind.) But then as they get older, they figure out that if they share, they don't have as much for themselves — especially when it comes to candy. If you don't know what I mean, try to take candy away from a six-year-old. You might find yourself missing an arm!

The nice thing about sharing FileMaker data is that you can share it and still keep it at the same time. FileMaker makes it easy to share your data. And you'll find many cases when you'll want to do so. Here are a few examples:

✔ Multiple employees need to share a products catalog.

✔ Sales personnel need to share a customer database.

✔ Your Aunt Sophie wants to share her recipe database with you.

✔ A dentist's office needs to share patient information.

✔ The local high school needs to allow teachers to share student information.

There are tons of reasons for wanting to share data. This is one of the major reasons for even having a database to begin with — for sharing information!

In this chapter, I explain some of the ways you can share a FileMaker database: by enabling access to the database across a network, by exporting your data to another format, or by sharing your FileMaker database with another database program. I also show you how to share outside data with FileMaker by importing it. If you're looking to share a database on the Web, you find out the details of exporting to HTML in this chapter, but you also need to check out Chapter 12, where I cover publishing and accessing a database on the Web in more detail.

Sharing a Database over a Network

You've just designed the coolest information database in FileMaker, and now you want to share it. Just how do you go about making a FileMaker database shareable?

One of the easiest ways to share a database is by enabling other FileMaker users to access that database on a computer across a network. (For a little background on what a network is, see the nearby sidebar, "The topic of topology.") Users can access the database through a shared folder on your computer or network. The computer where the database is saved is called the *host computer*. Users on various computers can access the database on the host computer and do whatever you allow them to do with that data (these users are sometimes called *clients*).

Because the FileMaker host computer is handling all the requests for data by the other computers, use the fastest computer available as the host.

If you decide to go this route, remember that FileMaker Pro sharing supports up to only five simultaneous users on a network. If you need to support more than five connections, check out FileMaker Server, which can support up to 250 simultaneous users.

Although you *can* have the database file on a remote computer or server (one accessed via the Internet rather than the local network) while hosting, that doesn't mean you should. I (and the folks at FileMaker) don't recommend it because doing so decreases the performance of the database and makes the database less secure.

The topic of topology

In order to share data, you need to have a method for allowing others to gain physical access to your data. Before the age of networks, I used a special method called Sneaker Net. I would write my data to a removable floppy disk (remember those?). Then wearing my best pair of sneakers, I would run my floppy disk over to the person who wanted to see my data. Fortunately, with the use of networking, we no longer have to be so physical about sharing our data.

When related to computer technology, the word *topology* generally refers to the physical structure of a computer network. You might hear your local computer geek utter phrases such as, "Our network utilizes a CAT-5 cabling system for Ethernet traffic in the local facility, fiber optics between the buildings, and various 802.11g wireless routers in key, hot-spot locations throughout the campus." Basically, he or she just described the topology of the computer network.

The following figure gives a simple example of a network configuration used in the home or a personal office.

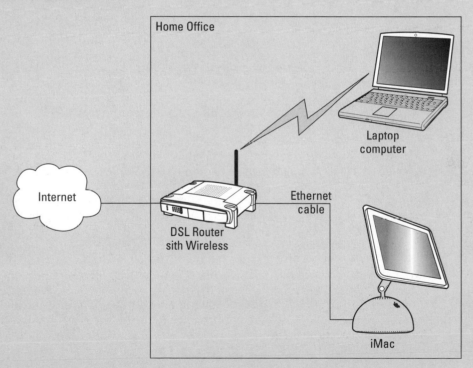

In this configuration, you could have your FileMaker database on the iMac computer and be able to use it from the laptop computer. (Providing you have a FileMaker license for both computers.) Or maybe you're working with a larger network topology, such as a business office, as shown in the next figure.

(continued)

(continued)

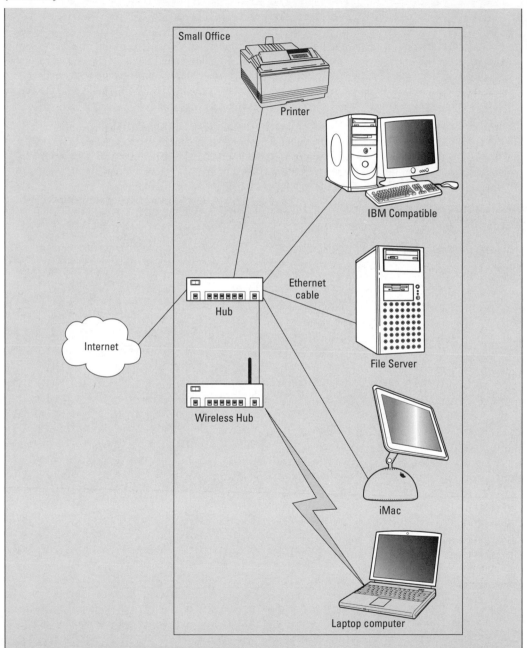

With this topology, the IBM PC, the iMac, and the laptop all have FileMaker installed, and they all connect to a FileMaker database file residing on the file server via the use of a shared disk folder. This is a very common approach used by many businesses.

Enabling sharing for the database

To share a FileMaker database over a network, the first step is to enable sharing for that database. When you do this, the computer where the database is saved becomes the host computer.

The host computer is responsible for controlling the connections to the database. If you exit FileMaker or turn off that computer, the other FileMaker users cannot connect to the shared database.

After you decide which computer should be the host, follow these steps to get you sharing data in a flash:

1. **Open the database that you want to make shareable in FileMaker Pro.**

    Just make sure that it's not a database with top-secret customer information like Social Security numbers, private phone numbers, or movie rental records.

2. **Choose Edit➪Sharing➪FileMaker Network (FileMaker Pro➪Sharing➪ FileMaker Network, if on a Mac).**

    The FileMaker Network Settings dialog box appears. This is where you configure the sharing options for the currently open database (see Figure 10-1).

FileMaker Network Settings	? X
FileMaker Network Settings	
Turn on Network Sharing to share your open files using TCP/IP.	
Network Sharing: ○ Off ● On	
TCP/IP Address: 192.168.16.15	
FileMaker access via FileMaker Network	
Currently open files	Network access to file
HeyLookAtMe-Shared.fp7	File: "HeyLookAtMe-Shared.fp7"
	● All users
	○ Specify users by privilege set Specify...
	○ No users
	☐ Don't display in Open Remote File dialog
	Send Message... OK Cancel

Figure 10-1: Configuring sharing options.

3. **In the Currently Open Files box, if there are two or more databases listed, select the database that you want to share.**

    I hate it when I accidentally share the wrong database file. (User error! Replace user, and try again!)

4. **For Network Sharing, select the On radio button.**

   This turns on the network sharing via TCP/IP for the current database.

   TCP/IP, which stands for Transmission Control Protocol/Internet Protocol, is a networking protocol used by just about everyone. It is basically an address scheme for assigning a networking address to every device attached to the network — similar to having an address on each house. In order for the mail carrier to deliver mail, he has to know the address. The same is true with TCP/IP — with it, the network communication devices know where to deliver the data when it is requested.

5. **In the Network Access To File area, select the All Users radio button.**

   For now, this turns on sharing for all the FileMaker users on your network. In Chapter 11, I cover how to define and configure User Accounts and Privilege Sets for limiting who can view and use shared data.

6. **Click OK to close the FileMaker Network Settings dialog box and save the changes.**

   Now wasn't that easy?

Connecting to a hosted FileMaker database

Now that you've hosted a FileMaker database, what about connecting to it? Again, you'll be amazed at how easy this is. FileMaker takes care of a lot of the work for you. Here's how to do it:

1. **Prior to connecting to the host computer, you do need to find out the TCP/IP address of that computer. In Windows, you can find out by entering `ipconfig` in a DOS window. On the Mac, you can find out by choosing ⇨**🍎**⇨Location⇨Network Preferences.**

   When you know the TCP/IP address of the hosting computer, the rest of the process is easy.

2. **In FileMaker, choose File⇨Open Remote.**

   The Open Remote File dialog box appears. Open Remote opens databases that aren't located on your local computer or on a locally accessible shared drive. (You can also do this by choosing File⇨Open, and then clicking the Remote button.) FileMaker Hosts (computers with FileMaker Network Sharing turned on and shared databases open) visible to your computer appear in the Hosts list box when the View drop-down list/pop-up menu shows Local Hosts.

3. **Click the Add to Favorites button.**

   The Edit Favorite Host dialog box appears. After you select a host as a Favorite, it appears in the Hosts box when you select Open Remote and choose Favorite Hosts. Selecting Favorite Hosts allows you to narrow the list of available hosts to just those that you frequent often (so you don't have to hunt for the one you want).

4. **In the Host's Internet Address text box, enter the TCP/IP address of the computer that is hosting the FileMaker database. Then enter a name for this connection in the Favorite Host's Name text box (see Figure 10-2).**

   This defines the address and the name of the host for viewing in the Hosts list in the Open Remote File dialog box when Favorite Hosts is chosen from the View drop-down list (pop-up menu on the Mac).

5. **If you want to limit what files are displayed when connecting to the host, you can select the Show Only These Files option in the File Settings frame, and then enter the names of the files that you want to be viewable.**

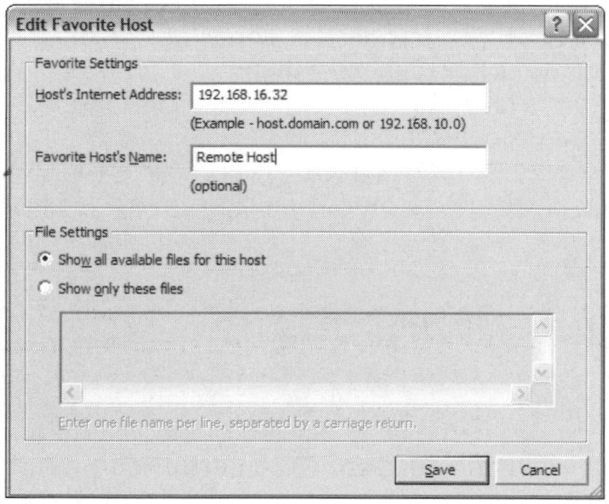

Figure 10-2:
Name your favorite host.

6. **Click Save.**

   The newly added host now appears in the Hosts list box and, when selected, a list of the available files appears in the Available Files list.

7. **Select the file that you want to connect to from the Available Files list.**

Notice that the full TCP/IP address, path, and filename appear in the Network File Path box. Instead of using the Hosts list, you can enter the full path to the host in this box. The format should always be:

```
fmnet:/TCPIP address/filename
```

For example:

```
fmnet:/192.168.16.32/HeyLookAtMe-Shared
```

8. Click the Open button to connect to the database.

You go through the rigmarole of defining the host only once. After that, all you have to do is choose File⇨Open Remote, click the Host, and then click the Open button. That's all there is to it.

Exporting Your Data to Other Formats

Not everyone has FileMaker Pro. It's a shame, too! But then, not everyone is as bright as you and I. For those instances when you need to share your FileMaker database with nonFileMaker users, various options are available. In this section, I explain what those options are and when you might use them. Then I explain how you do the actual exporting.

The process for doing an export is mostly the same for all the formats. So, although it would be cool to show how each one is exported and viewed in the target application, I focus on just the most popular formats — Excel and HTML.

Understanding your options

In FileMaker, you can export to a lot of different formats. Table 10-1 lists the available formats for exporting data and offers a quick description of each, along with an example of when you might use a particular format. (But some you might never use.) You also see an Extension column in the table that tells what filename extension is used for files of the specified type.

Table 10-1	Database Export Formats	
Extension	*Format*	*Description*
.tab	Tab-separated text	Very common format for text-based data files. In the exported file, tabs separate fields in your database. Most data-related applications support this format, so it's good when you need to import textual data.

Extension	Format	Description
.csv	Comma-separated text	Another common format for text-based data files. Commas separate fields. Most data-related applications support this format, so it's also good when you need to import textual data.
.slk	SYLK file, or symbolic link file format	This spreadsheet format originated with an application called Multiplan, and various spreadsheet applications still support it. If you have such a spreadsheet application, this format will come in handy.
.dbf	dBASE file	This format originated with the dBASE database application. It is now widely adopted throughout the industry as a data format. dBASE is a good option when you have a database application that supports dbf.
.dif	DIF, or data interchange format	This spreadsheet structure originated with the first spreadsheet application: VisiCalc. It is still widely supported by various applications. Choose DIF when your choice is between DIF and one of the text-based options.
.wk1	Lotus 1-2-3	One of the first spreadsheet applications on the market was Lotus 1-2-3, which is similar to Microsoft Excel. Look to this option when using an application that supports it.
.bas	BASIC	Most BASIC programming languages use this BASIC file structure, so try this option when writing your own BASIC language database application.
.mer	Merge file	The merge format is for creating a merge file, so you can use your FileMaker data with Microsoft Word or other word-processing applications. For example, export data to this format when you need to merge contact information in FileMaker with a letter you create in Microsoft Word.

(continued)

Table 10-1 *(continued)*

Extension	Format	Description
.htm	HTML table	Exporting to this format turns a FileMaker table into an HTML-based table of the data. Very handy when you need to display static data, for example, on a Web site. See the upcoming section later in this chapter for more detail about exporting to this format. See Chapter 12 for more about putting data on the Web.
.fp7	FileMaker Pro	You might be thinking, "Why bother? Isn't this the same as saving?" Not really. The export to a FileMaker Pro file enables you to select which layout, tables, and fields to export. So, for example, you can create a *projection* (subset of your table's field) for use by others (for example, not exporting salary information).
.xml	XML file, or Extensible Markup Language	This newer standard for formatting is being widely accepted throughout the computer industry. You might want to export to this format if you're not sure how the recipient intends to use the data.
.xls	Excel file	This option can transform a table into a worksheet in a Microsoft Excel workbook. Often used when you want to perform "what-if" calculations involving the data or chart the data.

Exporting to Microsoft Excel

Just about everyone either has Microsoft Excel or uses an application that supports the Excel format, such as OpenOffice. As such, sharing your data is easy if you export it to the Excel format. Here are the steps to do it:

1. **Open the FileMaker database that you want to export, and choose File⇨Export Records.**

The Export Records To File dialog box appears.

2. **In the File Name text box, enter the name that you want to give the exported database file, without the extension.**

   FileMaker automatically adds the correct extension for the filename when the file is saved.

3. **From the Save As Type drop-down list/pop-up menu, select the XLS file type. Then click Save.**

   FileMaker now shows the Excel Options dialog box for gathering information specific to the creation of the Excel formatted file.

4. **Leave the check box selected for Use Field Names As Column Names In First Row.**

   This places the field names at the top of each column in the exported spreadsheet.

5. **Type the names that you want to use for the Worksheet and Title. Then type the Subject of the exported file and the Author name. Click the Continue button.**

   This information is specific to the use of Microsoft Excel. Although optional, it is wise to at least enter a Worksheet and Title name.

   After you click Continue, you see the Specify Field Order For Export dialog box. This is for defining which tables and fields to export and the field order for the export.

6. **In the list box in the upper left, select the layout that you want to use for the source of the data to be exported.**

   This option lets you specify which table you want to export.

7. **Click the Move All button in the center of the dialog box. Or you can highlight which fields you want to include in the export. Click the Move button to move the fields to the right side of the dialog box.**

8. **If you'd like, you can select a field for grouping the exported fields — click the check box next to the Group field (in the Group By box).**

   You see Group fields if you have a field that uses a value list for setting the contents of the field. For example, if the field uses a Yes/No value list, that field shows up in the Group By list. If selected, your export is grouped by Yes and by No.

9. **You can set the order of the fields by using the ↑ or ↓ to drag the fields into the desired position in the Field Export Order box.**

   This is another cool feature, especially if the required export file needs to have a different order than what your native FileMaker database table uses.

10. **If you want to use the same formatting for the exported fields that you have in FileMaker, select the check box next to Apply Current Layout's Data Formatting To Exported Data.**

This uses the sizing of the fields for the exported data, which saves you from having to go into Excel and manually resize the columns to match the field sizes. Figure 10-3 shows a sample of export configuration.

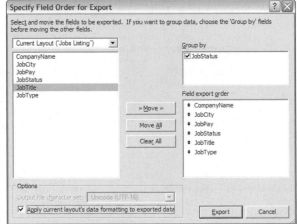

Figure 10-3: These settings tell FileMaker how to perform the export.

11. **Now that all the options look good, click the Export button.**

The data is exported to the Microsoft Excel format. Here's a screen shot of the result. (See Figure 10-4.)

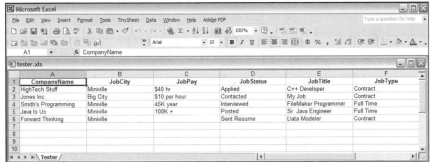

Figure 10-4: My Excel file looks just like I want it.

Exporting to HTML

This is a great feature for viewing your data as a Web page or for giving the data to a Web developer. The steps are very similar to the Excel export steps.

1. **Repeat the same steps as with the Excel export (in the preceding "Exporting to Microsoft Excel" section) with the following exceptions:**

   - **In Step 3, select the HTM file type.**

   - **In Step 10, you can also set the Output File Character Set Type (in the Options frame), depending on the character set that you want for your HTML file.**

2. **When you're satisfied with the Export options, click the Export button.**

   Because this is in HTML, you can edit the file with your Web development tools to make it look even nicer. Figure 10-5 shows the exported file in the Firefox Web browser.

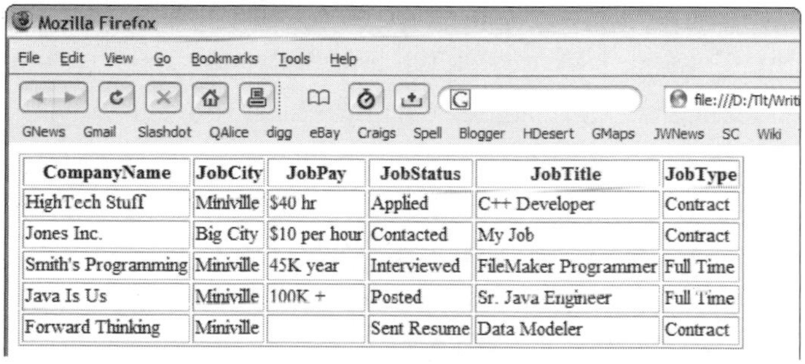

Figure 10-5: Exported data in HTML.

CompanyName	JobCity	JobPay	JobStatus	JobTitle	JobType
HighTech Stuff	Miniville	$40 hr	Applied	C++ Developer	Contract
Jones Inc.	Big City	$10 per hour	Contacted	My Job	Contract
Smith's Programming	Miniville	45K year	Interviewed	FileMaker Programmer	Full Time
Java Is Us	Miniville	100K +	Posted	Sr. Java Engineer	Full Time
Forward Thinking	Miniville		Sent Resume	Data Modeler	Contract

Importing Data from Other Sources

"Data never goes away! It just migrates to the next platform!" I can't remember who said this, but they evidently never suffered a hard drive failure with no backup. But in a sense, this person is correct. What is often called *legacy data* is information (in a database) that originally resided on an older computing platform. Often, the data is in an application that has outgrown its usefulness. For example, have you ever tried to maintain a contact management list in a spreadsheet? It might work fine for 30 contacts, but it could be a pain to maintain with a thousand. So, as a FileMaker user/developer, you might encounter situations where you'll need to migrate data from another system into FileMaker.

Excellent data from Excel

Microsoft Excel is a great tool, as far as spreadsheets go. But as a database-management tool . . . well, it's just not designed for that purpose. So, if you're stuck with an Excel spreadsheet with a lot of data in it, how do you get it into FileMaker? It's a lot easier than you might think. The following steps show you how to do this.

If you don't have an Excel spreadsheet to test this out with, you can download the `Customers.xls` file from the Web site mentioned in the Introduction.

1. **Click the New Database tool on the FileMaker toolbar.**

    The New Database dialog box appears.

2. **Select the Create A New Empty File radio button and click OK.**

    FileMaker now shows a file selection dialog box for entering the name that you want to use for the new database.

3. **In the File Name text box, enter the name that you want to use for the database. (If you're using the `Customers.xls` file, just use Customers as the filename.) Then click the Save button.**

    The Define Database dialog box appears, as shown in Figure 10-6.

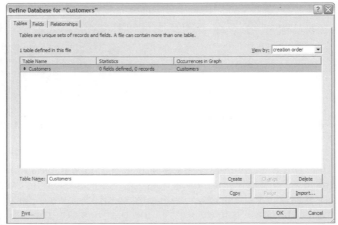

Figure 10-6:
Define
Database
dialog box.

4. **Click OK.**

    You now have a blank FileMaker database.

5. **Choose File➪Import Records➪File.**

The Open File dialog box opens. Now you need to tell FileMaker what type of file you want to import.

6. **In the Files Of Type drop-down list (Show pop-up menu on the Mac), select the Excel Files (*.xls) option.**

    A list of Excel files appears.

7. **Select the Excel file that you want to import, and then click the Open button. When the Specify Excel Data dialog box appears, you can opt to import specific sheets or named ranges of the Excel file. Make your choice depending upon how your Excel file has the data stored and click Continue.**

    The Import Field Mapping dialog box appears. This dialog box lets you define which fields you want to import into your database. However, before you can do the import, you need to define the fields for your database.

8. **Move the Import Field Mapping dialog box to the far left side of the screen, and click the Define Database button. After the Define Database dialog box appears, drag it to the right side of the screen.**

    As shown in Figure 10-7, the Import Field Mapping dialog box is on the left and the Define Database dialog box is on the right. This allows you to view the field names in the Excel file while you define the field names for the FileMaker database.

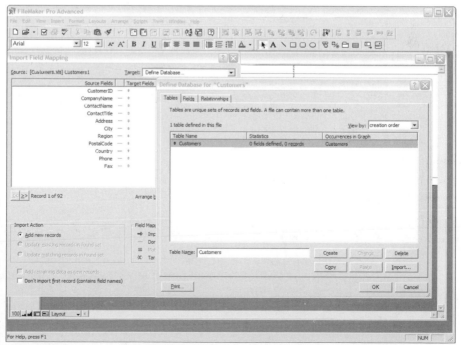

Figure 10-7:
Define
Database
and Import
Field
Mapping
dialog
boxes.

9. **Click the Fields tab, and create the fields with the same names as shown in the Import Field Mapping dialog box. Click OK when you're done adding the fields.**

   You don't have to use the same field names exactly as shown in the Import Field Mapping dialog box, but for now, it makes it easier to demonstrate how to do the import. If you need a refresher on creating fields in your database, just refer to Chapter 2.

10. **If your Excel spreadsheet has field names in the first row, click the Don't Import First Record (Contains Field Names) check box.**

    Notice, in Figure 10-8, that arrows point from the Excel fields to the FileMaker fields. By clicking an arrow (turning it off), you can tell FileMaker *not* to import the field. Also, by using the up/down arrows next to the FileMaker Target Fields, you can change the order of the fields. Move the arrow up or down into the desired position.

Figure 10-8:
Fields match and are ready for import.

11. **Click the Import button.**

    FileMaker imports the records. When done, it will show a Import Summary box with a count of how many records were imported, or skipped due to errors.

If you have your FileMaker preferences set to automatically add newly created fields to a layout, you're good to go; otherwise, you'll need to add the new fields to a layout in order to view the data in FileMaker Pro.

Getting text into your database

In many situations, when you've been given a data file that came from a main-frame computer system, it has been exported into a *tab-delimited* format. This means that tabs separate the fields. A sample of what this can look like is shown in Figure 10-9.

Figure 10-9: Tab-separated fields in a text file.

The process for getting this data into FileMaker is exactly the same as the process in the earlier "Excellent data from Excel" section — except for one minor step. In Step 6, instead of selecting the Excel option, you select the Tab-Separated Text Files option. All the other steps are the same.

Taming the dreaded comma-separated variable file

Once again, something that's usually a major pain to do in other programming environments is very easy in FileMaker. The comma-separated variable file, or CSV, is one of the most common types of data formats used for exporting and importing data from one database to another. In fact, just about every database and spreadsheet application that I know of supports the CSV format — including FileMaker. It handles the importing of CSV data the same as it handles Excel and tab-separated data.

To import a CSV file, follow the same steps used for importing the Excel spreadsheet in the "Excellent data from Excel" section earlier in this chapter. However, in Step 6, use the Comma-Separated Text Files option.

When importing data from other types of files and databases, FileMaker limits you to importing into a single table at a time. Therefore, if you want to import multiple tables and define a relationship between tables, import each table individually, and define the relationships manually. Trying to do this complex process automatically would require a sophisticated use of Artificial Intelligence. We might see this feature in future versions of FileMaker, but for now, importing is on a per table basis.

Importing from SQL via ODBC, and other strange acronyms

Are you afraid? Does the mere mention of the three-letter acronym S-Q-L send shivers down your spine, making you dread having to use an arcane set of incantations to manage your data? Well, it shouldn't. SQL stands for Structured Query Language. It is *the* most widely used method of database management in the world today and FileMaker's SQL import will help you with forming your incantation(s). As such, you need to understand how to import SQL data into FileMaker.

A very important piece of this process involves the use of a four-letter word — ODBC. ODBC stands for Open Database Connectivity, which is an industry standard for database connectivity drivers, regardless of the type of programming language or environment. As shown in Figure 10-10, multiple FileMaker Pro systems can talk to a back-end SQL database via the use of ODBC and a network.

Prior to trying out a connection to a SQL database, you need to have access to a SQL database — and you need an ODBC driver installed. If you want to do a test on your local system, you can get MySQL and MyODBC at www.mysql.com. You can find documentation there on how to install and configure MySQL and the MyODBC software.

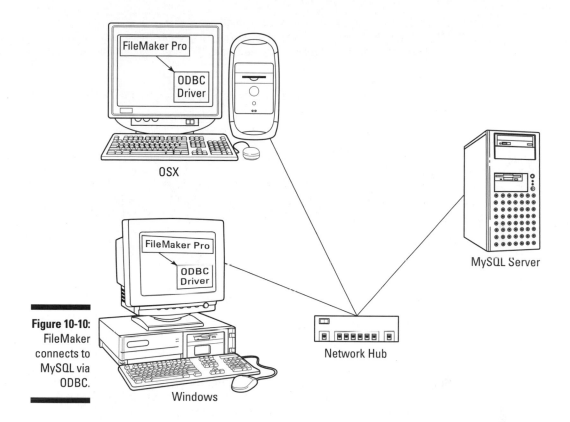

In the following steps, I'm connecting FileMaker to a MySQL database running on my local computer. The steps are the same for any other SQL database via ODBC, with the exception of the name of the ODBC driver, the database name, and the table name.

1. **Click the New Database tool on the FileMaker toolbar.**

   The New Database dialog box opens.

2. **Select the Create A New Empty File radio button, and click OK.**

3. **In the File Name text box of the dialog box that appears, enter the name that you want to use for the database and click Save.**

   For the MySQL test, type **keywords** as the database name.

   For the purpose of testing with a local MySQL database, you'll be connecting to one of the internal, system-database tables that installs with MySQL.

 4. **Click OK.**

   You now have a blank FileMaker database.

 5. **Choose File⇨Import Records⇨ODBC Data Source.**

   The Select ODBC Data Source dialog box appears with a list of available ODBC Data Sources, as shown in Figure 10-11.

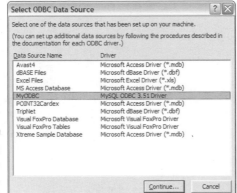

 6. **Select the correct ODBC Data Source for the SQL database that you are connecting to. For the local MySQL database, select the MyODBC Data Source. Then click the Continue button.**

   The SQL database asks you for your assigned user ID and password.

 7. **Enter your assigned user ID and password, and click OK.**

   This is the user ID and password that you assigned to yourself when you installed the SQL database. If someone else installed SQL, or if it's a remote SQL database on a network, you need to contact the database administrator for the correct user ID and password — and also make sure that it's okay for you to connect to the database. (DBAs tend to get picky about who's doing what to their databases!)

   As shown in Figure 10-12, the SQL Query Builder appears. You use this dialog box to enter the SQL query for retrieving data for your import into FileMaker.

 8. **In the SQL Query box, enter the query that you want to execute. Then click the Execute button.**

   For the MySQL example, enter the query that you see in Figure 10-12.

   After you click Execute, the Import Field Mapping dialog box appears.

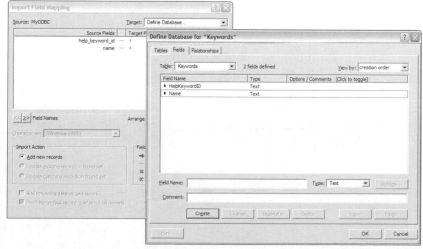

Figure 10-12:
SQL Query
Builder.

9. **Move the Import Field Mapping dialog box to the far left side of the screen, and click the Define Database button. After the Define Database dialog box appears, drag it to the right side of the screen.**

   As shown in Figure 10-13, the Import Field Mapping dialog box is on the left and the Define Database dialog box is on the right. This allows you to view the field names in the SQL table while you define the field names for the FileMaker database.

Figure 10-13:
Import Field
Mapping
and Define
Database
dialog
boxes.

10. Click the Fields tab, and create the fields with the same names as shown in the Import Field Mapping dialog box. Click OK when you're done adding the fields.

You don't *have* to use the same field names as shown in the Import Field Mapping dialog box, but for now, it just makes it easier to demonstrate how to do the import. If you need a refresher on creating fields in your database, just refer back to Chapter 5.

In Figure 10-14, notice that arrows point from the SQL table fields to the FileMaker fields. By clicking an arrow, you can tell FileMaker *not* to import the field. Also, by using the up/down arrows next to the FileMaker Target Fields, you can change the order of the fields. Move the arrow up or down into the desired position.

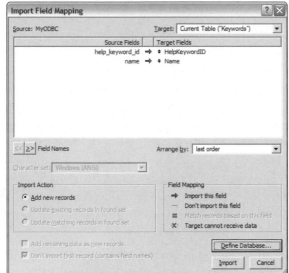

Figure 10-14:
Fields match
and ready
for import.

11. Click the Import button.

FileMaker imports the records. When done, the Import Summary box shows how many records were imported, or skipped due to errors. You can then create layouts and add functions for your imported database table. Figure 10-15 shows a screen shot of a table layout with the imported data.

HelpKeywordID	Name
0	MIN
1	JOIN
2	SERIALIZABLE
3	REPLACE
4	RETURNS
5	MASTER_SSL_CA
6	NCHAR
7	COLUMNS
8	WORK
9	DATETIME
10	MODE
11	OPEN
12	INTEGER
13	ESCAPE
14	VALUE
15	GEOMETRYCOLLECTI
16	DROP
17	SQL_BIG_RESULT
18	EVENTS
19	MONTH
20	REGEXP
21	DUPLICATE
22	LINESTRINGFROMTEX
23	UNLOCK
24	INNODB
25	YEAR_MONTH
26	LOCK
27	NDB
28	CHECK
29	FULL
30	INT4
31	BY
32	NO
33	MINUTE
34	DATA
35	DAY
36	RAID_CHUNKSIZE
37	SHARE

Figure 10-15:
Imported
SQL data.

Importing XML data

XML sounds like a new model of a Jaguar sports car. Actually, it's another data-storage format — the Extensible Markup Language. Though the standard has been around for a little while (since 1998), it's really been more widely adopted as a standard format for storing data since 2002 and its promotion by Microsoft and Apple as their standard for arbitrary data storage. That data can be documents, databases — just about any type of information.

The process of importing XML data is very similar to the process for importing from Excel, with a few minor differences. The following steps import an XML document into FileMaker:

An example XML file, `Customers.xml`, is available from the Web site listed in the Introduction.

1. **Click the New Database tool on the FileMaker toolbar.**

   The New Database dialog box opens.

2. **Select the Create A New Empty File radio button, and click OK.**

   FileMaker shows the Create a New File Named dialog box for entering the name that you want to use for the new database.

3. **In the File Name text box, enter the name that you want to use for the database. (If you're using the `Customers.xml` file, just use Customers as the filename.) Click the Save button, and then click OK.**

   You now have a blank FileMaker database.

4. **Choose File⇨Import Records⇨XML Data Source.**

   The Specify XML And XSL Options dialog box opens, as shown in Figure 10-16. Now, you need to tell FileMaker what type of file you want to import. Your choices are:

   - *File:* Import from an XML file.

   - *HTTP Request:* Import from a Web address.

   - *Use XSL Style Sheet:* Apply formatting to associated XML data.

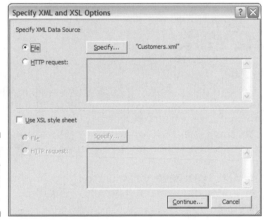

Figure 10-16: Specify XML and XSL options.

An extensive explanation of XML is beyond the scope of this book. To find out more about the XML format, take a look at *XML All-in-One Desk Reference For Dummies* by Richard Wagner and Richard Mansfield (Wiley Publishing).

5. **Click the File radio button, and then select the XML file that you want to import. Click the Open button, and then click the Continue button.**

The Import Field Mapping dialog box appears.

6. **Move the Import Field Mapping dialog box to the far left side of the screen, and click the Define Database button. After the Define Database dialog box appears, drag it to the right side of the screen.**

   Now you can view the field names in the XML file while you define the field names for the FileMaker database.

7. **Click the Fields tab, and then create the fields with the same names as shown in the Import Field Mapping dialog box. Click OK when you're done adding the fields.**

   You don't *have* to use the same field names as shown in the Import Field Mapping dialog box.

   By clicking an arrow, you can tell FileMaker not to import the field. Also, by using the up/down arrows next to the FileMaker Target Fields, you can change the order of the fields. Move the arrow up or down into the desired position.

8. **Click the Import button.**

   FileMaker imports the records. When done, the Import Summary box shows how many records were imported, or skipped due to errors.

Linking to Other FileMaker Databases

Having the ability to link to other FileMaker databases is a very powerful feature of FileMaker. By linking, you can share not only data, but also scripts and value lists. The ability to link to other databases is done via the use of file references. In the following sections, you find out how to set up and use file references.

Setting up a file reference

File references are easy to set up, as shown in the following steps:

1. **Open any database that you want to start with.**

   If you can't decide which one to start with, feel free to use the Hey, Look at Me! database (which you can find on this book's companion Web site; see the Introduction for details). Or try the Customers database created during the import earlier in this chapter.

2. **Choose File➪Define➪File References.**

The Define File References dialog box appears, which is where you define the links to the other FileMaker database.

3. **Click the New button.**

This opens the Edit File Reference dialog box, which is where you create and/or edit any links to other FileMaker databases.

4. **Click the Add File button. Browse to the location of the Templates folder in your FileMaker folders. Open the Home-General folder, and select the database to which you want to link. (I select Contact Management.) Click the Open button, and then click OK.**

This defines a file reference to the Contact Management database, as shown in Figure 10-17.

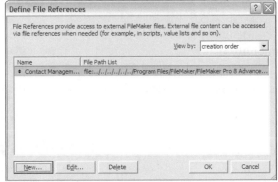

5. **Click OK.**

You are now linked to the Contact Management database. The tables, scripts, and value lists can be used within your current database. Keep your database open while you cover the next topic to see how to use a linked FileMaker database.

Using a file reference

After you've added a file reference to your current database (see the preceding section), you can use that reference in many different areas. For example, the following steps show you how to access a table in the linked database:

1. **In the database in which you created the file reference, switch to layout mode. Then click the Define Database tool on the FileMaker toolbar.**

Chapter 10: Share (Data) and Share Alike **221**

The Define Database dialog box appears.

2. Click the Relationships tab.

As a default, you'll see the tables that are defined in your currently open database. In the next step, you'll see how you can add a table from the linked database.

3. Click the Add Table tool at the bottom-left corner of the dialog box.

This tells FileMaker that you want to insert a new table into the Relationships view. The Specify Table dialog box appears, as shown in Figure 10-18.

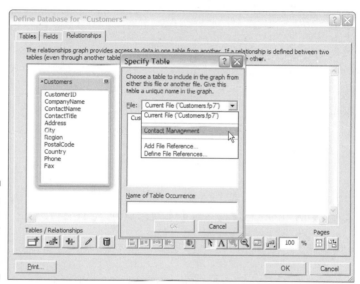

Figure 10-18: Specify a table for relationships.

4. As shown in Figure 10-18, open the File list and select the Contact Management database. Click OK.

As shown in Figure 10-19, you now have a second table in your relationship view. The italic text at the top of the table is an indication that the table linked via a file reference.

You'll find that there are many areas in FileMaker where you can select the names of tables, scripts, and value lists. In those selection boxes, if you have file references, you'll see the items that are available, just as if they were a part of your current database.

REMEMBER

If you use file references in your database applications and plan on distributing your database, you must also distribute the database files that you use in your file references.

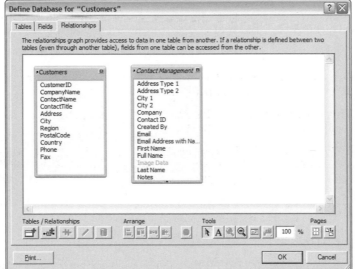

Figure 10-19:
File References show up in the Relationships Graph.

Sharing Data with Another Database System via ODBC/JDBC

With the plethora of database applications in the industry, at times, you just have to share with a database system that isn't FileMaker — such as Microsoft Access, 4th Dimension, and FoxPro. Well, the good news is that as long as those other applications support ODBC (Open Database Connectivity) or JDBC (Java Database Connectivity), they can connect to your FileMaker database.

TECHNICAL STUFF

ODBC and *JDBC* are two standards for defining an interface (database drivers) for connecting to databases, regardless of platform or database application. *ODBC* stands for Open Database Connectivity and *JDBC* stands for Java Database Connectivity. Most database application systems in the industry today support these two standards.

The ODBC/JDBC drivers do not automatically install when you install FileMaker Pro. For instructions on how to install these drivers, see the electronic documentation on your FileMaker Pro CD. Look for the file called `FM8_ODBC_JDBC_install.pdf`, and follow the instructions included in that document.

Even though ODBC and JDBC sound like four-letter words with a lot of complexity behind them, FileMaker makes it easy to share your database via these standards. Here are the steps:

1. **Open the FileMaker database that you want to make available via ODBC/JDBC. Choose Edit⇨Sharing⇨ODBC/JDBC.**

   This opens the ODBC/JDBC Sharing Settings dialog box, which is very similar to the standard FileMaker Sharing dialog box.

2. **Click the On radio button for the ODBC/JDBC Sharing, select the file that you want to share in the Currently Open Files list, and select All Users in the ODBC/JDBC Access To File frame.**

   This provides access to your database for all users. I cover how to set up specific user security in Chapter 11.

3. **Click OK.**

4. **Set up a link to the FileMaker database in whichever database program you want to use. Then you're ready to start sharing the file.**

   That's all there is to it. Nothing too complex or difficult. Just as a test under Windows, I created an ODBC data source for connecting to FileMaker Pro. Then, using Microsoft Access, I created a blank database and established a link to the Hey, Look At Me! database (see Figure 10-20). Although explaining how to configure another database program is beyond the scope of this book, you can check that program's help files or documentation. Figure 10-21 shows how my FileMaker database looks in Access.

Figure 10-20: ODBC-linked tables in MS Access.

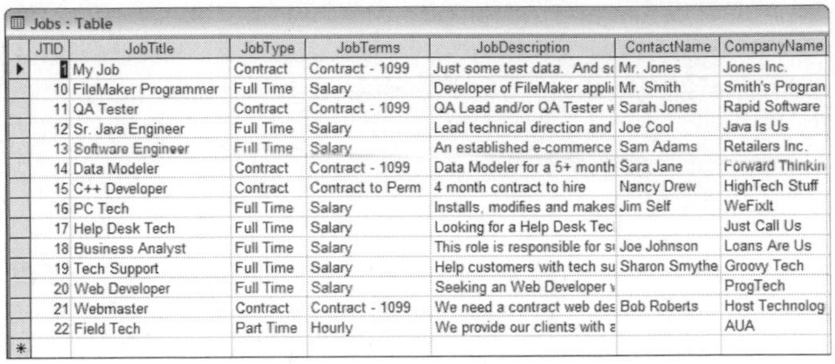

Jobs : Table

JTID	JobTitle	JobType	JobTerms	JobDescription	ContactName	CompanyName
1	My Job	Contract	Contract - 1099	Just some test data. And s	Mr. Jones	Jones Inc.
10	FileMaker Programmer	Full Time	Salary	Developer of FileMaker appli	Mr. Smith	Smith's Progran
11	QA Tester	Contract	Contract - 1099	QA Lead and/or QA Tester w	Sarah Jones	Rapid Software
12	Sr. Java Engineer	Full Time	Salary	Lead technical direction and	Joe Cool	Java Is Us
13	Software Engineer	Full Time	Salary	An established e-commerce	Sam Adams	Retailers Inc.
14	Data Modeler	Contract	Contract - 1099	Data Modeler for a 5+ month	Sara Jane	Forward Thinkin
15	C++ Developer	Contract	Contract to Perm	4 month contract to hire	Nancy Drew	HighTech Stuff
16	PC Tech	Full Time	Salary	Installs, modifies and makes	Jim Self	WeFixIt
17	Help Desk Tech	Full Time	Salary	Looking for a Help Desk Tec		Just Call Us
18	Business Analyst	Full Time	Salary	This role is responsible for s	Joe Johnson	Loans Are Us
19	Tech Support	Full Time	Salary	Help customers with tech su	Sharon Smythe	Groovy Tech
20	Web Developer	Full Time	Salary	Seeking an Web Developer v		ProgTech
21	Webmaster	Contract	Contract - 1099	We need a contract web des	Bob Roberts	Host Technolog
22	Field Tech	Part Time	Hourly	We provide our clients with a		AUA

Figure 10-21: Linked Jobs Table in MS Access.

Generating the Ultimate Database Report

With all this importing, exporting, linking, editing, massaging, printing, managing, and all those other types of *-ing* words, there's one thing that's real handy to have around — a nice, detailed description of the database application. Well, it just so happens that FileMaker Pro Advanced provides a wonderful tool for doing just that — it's called the Database Design Report. Among the more useful applications for this feature are the following:

- Documenting all the layouts, tables, fields, relationships, scripts, and so on in your database.
- Tracking how changing one item (for instance, a field definition) impacts other parts of your database that reference that item.

Here's how to use it:

1. **In FileMaker Pro 8 Advanced, open any FileMaker Pro database application about which you want a detailed report. Then from the Tools menu, choose Database Design Report.**

   This shows the Database Design Report dialog box for setting the options.

2. **Select the desired file from the Available Files list.**

   When the file is selected, the Include Fields From Tables list shows the available tables in that file.

3. **Select the tables that you want to include in the report. Then in the Include In Report box, select the items that you want to have in your report.**

   As you can see, the list is pretty extensive. If you plan on generating a report with all the options enabled and printing it, you better be prepared to have a lot of paper.

4. **Select the format that you want for the report (HTML or XML), and then decide under File Handling if you want to automatically open the report (automatically opening the report is the default). Click the Create button to generate the report.**

   FileMaker asks you where you want to save the generated report file.

5. **Set your desired filename and file type, and click Save.**

   If (in Step 4) you left a check in the Automatically Open Report When Done box, your default Web browser opens with the generated HTML or XML file. Then sit back and be prepared to do a *lot* of viewing! This report is extensive. It contains just about everything that you would want to know about your database.

Chapter 11

Batten Down the Hatches! Keeping Your Data Safe

. . . .

In This Chapter

▶ Creating and managing user accounts

▶ Using privilege sets

▶ Using extended privileges

▶ Thinking about FileMaker security guidelines

. . . .

*W*hen I was in junior high school, I had a big interest in chemistry. I carried a small, hard-bound notebook that I kept chemical formulas in. (Yeah, I was kind of geeky that way.) I treasured that little notebook. Then one day it just disappeared. I was devastated. I had spent so much time filling its pages with formulas and molecular structures, and then it was gone. I never did get it back, although I did discover that another student had taken it.

Unfortunately, we have to be very careful about what we do with sensitive information. Especially, with data being available via the Internet, the issue of security is a hot topic. I've seen various news reports about how someone gained access to thousands of customer credit card records, student records in school databases, and records of online banking transactions.

Fortunately, FileMaker Pro has an extensive set of security methods for helping you keep your information safe — not just in the manner of user IDs and passwords, but also through the use of what's called *privilege sets* and *extended privileges*. In this chapter, I cover what these are and how you can use them for securing your data.

Introducing FileMaker Security Methods

FileMaker Pro 8 provides three different methods of data security. These are:

- ✔ **User accounts:** A protected FileMaker file requires a user account and password for access to the file. This is the form of security that most computer users are accustomed to. You enter your user ID and password, and then you're allowed access to the data.

- ✔ **Privilege sets:** A *privilege set* is a definition of levels of security within a database. It defines what level of authorization allows access to layouts, menus, tables, records, and fields within the database. FileMaker assigns a default set of privilege sets to each database when it is created. You can use privilege sets to determine, for example, that only certain groups of employees can access salary information.

- ✔ **Extended privileges:** These define how access to the database is extended to external access methods, such as ODBC/JDBC, Instant Web Publishing, FileMaker Mobile, and so on. If you enable this type of sharing (which I explain how to do in Chapter 10), you likely want to have a look at extended privileges.

Together, these three methods of implementing security provide a rock-solid process of controlling who can gain access to the data and how they are allowed to view or use that data.

Defining User Accounts

Each FileMaker database file is automatically created with two user accounts: admin and guest. Unless you tell FileMaker otherwise, it uses the admin account for opening your databases, which uses the Full Access privilege set. This means that the admin account can do just about anything — modify layouts, edit scripts, modify field definitions, you name it.

If you're going to be sharing your database with other users and you're concerned about the safety (integrity) of the data, you need to consider creating a user account for everyone who uses your database.

If you are concerned about security for your data — due to the use of a network and/or your database contains sensitive information — the very first thing that you should do is change the password for the admin user account. (See "Changing the admin password" later in this chapter for details.) Many compromises of secure data happen when administrative accounts still have default passwords.

Creating a user account

Here are the steps for creating a new user account:

1. **Open the database for which you want to set up a user account.**

   Keep in mind that when you do this on a new database or a database that has no user accounts configured, the default account for opening the database is the admin account with Full Access as the privilege set authority (as shown in Figure 11-1).

2. **Choose File⇨Define⇨Accounts & Privileges.**

   The Define Accounts & Privileges dialog box appears. You see the two default user accounts listed — Admin and Guest — and their assigned privilege sets.

3. **Click the New button.**

   The Edit Account dialog box appears, as shown in Figure 11-1.

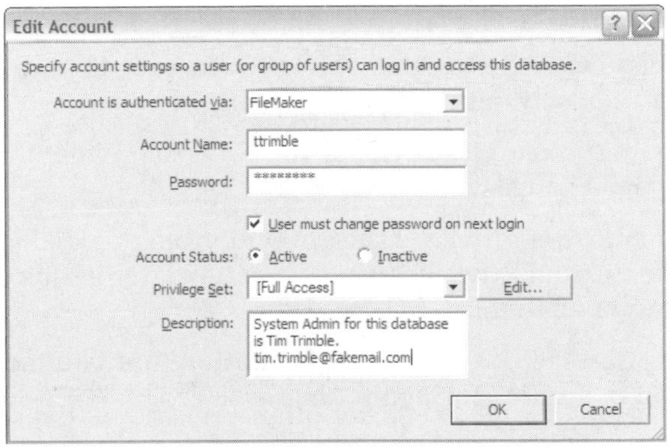

Figure 11-1:
Edit an account for a user.

4. **Leave the Account Is Authenticated Via field set at the default (FileMaker).**

   This tells FileMaker that *it* is responsible for enforcing security.

   The other option in this drop-down list is External Server, which uses the network authentication server — such as Open Directory (Mac) or Windows Domain. See the FileMaker online help for more information if you want to use this feature.

5. **Type the user account name in the Account Name box, and type the desired password in the Password box.**

Security is only as good as the ability of the hacker to decipher the user ID and password. Be sure to use a password that is not easy to figure out. See "FileMaker Security Guidelines," later in this chapter, for assistance on assigning passwords.

6. **If you want the user to change her password the next time she logs in to the database, select the User Must Change Password On Next Login check box.**

Many database administrators use a generic password when they create new user accounts, and they let the user pick her password for using the database.

7. **Select the appropriate radio button for making the new user account Active or Inactive.**

Sometimes the database administrator wants to create a bunch of user accounts for the database but leave them inactive until the actual user is ready to begin using the database.

8. **Select the appropriate privilege set for the user.**

   • *Full Access:* Choose this option for yourself as the database administrator.

   • *Data Entry Only:* Choose this option if you want to permit the user to enter only new data into the database.

   • *Read Only:* Choose this option if you want to prevent the user from making any changes in the database.

You can create Custom privilege sets, but not from this dialog box. See the "Using the Custom Privilege feature" section later in this chapter for more information on that.

9. **In the Description Field, enter any information that you feel will be helpful to you in administering the database.**

Some administrators like to put the user's phone number or e-mail address in this field. That way, administrators can contact the user if they need to make changes to the security levels or the login/password information.

10. **Click OK to save the new user account information, and then click the next OK button to close the Define Accounts & Privileges dialog box, if you're done entering new user accounts.**

Be sure to have the user test his new user account for logging into the database.

11. **If the Confirm Full Access Login dialog box appears, enter the user account ID and password for the account that you want to use for the administrator.**

FileMaker might ask you to Confirm Full Access Login for making sure which user account to use for providing administrative access to the current database.

Enabling logins for the database

After you have taken the steps to create user accounts for the database, you need to make sure that FileMaker will ask for the login ID and password when users load the database. As a default, FileMaker assigns the admin account to automatically log in when loading the database. Here are the steps for disabling the automatic login:

1. **With the desired database open, choose File⇨File Options.**

   The File Options dialog box appears, with the Open/Close tab contents displayed.

2. **Deselect the Log In Using check box and click OK.**

   This turns off the automatic login to the database. Now, when the database is loaded, it asks for a user ID and password.

Changing the admin password

Because FileMaker assigns the admin user account to all newly created databases without a password, it is important that you change the password if you want the administrator account to be secure. Here are the steps for changing the password:

1. **With the desired database open, choose File⇨Define⇨Accounts & Privileges.**

   This opens the Define Accounts & Privileges dialog box with a list of all the assigned user accounts for the current database.

2. **Highlight the admin user account, and then click the Edit button.**

   The Edit Account dialog box for the admin user account appears.

3. **Type a password for the admin.**

   Be sure to use a password that is hard for someone to casually figure out. Feel free to enter a Description if you want.

4. **Click OK to save the changes, and then click the next OK button to close the Define Accounts & Privileges dialog box.**

   FileMaker now asks you to confirm the Full Access Login for the database.

5. **Type the user ID and the password for the admin user account that you just edited. Then click OK.**

   Your admin user account now has a secure password for the currently open database.

Using Privilege Sets

Don't you just hate it when your mom takes away your privileges? "No dessert for you tonight, young man!" Only now, the phrase is, "No Internet access for you!" But the response is still, "Aww, mom!" But now, it's your turn to determine who can do what, and when. With FileMaker, as the database administrator, you can give and take away privileges with your database.

Even though a user has a user ID and password for a database, it does not give her full control over the database (unless she's the administrator). It all depends on the privilege set assigned to that user ID. As a default, FileMaker has the following privilege sets:

- ✔ **Full Access:** User has full read, write, create, and delete permissions and the ability to destroy any data at will.

- ✔ **Data Entry Only:** User can enter data but can't delete data.

- ✔ **Read-Only Access:** User can do just what it says: read and view data. The user is not permitted to create data, delete data, or make any changes.

These two privilege sets might be enough for the casual FileMaker user who builds databases for personal use. However, in many instances, you will want to use more customized privilege sets. Here are a few examples of why you might need more privilege sets for your databases:

- ✔ Some of the information in your database needs to be changeable by other users. However, you also have some data in the same database that can be viewable but has to be protected from any changes.

- ✔ You have a layout that contains both read-only fields and editable fields.

So, you need to be able to create your own privilege sets to meet your specific needs for data protection.

Creating a privilege set

FileMaker provides a detailed process for creating and managing your privilege sets. Here are the steps for creating a new privilege set:

1. **With the desired database open, choose File⇨Define⇨Accounts & Privileges.**

   This opens the Define Accounts & Privileges dialog box with a list of all the assigned user accounts for the current database.

2. **Click the Privilege Sets tab.**

This shows a list of the currently defined privilege sets. If this is your first time in this area, you should see just the three, default privilege sets.

3. **Click the New button.**

   You see the Edit Privilege Set dialog box, shown in Figure 11-2, which offers a whole buffet of options.

4. **Type the desired Name for your new privilege set.**

   Even though you have a Description field, it's a good idea to use a name that describes the type of privileges that you are setting up. For example, if you're setting up privileges for editing layouts but not the data, you might name the privilege set **Layout Editor Only**.

5. **Type a Description that gives a little more detail about the privilege set you're creating.**

   The description can provide more details about what data access rights this privilege set is for.

6. **In the Data Access And Design area, select the Records option that you want to assign to your new privilege set.**

   The available options for Records are:

   - **Create, Edit, And Delete In All Tables:** Has full access and control over the data in all the database tables.

   - **Create And Edit In All Tables:** Can create and edit data but can't delete any data.

   - **View Only In All Tables:** Can view the data but can't make any changes.

- **All No Access:** Has no access to any of the data in any of the tables. This is rarely a useful option, but might come in handy if you want to have scripts and dialogs be the interface in a kiosk-like setting (maybe to print visitor badges).

- **Custom Privileges:** Has customized settings for the table access. The next section, "Using the Custom Privilege feature," discusses how to use this feature.

7. **For the Layouts option, select the desired access rights for the database layouts that you want for your privilege set.**

   The available options for Layouts are:

   - **All Modifiable:** Can create, delete, and make changes to the layouts.

   - **All View Only:** Can only view the layouts. Can't make any changes.

   - **All No Access:** Can't do anything with the layouts. Setting this option precludes a user's ability to enter Layout mode.

   - **Custom Privileges:** Has customized settings for the layout access. The following section, "Using the Custom Privilege feature," discusses how to use this feature.

   In the example of the Layout Editor Only privilege, you'd want to set this option to All Modifiable.

8. **In the Value Lists option, you can select the desired access rights for the value lists that you want to assign to this privilege set.**

   The options for Value Lists are:

   - **All Modifiable:** Can create, delete, and make changes to the value lists.

   - **All View Only:** Can view the value lists but can't make any changes.

   - **All No Access:** Can't do anything with the value lists.

   - **Custom Privileges:** Has customized privileges, which are not covered by the previous options. The following section, "Using the Custom Privilege feature," discusses how to use this feature.

   With the Layout Editor Only privilege, you might want to set this option to All Modifiable because doing layout design can require the creation and use of value lists.

9. **For the Scripts option, select the desired access rights for the Scripts in your database.**

   The available options for Scripts are:

   - **All Modifiable:** Can create, delete, and make changes to the scripts in your database.

- **All Executable Only:** Can execute scripts but can't create or change scripts.

- **All No Access:** Can't access any of the scripts.

- **Custom Privileges:** For creating custom privileges which are not covered by the previous options. The following section, "Using the Custom Privilege feature," discusses how to use this feature.

With the Layout Editor Only example privilege, you would want to leave the Scripts option set to All No Access to prevent any changes to the scripts.

10. **The Extended Privileges area shows the set of extended privileges that are currently defined. Select the ones that you want to have in your new privilege set.**

These control access to your data via other applications. I cover these in a little more detail in "Managing Extended Privileges" later in this chapter.

11. **In the Other Privileges frame, select the options you want for your privilege set.**

These options are:

- **Allow Printing:** When selected, you are allowing the user with this privilege set to print from your database.

- **Allow Exporting:** If you want to permit the exporting of the data in your database to other platforms (such as MS Excel), select this option.

- **Manage Extended Privileges:** Check this to allow this privilege set to give access to the extended privileges for the database.

- **Allow User To Override Data Validation Warnings:** Ooooo, be careful here. When selected, this allows the user with this privilege set to circumvent the use of any data validation that you have set up in your layouts.

- **Disconnect User From FileMaker Server When Idle:** If your database is hosted on a FileMaker server, when selected, this automatically disconnects the user from the FileMaker server when the connection has been idle for a specific period of time.

- **Allow User To Modify Their Own Password:** When selected, this allows the user to change his password. This also allows you to define how often the password should be changed and the length of the password.

- **Available Menu Commands:** From the drop-down list, you can choose which menus are available to the privilege set you are defining.

Figure 11-3 shows how this dialog box looks after making a few changes.

12. **Click OK to save your changes.**

The list of privilege sets is updated with your new privilege set.

Using the Custom Privilege feature

In the preceding section on creating a privilege set, one of the available options in the Data Access And Design frame of the Edit Privilege Set dialog box (refer to Figure 11-3) is the Custom Privilege option. Basically, this option enables you to create very specific privilege sets. Here's how to take advantage of this cool feature:

1. **With the desired database open, choose File➪Define➪Accounts & Privileges.**

This opens the Define Accounts & Privileges dialog box with a list of all the assigned user accounts for the current database.

2. **Click the Privilege Sets tab.**

This shows a list of the currently defined privilege sets. If this is your first time in this area, you should see just the three default privilege sets (Full Access, Data Entry Only, and Read-Only Access). If you've created a privilege set, which I explain in the preceding section, you see that here, too.

3. **Select the privilege set that you want to customize, and click the Edit button. (Or, you can edit it by double-clicking the desired privilege set.)**

If you created a privilege set for the Layout Editor Only example earlier in this chapter, that would be a good one to play with for this exercise. Alternatively, you could duplicate one of the existing privilege sets and make your modifications to the copy.

After you select a privilege set, the Edit Privilege Set dialog box appears.

4. **In the Data Access And Design frame, click the arrow for the Records drop-down list and select Custom Privileges.**

   You should see the Custom Record Privileges dialog box. This has a list of the tables currently in your database, along with columns for the various access rights available for those tables.

5. **Select any of the tables in the list.**

   When a table is selected, the Set Privileges items become available at the bottom of the dialog box.

6. **For each privilege option, select the type of privilege that you want to assign for the currently selected table.**

   In most of the drop-down lists, the options are Yes, No, and Limited. The Limited option is a very powerful feature that lets you use the Calculation Editor for defining the criteria by which access to the table is permitted. For example, you can set your table up so that it can be edited on only the standard business days of the week. To do that, you select the Limited option, and then in the Calculation Editor you build a formula that equals any of the five business days.

7. **After you have defined your Custom Privilege parameters, click OK to save your changes.**

   Yes, it's pretty geeky, and you might want to play with this feature a little in order to get the hang of it. But after you become comfortable with this feature, you'll be amazed at how much control this can give you over securing access to your database.

Managing Extended Privileges

Nope. Sorry, but this extended privilege does not mean that you get to have extra dessert or stay out partying with your posse. This extended privilege means that you're extending the privileges of access to your database to and from other applications.

An *extended privilege* is basically an interface to another data format. The extended privileges listed in Table 11-1 are included with FileMaker. (The Keyword is used by FileMaker for identifying the interface being used for the extended privilege.)

Table 11-1	Included Extended Privileges
Keyword	**Description**
fmiwp	This extended privilege provides an interface for Instant Web Publishing. If you plan on publishing your FileMaker application to the Web, you need to make sure that your privileges include this.
fmxdbc	In order for your FileMaker database to be available via the use of ODBC/JDBC, this extended privilege needs to be included in your privilege set for the database.
fmapp	This provides sharing of your database via the FileMaker Network. This is the configuration for hosting the database application from one workstation — the other workstations become clients and share the database.
fmmobile	If you decide to interface your FileMaker database with FileMaker Mobile for Palm OS and Pocket PC devices, include this extended privilege in the privilege set for your users.
fmxml	This interface is for publishing your database to the Web as XML. In order to use this extended privilege, you need to have FileMaker Server Advanced installed.
fmxslt	Similar to the XML interface, this is for publishing the database to the Web. Again, this requires the use of FileMaker Server Advanced.

Adding an extended privilege to a privilege set

In order to use one of these extended privileges, it's just a matter of selecting which one you want to use in your privilege set. To do so, follow these steps:

1. **With the desired database open, choose File➪Define➪Accounts & Privilege.**

   This opens the Define Accounts & Privileges dialog box with a list of all the assigned user accounts for the current database.

2. **Click the Privilege Sets tab.**

   This shows a list of the currently defined privilege sets. If this is your first time in this area, you should see just the three default privilege sets. If you've created custom privilege sets, you see those, too.

3. **Select the privilege set to which you want to add an extended privilege, and click Edit. (Or, you can edit it by just double-clicking the desired privilege set.)**

   This shows the Edit Privilege Set dialog box with all the options for the currently selected privilege set. In the bottom, left frame (the Extended Privileges frame), you see a list of all the available extended privileges.

4. **Select the extended privileges that you want to include in your privilege set by clicking the associated check box. After you have selected the ones you want, just click OK to save your changes.**

   Now, when you assign this privilege set to any of your database users, they will have the ability to interface with the data systems that you selected.

Adding a new extended privilege

Aside from the default extended privileges that are provided with FileMaker, the only time that you'll need to add a new extended privilege is when a third-party developer provides a new application tool. Usually, this is for a database, spreadsheet, or reporting tool that you want to interface with FileMaker.

Many third-party application tools on the market provide additional capabilities to FileMaker, such as the plug-ins from Troi Automatisering. This is one method that those applications can utilize for providing a way to communicate with FileMaker.

Here's how easy it is to add a new extended privilege to FileMaker:

1. **With the desired database open, choose File➪Define➪Accounts & Privileges.**

   This opens the Define Accounts & Privileges dialog box with a list of all the assigned user accounts for the current database.

2. **Click the Extended Privileges tab.**

   This shows the list of extended privileges that are currently installed in FileMaker and which privilege sets are currently using them.

3. **Click the New button.**

4. **Type the Keyword for the extended privilege, and then type an appropriate description.**

   The documentation for the application that you're adding for the extended privilege tells you what the Keyword name should be.

Just think of the Keyword as being the secret password that FileMaker has to communicate to the external application in order to get permission to share data with that application.

5. **Select the privilege sets that you want this extended privilege to be used for.**

   This automatically turns on this extended privilege for the selected privilege sets.

6. **Click OK to save your changes.**

FileMaker Security Guidelines

Remember that when you create a new database within FileMaker, as a default, the file is unprotected. When the database opens, it does so with the admin privilege set, which grants any user the ability to do whatever he wants with the data.

If you're planning on designing and implementing a FileMaker database for multiple users on a network and/or via an extended privilege interface, it is vital that you give a lot of thought and consideration to how you want to implement your security settings.

To assist with this process, the FileMaker folks have written a comprehensive document about implementing security. I highly recommend that you visit the FileMaker Web site at `www.filemaker.com/support/downloads/index.html` and do a search on "security guidelines."

Chapter 12

Putting Your Databases on the Web

*I*f you're not on the Internet, you're in the dark ages! Your friends treat you like you have a disease. You don't get invited to the trendy coffeehouses. And even your pet cat walks away when you try to get cuddly. Oh, I forgot — the cat always does that, even if you are online.

So FileMaker includes a set of great capabilities for publishing your database applications on the Web — not only because FileMaker folks thrive on going to the trendy coffeehouses, but also because these capabilities enable you to interact with your FileMaker database without having to run a copy of FileMaker. And putting a database on the Web is an easy way to give Linux users access to your database as well, through their browsers. One popular use of this functionality is to publish a product catalog with an order form.

Designing Layouts for the Web

If your FileMaker database application is to be used via the Web, you need to know this ahead of time so that you can design it for the Web. Not all the layout and scripting capabilities of FileMaker work via the Web. Additionally, you might need to make a few design decisions differently for Web-hosted databases, because the toolbar options for a Web database are slightly different from that of a network-shared database.

Keeping a layout Web friendly

Take the following points into consideration when designing your layouts for the Web:

- FileMaker uses CSS (cascading style sheets) for presenting the layout in web browsers. *CSS* is a Web markup standard that allows Web designers to layout a Web page with special, dynamic effects. However, CSS also creates certain limitations that are not a factor with nonWeb FileMaker applications. Most important, CSS can cut off text in a layout, so you need to leave more white space around elements.

  For a more general understanding of CSS, check out *CSS Web Design For Dummies,* by Richard Mansfield (Wiley Publishing).

- Web browsers don't support the layout parts of header, footer, and summary, so you can't use these elements in Web-based layouts.

- The use of various text formats isn't supported in Web-based layouts. For example, vertical alignment and double underlines are not supported.

- When using check boxes or radio buttons, arrange them horizontally for the best appearance. Also, allow for a large enough display area for these controls because the browser-based controls might appear larger than what is in the FileMaker layout designer.

- Buttons can't have rounded corners. Well, actually, they can have rounded corners in the layout designer, but they appear as square corners in the browser.

- Items that don't appear in the browser are fill patterns, pen patterns, ovals, and diagonal lines.

- If you are including pictures in your layout, use the GIF format. You'll be much happier — trust me!

- FileMaker spoils us by allowing fields to automatically expand when the field contents are greater than the layout field size. However, when used in a browser, the fields don't expand. Always allow enough room for the display of your field data in the browser.

- Container, summary, or global fields can't be searched in a browser environment.

- Speaking of Container fields, browser users can't add movies, sounds, or graphics to the Container field. Also, they can't play sounds or display OLE objects in the Container field.

- When using List or Table views, the current record is always displayed as the first record at the top.

Be sure to conduct regular reviews of your layout in all the target browsers while you are designing, to ensure that it will appear correctly. *Target browsers* are the browsers your visitors use to access your page.

Checking out the browser interface

When you're using a browser for viewing a FileMaker database, the tool panel looks a bit different than when you're directly using FileMaker (see Figure 12-3 a little later in this chapter). The FileMaker folks have provided a tool panel that offers the right amount of functionality specifically for use in a browser environment. Table 12-1 describes the available functionality of the browser-based tool panel. Of course, just as in a nonWeb database, you can hide the Tools panel.

Table 12-1	FileMaker Browser Tool Panel	
Tool	*Name*	*Description*
	Home	Returns to the FileMaker database home page.
	Browse Mode	Selects Browse mode.
	Find Mode	Selects Find mode.
	Current Mode	Shows what mode the current layout is in.
	Revert Changes	Reverts any changes that were made to the current record.
	New Record	Creates a new record.
	Edit Record	Edits the current record.

(continued)

Table 12-1 *(continued)*

Tool	Name	Description
	Duplicate Record	Makes a duplicate of the currently displayed record.
	Delete Record	Deletes the current record.
	Sort Records	Displays the Sort Options dialog box, and lets you define the criteria for sorting the database.
	Show All Records	Cancels any find results, and shows all the records in the database.
	Show Additional Tools	Displays an additional toolbar with functions for Omit, Omit Multiple, and Show Omitted.
	Omit Record	Omits the current record from the current result set (listing of records).
	Omit Multiple	Omits multiple records from the current result set.
	Show Omitted	Shows the records that have been previously marked as Omitted.
	Close Additional Tools	Closes the additional toolbar with the Omit, Omit Multiple, and Show Omitted functions.
Layout: Jobs Listing	Layout List	Lets you select which layout you want to see.
View as: List	View As	Lets you select how you want to view the current layout — as a form, list, or table.
1 - 14	Record/Page Position	Displays a selector for moving through the records or pages of the layout.

Tool	*Name*	*Description*
Record: [1]	Record Number	Accepts the number of the record that you want to see.
[>>]	Go To Record	Goes to the record number entered in the Record field.
Found Set: 14	Found Set	Shows how many records are in the current result set.
(magnifier icon)	Modify Last Find	Allows you to make changes to the last Find request that you made.
Total Records: 14	Total Records	Shows the total record count for the entire table, including omitted records.
Unsorted	Sort Mode	Shows whether the records are sorted or unsorted.
[Log Out]	Logout	Logs out from the current database, and returns to the FileMaker database home page.
(icon)	Add New Request	Adds a new Find request while in Find mode.
(icon)	Duplicate Request	Makes a duplicate of the current Find request while in Find mode.
(icon)	Delete Request	Deletes the currently displayed Find request while in Find mode.
Request: [1] [>>]	Select Request	Allows you to select which Find request you want to view by entering the number and clicking the Go To button. (Find mode only.)
Total Requests: 1	Total Requests	Displays the total number of Find requests currently available while in Find mode.

(continued)

Table 12-1 (continued)

Tool	Name	Description
Omit ☐	Omit Request	Toggles the Omit flag for the currently displayed Find request. When selected, the current Find request omits records matching the entered criteria. (Find mode only.)
Symbols ▾	Symbols List	Displays a list of symbols that can be used for building the Find criteria while in Find mode.
Perform Find	Perform Find	Executes the Find based on the currently entered criteria. (Find mode only.)
Extend Found Set	Extend Found Set	Allows you to expand the current Find results to include additional criteria. (Find mode only.)
Constrain Found Set	Constrain Found Set	Allows you to reduce the current Find results by entering more-specific criteria. (Find mode only.)

Script Writing for the Web

An associate whom I used to work with in an information systems department was a scriptwriter and an actor. As such, he had a great idea for a movie script called *GIGO* — which, in the computer industry, is an acronym for *garbage in/garbage out.* I won't give away the details about the script, but it was pretty funny. It also highlighted how a computer program is only as good as what you put into it.

When you're programming applications for the Web, you need to put a little more thought into your application than you do for a plain, old FileMaker program that runs on FileMaker. If you don't give any consideration to how your program will work in a web browser, what you could end up with could be called garbage. The first step in programming an application for the Web is making sure that you use only the functions and features that are compatible with the Web. You also need to consider how a Web user (versus a user working with your application on a PC or Mac) will interact with the application you're designing. The following sections layout the details.

Choosing Web-compatible features

Fortunately, the FileMaker folks have taken steps to provide a programming environment that makes writing your applications for the Web easier. In the ScriptMaker environment, FileMaker lets you indicate that you want to use only the functions and features that are compatible with Web development. The following steps show how to use this feature:

1. **Load any FileMaker database that has some scripts in it.**

   You can experiment with these steps by using any of the sample databases that come with FileMaker.

2. **Choose Scripts⊅ScriptMaker.**

   A list of scripts that are in your current database appears.

3. **Select one of the scripts, and then click the Edit button. (Or just double-click the script that you want to look at.)**

   This shows the script code in the Edit Script dialog box, as shown in Figure 12-1. Notice the Indicate Web Compatibility check box under the list of script functions on the left.

4. **Select the Indicate Web Compatibility check box.**

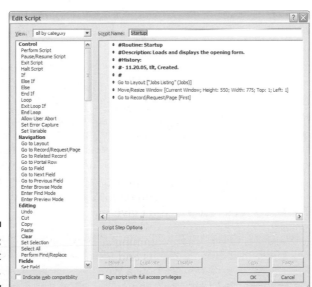

Figure 12-1:
Edit Script
dialog box.

When this box is selected, any functions that are *not* compatible with the Web are grayed out. Existing statements in the script also turn gray to show incompatibility with the Web. You can still select incompatible (or grayed out) functions and put them in your script code, but your script stops execution in the browser when it hits an incompatible statement (although it will continue to function when invoked locally or remotely in a nonWeb manner).

The Indicate Web Compatibility feature is merely a visual indicator of which statements don't function in a web browser. If you use incompatible functions, those functions still execute in the FileMaker environment. In fact, you can leave it on while writing scripts for nonbrowser execution.

Considering scripts for the Web application

If you're creating a database for the Web, you need to take into account a few online quirks of FileMaker and online FileMaker users:

- **Help users see changes in the browser.** Add a `Commit Records/Request` function to the end of any script that modifies data, because the browser does not reflect changes to the data until the changes are sent to the FileMaker web server. Use this with the following types of functions: `Cut, Copy, Paste, Copy Record/Request,` and `Copy All Records/Requests.`

  Remember buttons, too. Append the `Commit Records/Request` function to the end of any button script that performs a data-modifying action instead of assigning a single script step to the button.

- **Make sure Web-based users log out.** You can add the `LogOut` function to a button to exit from the database application, or you can provide a script that performs this function. Due to the nature of how the File-Maker web server opens additional windows for various functions (sorting, for example), a session can't be terminated while windows are still open. Proper termination can occur only via the use of the LogOut button, your own custom script, or a session timeout.

If both Web-based and workstation-based computers will access your database application, you have a few other bits of functionality to think about:

- You can use the `Get(ApplicationVersion)` function to determine what type of client is using your scripts. If the value is `FileMaker Web Publishing,` you can execute scripts that are specific to use via the Web.

✔ If you have Web-incompatible statements, tell FileMaker to ignore them in your Web application. Add the `Allow User Abort` statement and set it to `off` in your Web-based scripts. This forces the FileMaker Web server to skip over incompatible script statements and continue execution. As a default, the FileMaker web server halts execution of a script if it encounters an incompatible script statement.

✔ You can use security accounts and privilege sets to specify which scripts a user can execute via the Web and thus use a specific set of scripts for your Web-based interface. See the "Putting Your Database on the Web" section later in the chapter for details on enabling security accounts and privileges. Chapter 11 explains your options for setting these privileges.

Handling the two-faced script statements

Among your many options, some script statements that you can execute on a Web-based client don't behave the way you'd expect. They produce different results when executed on a workstation versus the Web. Table 12-2 highlights which script statements these are and how they function in a Web browser environment.

Table 12-2	Web-Based Script Statements Functionality	
Script Statement	*Functionality in a Web Browser*	*In a Desktop Application*
`Allow User Abort`	Handles unsupported script steps. Set to On to halt execution of unsupported script steps orset to Off to skip over the unsupported script steps.	Allows the user to abort script execution by pressing ⌘+. (Mac) or Esc (either Mac or Windows).
`Exit Application`	Executes a proper termination and shutdown of all application windows, closes the session, and returns to the FileMaker database home page.	Properly terminates all application windows and quits the FileMaker application.

(continued)

Table 12-2 *(continued)*

Script Statement	Functionality in a Web Browser	In a Desktop Application
New Window	Opens a new window within the current browser window. It does not create a new browser window. Only one window can be viewed at a time. Use the Close Window statement to close the current window and reveal the underlying window.	Opens a new FileMaker window.
Perform Script	Restricts you from performing scripts that are located in other files, unless the files are open and being shared via the Instant Web Publishing on the same host computer.	Performs the referenced script, unless you do not have sufficient access privileges.
Sort	Defines sort settings, which must be defined in the script, because they are not saved at the browser client.	Defines sort settings, defaulting to the last-used settings for the database.

Putting Your Database on the Web

To put your FileMaker creation on the Web, all you need to do is select a couple menu items, and your database is available via the Internet (or intranet). Here's how easy it is to do it:

1. **Load the database that you want to publish on the Web.**

   Keep in mind that your computer needs to be connected to either a local area network (for publishing onto the intranet) or be attached to the World Wide Web with a public TCP/IP address (to be published on the Internet).

2. Choose Edit➪Sharing➪Instant Web Publishing.

The Instant Web Publishing dialog box appears, as shown in Figure 12-2. As a default, Instant Web Publishing is turned Off. You can see the database that you selected in the Currently Open Files list.

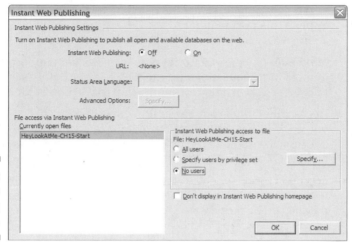

Figure 12-2:
Instant Web
Publishing
dialog box.

3. Select the On radio button.

When you do this, FileMaker grabs the TCP/IP address of your computer and displays it as the Web URL for the database.

4. Write down the number for your TCP/IP address.

Place this address in the web browser address bar for gaining access to your database.

When your computer is connected to the Internet, the TCP/IP address of your computer is either static or dynamic. A *static* address is an address that has been assigned permanently to your computer, and a *dynamic* address is one that is assigned to your computer automatically when you connect to the network. The dynamic address could be different every time you reconnect.

A *public* TCP/IP address means that your computer TCP/IP address is visible to any device on the World Wide Web. However, if you are behind a firewall or router, chances are that your TCP/IP address is hidden from the World Wide Web.

5. Click the Specify button, and select any Advanced options you need. Click OK when you're done.

The Advanced Web Publishing Options dialog box gives you a lot of control over who accesses your database and how. The following features are available:

- **TCP/IP Port Number:** As a default, browser calls to a web server use TCP/IP port 80 for connecting. If you want to make it harder for the casual user to connect to your database, you can assign a different port number. Then the users of your database will need to append this port number to the URL address, such as: 192.168.1. 15:99 (where 99 is the new port number).

- **Maximum Number Of Connections:** FileMaker supports a maximum of five connections via the Web to your database. If you use FileMaker Server, you can support up to 250 connections.

- **Accessible Only From These IP Addresses:** By checking this box, you are limiting the use of your database only to those TCP/IP addresses entered in the box — separate each address with a comma (,).

- **Logging Options:** The selected options determine what type of information is tracked when users connect to and use your database. The files created for the logging information are `application.log` and `access.log`.

- **Disconnect Inactive Accounts:** You can set the default number of minutes to wait before you disconnect a user from your database due to inactivity. I tend to set this option based on how many potential users I might have. If that number is higher than the max allowed, then I set it to around 30 minutes so that people can't just tie up a connection that someone else might need. If I don't expect to have a large number of visitors, I leave it really high. But others set this wait period higher or lower.

6. **In the Instant Web Publishing dialog box, select an option in the Instant Web Publishing Access To File Frame area.**

   The All Users option makes the database available to anyone who connects to your computer. Or select Specify Users By Privilege Set to set the security rights to the database. Chapter 11 explains the security settings options in more detail.

7. **Click OK to save your changes.**

   FileMaker is now acting like a web server and has published your database on the Web (Internet/intranet).

8. **Test your published database by loading your Web browser and entering the TCP/IP address that you wrote down in Step 4.**

   As shown in Figure 12-3, your database is now available via a Web browser.

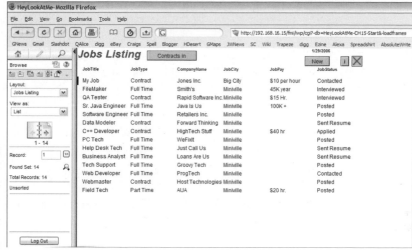

Figure 12-3:
FileMaker
published
database in
a browser.

You might wonder what the Don't Display In Instant Web Publishing Homepage option is all about. Why would you want to disable access to your database? Well, although you wouldn't want to do that when you're trying to publish your database to the Web, this is a quick way to turn off the database access to the Web so that you can make changes and/or updates to your database. Then, when you're done with your changes, you just have to uncheck this box, and the database becomes available again.

Part V
The Part of Tens

The 5th Wave   By Rich Tennant

In this part . . .

The final part of this book offers two top-ten lists that I hope you'll enjoy. In Chapter 13, check out the cool tricks you can do with FileMaker, such as adding graphics with pizzazz, making sure your layout is centered on any screen, and sending e-mails automatically right from FileMaker. Chapter 14 shows you how to make FileMaker even better with a list of ten handy add-ons.

Chapter 13

Ten Cool Things You Can Do with FileMaker

*Y*our mission, should you want to accept it, is to embark upon an endless journey, into the realm of creativity. You have been presented with the ultimate database developer's toolkit, called FileMaker. By using this toolkit, you are now tasked with discovering new ways to design, develop, and implement database applications. It is through your accomplishments with this toolkit that you can bring enlightenment to the world, the universe, or at least your next-door neighbor. To aid you in your quest for the perfect database applications, I present to you ten of my most coveted Cool Things that you can do with your toolkit. I now entrust you to guard these Ten Cool Things as I send you on your way.

Making Hidden Buttons

Button, button. Where is the button? Ah, the fond memories of playing that game as a kid. Little did I know I would find myself hiding buttons in software. You might be wondering, "Why would I ever have a need to hide a button on the layout in FileMaker?" First of all, I hide buttons so that the user doesn't know that they are there. And even if they do know that there is a hidden button, they tend to forget about it because it's not visible and its only use is for special occasions. Usually, those special occasions are for clearing out a bunch of data when testing, or for the display of diagnostic information about the database. Then there's the sneaky reason of embedding an "Easter egg" in the application, just for fun. Here are the steps for adding a hidden button to your layout:

1. **With your target database and layout loaded in FileMaker, go into Layout mode.**

   Preferably, you have a layout with some graphics or maybe some text on the layout. Usually, when I add a hidden button, I like to place it over some existing text or even just a letter — something not real obvious to the user if they're looking for hidden hot spots.

2. **Click the Button tool on the FileMaker Tool palette, and drag out the button outline in the position that you want to use for your hidden button.**

   Make sure the position is in a location that is going to be easy for you to remember, or you might find yourself hunting with the mouse later on.

3. **When the Specify Button dialog box appears, select the script or function that you want the button to perform when it is clicked.**

   If you currently don't have a script written for this button, you can select the Show Custom Dialog function and put a generic "Hello Neighbor" message in it to remind you that it is just a placeholder.

4. **A very important step is to make sure that the Change To Hand Cursor Over Button check box is *not* checked.**

   Because this is a hidden button, you don't want the mouse changing to a hand cursor when it is positioned over the button. That would be a dead giveaway that there is something clickable there.

5. **Click the OK button to close the Specify Button dialog box. Then click anywhere on the layout outside of the button.**

   Because the button is to be hidden, you don't need to enter a label on the button.

6. **Click the Pointer tool on the FileMaker Tool palette, and then click the button.**

   Now you're ready to tell FileMaker that you want an invisible button.

7. **Click the Pattern icon on the Fill controls (middle icon), and then select the transparent pattern (top-left corner), as shown in Figure 13-1.**

   You'll notice that the button has disappeared, but a black outline still surrounds the button.

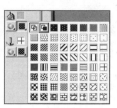

Figure 13-1:
Patterns in
the Fill
controls.

8. **Click the Pattern icon from the Pen controls (middle icon), and then select the transparent pattern (top left corner).**

   You now have a hidden button. Try it out in Browse mode.

Giving Your Layouts Pizazz with Graphics

One of the reasons that a Ferrari is so much more appealing than your neighbor's Volkswagen is that it just looks good! Well, yes, there is the aspect of horsepower and dollars, but when people see a Ferrari going down the street they all go, "Oooooh, ahhhh, wow, cool, . . . " and other mind-numbing exaltations.

It's fairly easy to get the same type of reaction when you add cool graphics to your FileMaker database application. If you don't believe me, compare Figure 13-2 to Figure 13-3.

Figure 13-2:
Research
Notes
database.

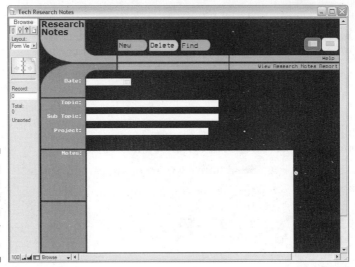

Figure 13-3:
Research
Notes
database
after
makeover.

Both of these screens are derived from the Research Notes sample database that comes with FileMaker. Figure 13-2 is the original layout. It looks okay, but it doesn't make your socks roll up and down. Figure 13-3 is the same screen, modified by yours truly with added graphics, a few font changes, and movement of the screen objects. It actually took less than a half-hour to make these changes.

To start, I created graphics for the background and for each button. If you want to experiment with graphics by trying my example layout, you can download the Chapter 13 files, which include the graphics used for doing the layout makeover shown in Figure 13-2, from this book's Web site (see the Introduction for details). Save the files in any folder that you plan on using for this example.

After you have your graphics files, here's how the makeover is done:

1. **Open the database with the layout you want to change.**

   If you're following my example makeover, locate the Research Notes.fp7 file (FileMaker\English Extras\Templates\Business-General) and load it in FileMaker. You'll see the screen shown in Figure 13-2. To avoid changing the original sample that came with FileMaker, choose File➪Save a Copy As, and save it in the same folder as your art files. (Feel free to give it a different name if you want. I named mine Tech Research Notes.fp7.) Make sure you close the current Research Notes.fp7 file and then load the file that you just saved in your example folder.

   Now you're back to the original detail layout form for the database. The layout name is Form View.

2. **Put the layout in Layout mode.**

3. **Choose Insert⇨Picture. Select your background graphic. (In my example, that's the `Background.tif` file.)**

   Now that you've added the picture to the layout, you'll notice that it is covering up everything else on the layout. Before you move it to the back, you need to first position the picture to the correct location.

4. **Drag the picture as far left and top as possible.**

   The picture should be covering the entire layout.

5. **Choose Arrange⇨Send to Back.**

   This places the picture behind all the other layout objects. Now you need to make sure that the picture will stay in one place while you move the other layout objects around.

6. **Choose Arrange⇨Lock.**

   This locks the picture object and prevents it from being moved. If you do decide that you want to move it around, you can just unlock it.

7. **Move the table fields and labels into the positions that are appropriate for the background image.**

   If you're experimenting with my example, just look at Figure 13-3 as a reference. You can also change the font type, size, and color to whatever you want, to make the fields easier to see.

8. **If your layout has existing buttons that you want to replace with graphics that act like buttons, first make a note of the functions that each button uses by right-clicking (Control+clicking on a Mac) each one and selecting Button Setup. Then delete the buttons you want to replace.**

   Because you're replacing the graphic buttons, you need to keep track of what functions and/or scripts the buttons use. In my example, I deleted the New, Delete, Find, and Help buttons.

   For my example layout, I wanted to tuck the new Help button into the thin horizontal bar that runs across the top of the layout. In this case, instead of using a graphic file, I added a text label over a specific area of the background. To create a text label named **Help,** position it over the background image, and then select the Go To Information Layout script as the button assignment. Right-click (Control+click on a Mac) the Help text, select Button Setup⇨Perform Script, and then select the appropriate script. The help script executes when the user clicks the Help label.

9. **To add the new button pictures, choose Insert⇨Picture.**

   In my example, the filenames are `New.tif`, `Delete.tif`, and `Find.tif`. Place all three buttons as shown in Figure 13-3. These are your new New, Delete, and Find buttons.

10. **For each graphic button, right-click (Control+click on a Mac), select Button Setup, and then select the correct function or script for that button (as you noted from the previous buttons).**

    These now have the correct functions for execution.

11. **Feel free to position and set the font format for any field labels so that they match your new layout.**

    I changed the <<Topic>> field object and the View Research Notes Report text, as shown in Figure 13-3. The <<Topic>> field object is just a non-editable copy of the Topic field. Whatever is entered in the Topic field also shows up in the <<Topic>> field object.

    In my example, I also repositioned the Form View and List View buttons. I liked the current look of the buttons so I just kept the current graphics.

There you have it. Snazzy graphics in a minimum amount of time.

Making Layout Titles and Text Dynamic

Here's a trick that I like to use for setting the title text of a layout when I need the ability to change the text, depending on a variable. For example, you can use this trick to add the name of the current user to your layout title. You do this by first adding a field for displaying a global text field containing your title to your layout. Then you use ScriptMaker to create the script that sets the desired value for the global text field. When you're done, the field displays the current user's name as part of the title.

Follow these steps to add the field:

1. **Select a database that you want to use for your dynamic text. Or you can create a blank database to use as an example. Make sure that the current layout is in Layout mode.**

    This trick requires the use of a global variable in a table, which you'll reference from your layout.

2. **Click the Define Database icon on the FileMaker toolbar.**

    The Define Database dialog box appears.

3. **Select a table to add a global field to, or just create a new table that you'll use for global fields.**

    In many of my database applications, I have a table named Globals that I use specifically for storing global values.

4. **Add a field named** LayoutTitle **as a text field.**

    Chapter 2 explains how to add fields in more detail.

5. **Select the LayoutTitle field, and click the Options button. In the Options dialog box that appears, select the Storage Options tab, and select the Use Global Storage check box. Click each OK button to save and exit the Define Database dialog box.**

   You now have a global field named **LayoutTitle** that can be used from any script, table, or layout in the database. To take advantage of this global field, you need to add this global field to your layout.

6. **Select the layout that you want to place this title on.**

7. **In Layout mode, click the Field tool on the Tool palette. Place the field in the desired location on your layout.**

8. **Select the table that has your global field from Step 4, and then select the LayoutTitle field (the name of your global field).**

9. **Make sure that the Create Label check box is deselected. Click OK to confirm your selection.**

   You should now see the ::LayoutTitle field on your layout. Feel free to set the desired size, position, and font.

Now that you have the global field on the layout, you need to have a script that sets the desired value for the global.

1. **Choose Scripts⇨ScriptMaker, and click the New button to create a new script.**

2. **Set the Script Name to** LayoutUpdate.

   This script is called when you want to update the text on the layout.

3. **Select the Set Field function from the function list.**

   Use this function to set a new value for the global field.

4. **Double-click the Set Field step in your script.**

   The Specify Field dialog box appears.

5. **Select the table with your global field, and select the LayoutTitle field. Click OK to close the Specify Field dialog box.**

   Your script step now shows the following:

   ```
   Set Field [tablename::LayoutTitle]
   ```

   tablename is the name of your table that holds the LayoutTitle field.

6. **In ScriptMaker, click the Specify button next to Calculated Result.**

   This opens the Calculation Editor, where you can set the value to be put in your global field.

7. **In the Edit window, enter the following:**

```
"Hello " & Get(UserName)
```

This is the value that's placed in the global field: the text Hello and the name of the current user.

8. **Click OK to close the Calculation Editor.**

The script step now looks like this:

```
Set Field [tablename::LayoutTitle; "Hello " & Get(UserName)]
```

9. **In the ScriptMaker window, select the Refresh Window function from the function list.**

This script step refreshes the currently active window and thus updates the LayoutTitle field on your layout. Your script now looks like this:

```
Set Field [tablename::LayoutTitle; "Hello " & Get(UserName)]
Refresh Window []
```

10. **Click the OK buttons to save your script and exit ScriptMaker.**

Your LayoutUpdate script is ready for use.

11. **On the layout with the LayoutTitle field, add a button by clicking the Button tool and dragging an outline for your button.**

12. **In the Button Setup dialog box that appears, select the Perform Script function, and then select the LayoutUpdate script. Click OK, and give your button a label.**

I called my button **Update Layout.** Very original, don't you think?

13. **Go into Browse mode and test your script by clicking the Update button.**

The layout now shows a nice greeting and your name, or the name of the current FileMaker user.

Reusable Layouts

The Custom Dialog function usually enables me to display any necessary information. However, sometimes I want to have more functionality or display only a subset of the fields for editing. In such cases, I create a form-style layout and use it for my special need, all the while leaving the parent form still displayed, as shown in Figure 13-4. A really trivial example would be a prompting form that asks for a catalog item number and then retrieves the record detail. Yes, this can also be accomplished by going into Find mode and doing a search, but not all your users are going to be FileMaker-savvy, so hiding the nitty-gritty from the user makes supporting a broad class of users much easier.

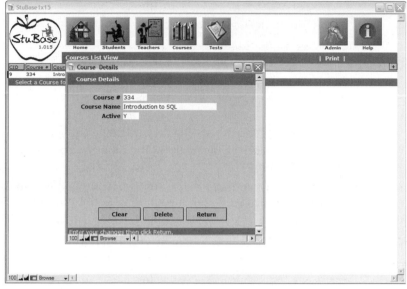

Figure 13-4:
A querying
form, asking
which
course's
record to
retrieve.

Here are the steps for creating and using a reusable layout:

1. **Create a new layout in your database application.**

   Don't worry about setting the size visually, because you'll do that via script code when you call the layout.

2. **Place any desired objects that you want to see (fields, text, buttons, and so on) on the layout. Be sure to add a button that lets the user close the layout and return to the parent layout.**

   If the content of the layout is *dynamic* (can display different prompts or text depending on usage), you should use global fields. Then you'll be able to load the global fields as needed before displaying the layout.

3. **Create your script file for calling the reusable layout. As always, you use ScriptMaker (Scripts⇨ScriptMaker) to create your script.**

   Here's a sample script that I use in one of my applications, followed by an explanation of each line. The script loads and displays a sub-layout while it keeps the parent layout on the screen.

```
Freeze Window
New Window [Name: "Details"; Height: 417; Width: 457; Top: 150; Left: 150]
Show/Hide Status Area [Hide]
Go to Layout ["CourseDetail" (tblCourses)]
Go to Field [tblCourses::CourseNumber]
```

   • Freeze Window turns off any updates to the current window.

- `New Window` creates a new window and allows the setting of the window title, dimensions, and position.

- `Show/Hide Status Area` turns on or off the Status area of the window. The Hide option turns off the status panel and Tool palette.

- `Go to Layout` calls the reusable layout by the name of the layout.

- With the layout showing, `Go to Field` sets the cursor focus on the first field. You include this line only if users change data on this layout. Otherwise, the `Go to Field` is not needed.

4. **Write your script code for exiting the reusable layout and returning to the parent layout.**

   I usually have a button on the reusable layout called Return or Close. Here's how I return to the parent layout, along with an explanation of each line:

   ```
   Commit Records/Requests []
   Close Window [Current Window]
   Refresh Window []
   ```

   - `Commit Records/Requests` saves any changes that were made. If you have fields on the layout that the user can edit, you need this line in your script.

   - `Close Window` closes the current window, which is the reusable layout.

   - `Refresh Window` tells FileMaker to update the parent window and turns off the Freeze Window setting.

After you get the hang of creating and using a reusable layout form, you'll soon discover many ways to use this trick in your database applications. Now, just exit from ScriptMaker, and give your new tool a test run.

Showing Movies in FileMaker

One of the amazing tricks of FileMaker is the ability to play various types of multimedia that is stored in the database. Because FileMaker can do this, you can create databases of videos, sounds, and music easily. Follow these steps to see just how easy it is:

To take advantage of this feature in FileMaker, you should have QuickTime installed on your computer. You can get a free download of QuickTime by visiting www.apple.com and then clicking the QuickTime tab.

1. **Select the database and layout that you want to put a movie in. (Or just create a new database.)**

2. **Click the Define Database icon on the FileMaker toolbar.**

   The Define Database dialog box appears.

3. **In the Define Database dialog box, add a field to the table for your layout, choosing Container from the Type drop-down list (pop-up menu on a Mac) or pressing Ctrl+R (⌘+R on a Mac).**

   The Container field is a general all-purpose field for holding multimedia and files that use Object Linking and Embedding (OLE).

4. **Add the Container field to your layout if you don't have your Layout preferences set to Add Newly Defined Fields To Current Layout.**

   Make sure that you place and size the field big enough to be able to see the movie.

5. **Select the Container field and choose Format⇨Graphic. In the Graphic Format dialog box, select the desired options for how you want the movie to be displayed in the field. Click the OK button to save the options.**

   Personally, I prefer to reduce the image to fit the frame of the field, and I set the Alignment to Center.

6. **Switch to Browse mode.**

7. **Add a record to the database by choosing Records⇨New Record or by pressing Ctrl+N (⌘+N on a Mac).**

8. **Right-click (Control+click on a Mac with a one-button mouse) the Container field, and from the context menu, choose Insert QuickTime.**

   If you're running Windows, you can also use the Insert Object option for selecting a media clip or video clip.

9. **In the dialog box that appears, locate a media file for the movie that you want to add. With QuickTime, this can be an AVI or a MOV file.**

   After you've loaded the file in FileMaker, the playback controls appear in the Container field. Then you can just click the Play button to view the movie, as shown in Figure 13-5.

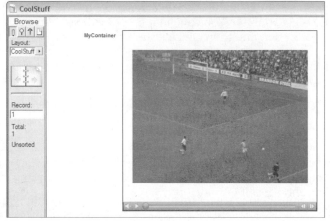

Figure 13-5:
Movie
playback in
a Container
field.

Using Auto Start & End Script Code

Using Auto Start script code is a very handy trick for adding script code to the launching of your database application. This gives you a huge amount of control over how your application launches and behaves. For example, you might want to initialize some global fields or variables, or maybe you want to check on data that is time sensitive at startup. Here's how to do it:

1. **Select the database application that you want to assign auto-execution script code to.**

   Be sure to select a database that has some script code already. Or you can create some script code as an example.

2. **Choose File⇨File Options.**

   The File Options dialog box appears.

3. **Select the Perform Script check box, and then select the script that you want to execute.**

   If you also want to execute a script when the database is closed, select the Perform Script check box in the When Closing This File area.

4. **Click the OK button to save your changes.**

   You can test it by closing your database and then reopening it. As soon as your database loads, the selected script code executes.

Sending E-Mail from FileMaker

Sending e-mail from FileMaker is really handy when you have a database containing contact information, such as e-mail addresses. For example, if you have a customer database for a bookstore, you could send out an e-mail to all Tom Clancy fans (customers who have purchased Mr. Clancy's novels in the past) when a new Jack Ryan title comes into stock. Check it out:

1. **Open your database with the contact information, and go to a record of someone to whom you want to send an e-mail.**

   Or you can use the Contact Manager database that comes with FileMaker and just fill in some data — like I did in Figure 13-6.

Figure 13-6: Contact Manager with the Author record.

2. **Choose File⇨Send Mail.**

   You'll see the Send Mail dialog box, which has all the necessary fields for the e-mail message. However, what you want to do is grab the address and other information from the current record.

3. **Click the arrow at the right of the To: field and select the Specify Field Name option.**

   This displays a list of fields in the current layout. One of these fields should contain the e-mail address that you want to send to.

4. **Select the field that holds the e-mail address, and then click the OK button.**

The name of the table and the e-mail address field name are placed in the To: field.

5. **If there are any other fields in the record that you can grab data from, use the same process as Step 4 to select the field that you want to use for the data.**

Or you can manually fill in the information in the rest of the fields.

6. **If you have a file that you want to attach to the e-mail, select the Attach File check box, and then click the Specify button to select the file that you want to attach.**

The name of the attached file appears to the right of the Specify button.

7. **Click the OK button to send your e-mail.**

FileMaker uses your default e-mail application for sending the e-mail.

Launching a Web Site with FileMaker

One popular trend in software products is using Web sites to provide technical support and online help information. The nice thing about doing this is that you can update the content on the Web site without sending new versions of the software to the users. This is just one example of what you can do with FileMaker's ability to call and launch a Web site from within your database application. Here's how:

1. **Select and open a database that has any text fields in it.**

You can use the Contact Manager database that comes with FileMaker because the Notes field can hold a URL address for a Web site.

2. **Select any text field on the layout that contains a Web site address, or just enter a Web site in that field.**

Make sure that you include the `http://` at the beginning of the URL. This ensures that FileMaker knows that this is a Web site address.

3. **The user can right-click (Control+click on a Mac with a one-button mouse) in the field with the URL. From the context menu that appears, they would then choose Open http://*www.websiteaddress.com* (where *websiteaddress.com* is the URL in the text field).**

4. **But, you can make this process much easier by adding a button to the layout (adjacent to the field with the URL). This button's script should contain the Open URL script step, and that step's specification should tell FileMaker to retrieve the data from the field in Step 2 to use as the URL.**

FileMaker launches the customer's default web browser and loads the Web site for the URL.

Changing a Field Background Color

It sure would be nice if you could use script code to change the color of a field on a layout — but, currently, you can't. (Hey, FileMaker Inc. — you listening?) However, you can try a trick that makes it appear that way. I demonstrate this with just a few colors. It's a little bit of work and requires some script code, but the effect is well worth the effort. First you set up a globals table that contains the colors. Then you create a layout with global container fields that fill with your colors and overlay those global fields with transparent data fields. Script code then loads the desired color into your global (background) field based upon the value in your transparent (foreground) data field.

To set up the globals table, follow these steps:

1. **Select and open a database that you would like to add the field background colors to.**

   If you don't have one, you can use any of the sample databases that come with FileMaker. For some reason, I like to torture the Contact Management database when trying out new stuff.

2. **Go into Layout mode and click the Define Database icon on the FileMaker toolbar.**

   You're going to need to create some global fields for holding the colors.

3. **Create a new table and call it *Globals* — or any other name that you would like to use for the table holding your global variables.**

   Personally, I like using the name *Globals* because it clearly shows what the purpose of the table is.

4. **Add the following three fields to the Globals table and set the listed attributes:**

Field Name	Type	Attributes
BlueBG	Container	Set the storage to global
GreenBG	Container	Set the storage to global
Background1	Container	Set the storage to global

   The first two fields hold the actual colors and the Background1 field will be the field you place on the layout for your script to fill.

5. **Using your favorite graphics editor, create two pictures of a solid color — one light blue and the other light green. Use a small size for the picture. Save in a common format (.jpg, .gif, .tif, and so on).**

   I like to use a 20-x-20 pixel picture, and I just give it a generic name, like Green.jpg or Blue.jpg.

6. **Back in FileMaker, create a new, blank layout with the Globals table as the associated table.**

   The only purpose of this layout is to allow you to set your colors in the global fields. You don't want to have this layout visible to your users, so be sure to turn off the Include In Layout Menus option in the Layout Setup dialog box.

7. **Add the BlueBG and GreenBG fields to the layout by using the Field tool.**

8. **Select both of the fields and choose Format➪Graphic.**

9. **In the dialog box that appears, set the Image To Fit Frame option to Enlarge, and deselect the Maintain Original Proportions check box. Then click OK to save.**

   This ensures that the inserted picture fills the full size of the field.

10. **Switch the layout to Browse mode. Right-click (or Control+click on a Mac) the BlueBG field, and then select Insert Picture. Select the Blue picture that you created. Repeat for the GreenBG field with the Green picture.**

    You now have two global fields with a color picture in them for use as your background colors.

Phase two of this task involves setting up your layout so that it can use the globals table to switch colors. Here's what you need to do:

1. **Open the layout with data fields that have colors that you want to change.**

2. **Switch to Layout mode.**

   Now, you're almost ready to add the Background1 global field to your layout. But first, you need to set the target fields to have a transparent background.

3. **Select the fields that you want to use the background colors with. Select the transparent pattern (top left) from the Pattern icon in the Fill control.**

   This sets the data fields to have a transparent background.

4. **Click the Field tool, and add the Background1 field on top of one of the target data fields.**

5. **Resize the Background1 field to match the dimensions of the data field.**

6. **Right-click (Control+click on a Mac with a one-button mouse) the field and select the Graphic option. Choose Enlarge from the Image To Fit**

Frame drop-down list (pop-up menu on a Mac), and turn off the Maintain Original Proportions check box. Click OK to exit.

7. **Choose Arrange⇨Send Backward.**

This places the Background1 field behind the data field. Because the data field has a transparent background pattern, the Background1 field shows through. Did your socks just roll up and down as you realized how this is going to work? Good!

8. **Repeat Steps 4–7 for each data field that you want to have the color background.**

Now you just need to do a little script writing.

9. **Go into ScriptMaker and create a new script called** UseGreen.

10. **Add the SetField function to the script. Select the Globals:: Background1 field as the target field, and select the Globals:: GreenBG field as the Calculated Result. Click OK to save the script.**

This script code copies the Green picture into the Background1 global field.

11. **Create another script named** UseBlue, **and use the same parameters I mention in Step 10 but for the BlueBG field. Then exit out of ScriptMaker.**

You now have two scripts for setting your colors. Now, you need a way to test this new background feature.

12. **On your layout, add two buttons to the layout: one labeled** Blue **and one labeled** Green.

13. **In the Button Setup dialog box that appears when you add the buttons to the layout, have the Blue button call the** UseBlue **script (via the Perform Script function) and have the Green button call the** UseGreen **script (via the Perform Script function).**

Getting excited yet? I am, and I already know how to do this!

14. **Switch to Browse mode and test out your buttons.**

Is that cool or what!? You might need to play with resizing and positioning of the Background1 field to get it to fit the data field dimensions.

Now that you know how to use this, you can build a full set of global variables with all kinds of colors. This is a great feature for highlighting a field that needs special attention from your users. Just don't get too carried away or your users will get lost in all the colors.

Running Another Application

Although it's nice to know that FileMaker can do a lot of different things, at times, you simply need to invoke another application, such as a graphics editor or a spreadsheet program. FileMaker can humbly do just that for you. This is actually quite easy and is done via the use of a single script step, as follows:

1. **Select and open the database in which you want this "launch another application" capability.**

   Or for testing, just use one of the FileMaker sample databases.

2. **Go into ScriptMaker. Create a new script, and then add the Send Event function to the script.**

   This function sends an event to the operating system.

3. **Make sure the File radio button is selected, and then click the Specify button.**

   The Send Event Options dialog box appears.

   The Specify File window appears. This provides the ability to launch multiple applications.

4. **For executing an application, choose the Open Application option from the Send The _____ Event With drop-down list (pop-up menu on a Mac). Select the application that you want to launch.**

5. **Click the Add File button, and then select the program that you want to run.**

   After you've selected the program, the file, along with the path, appears in the Specify File window.

6. **Click OK to save your changes, and then exit out of ScriptMaker.**

   You now have a script that launches the application when called.

7. **Feel free to test this out by adding a button to your layout that calls the newly created script.**

   The application loads and runs. Just don't use this function to call Microsoft Access. Yeah, it works, but it just doesn't seem like the right thing to do.

Chapter 14

Ten (Or So) Items to Aid Your FileMaker Development

In This Chapter

▶ Obtaining FileMaker tips and techniques

▶ Acquiring FileMaker add-ons

▶ Augmenting your inner graphic artist

▶ AppleScripting your FileMaker application

FileMaker Pro is a powerful tool — one for which people (and companies) keep coming up with new uses and techniques. Some of the techniques are so novel that the folks at FileMaker probably didn't consider or visualize the possibilities. Although the developers at FileMaker couldn't possibly foresee everything users might want to do with their product, they did realize that users would want to extend FileMaker functionality. That's why they enabled FileMaker to work with both plug-ins and (for Mac users) AppleScript.

As with other popular applications, such as Adobe's Photoshop, a cottage industry has emerged around FileMaker Pro, and FileMaker, Inc. has nurtured this symbiotic industry through the FileMaker Solutions Alliance (FSA). In this chapter, I point out some interesting informational resources, some plug-ins (and their providers), and some AppleScript resources — all of which are available to help you get even more out of FileMaker Pro than you might have thought possible.

Checking Out Online Resources for FileMaker Pro

These first items are good sources of FileMaker information, so you can keep up-to-date and find answers to questions. The publications and Web sites in the following sections present tips and techniques from people who use FileMaker every day as their source of livelihood.

FileMaker Pro mailing lists and newsgroups

`www.filemaker.com/support/mailinglists.html`

On this Web page, you'll find links to a wide variety of e-mail mailing lists, Web-based discussion lists and forums, and Usenet newsgroups devoted to FileMaker Pro and add-ons to FileMaker Pro.

FMNewswire

`www.fmnewswire.com`

FMNewswire is a great central nexus for all things FileMaker. The main page is, essentially, a headlines page of announcements made by FileMaker, Inc. and the developers and vendors of FileMaker-related products. If you're interested in one-stop shopping for the latest FileMaker announcements, this Web site is a leading candidate.

FileMaker Magazine

`www.filemakermagazine.com`

ISO Productions' FileMaker Magazine is an electronic publication where you can find all kinds of practical, hands-on information about getting the most out of FileMaker. Registration is free, but you have to pay a subscription fee ($25 quarterly) to access the instructional videos, various developer tools, and the full text of articles. With this subscription, you also get discounts on many third-party FileMaker products.

FileMaker Magazine has been around since 1995 and is the "baby" of an avid FileMaker Pro developer named Matt Petrowsky (headquartered in Livermore, California).

comp.databases.filemaker

comp.databases.filemaker is an active Usenet discussion list where you can post questions or answers to questions about all things FileMaker.

Predating the World Wide Web by over a decade, Usenet is a huge and very active part of the Internet. Usenet is accessed via newsreader clients via what is called the *NNTP* (Network News Transfer Protocol). You almost certainly have such a client, even though you might be unaware of it. Outlook and Outlook Express (Windows) include newsreader capabilities, as does Entourage on the Mac, but there are many others including Forte Agent and XNews on Windows as well as MT-Newswatcher, Hogwasher, and Unison on the Mac.

You can also access newsgroup articles via Google Groups (groups. google.com), but a dedicated news client offers more flexibility, such as seeing the headers for more postings at one time and quicker response times. Additionally, news clients make posting your own queries and responses easy, a cumbersome task at best via Google Groups.

Newsgroups — and there are well over 100,000 of them as I write this chapter — are organized in tree-like hierarchies. Some of the major roots in this structure include rec (for newsgroups on recreational activities, such as hiking, racing, bridge, and so on), talk (for debating and philosophical discussions — some of these, such as the talk.politics groups, can get really heated) — and of course, comp (for computer-related discussions).

Plugging into FileMaker Pro

You've almost surely encountered plug-ins, whether you're 100 percent aware of that fact or not. Web browsers implement much of their functionality via plug-ins. Viewing Flash animations, watching QuickTime or Windows Media video, or perusing PDF files without leaving your browser are all implemented via web browser plug-ins. Likewise, Adobe's Photoshop application is famous (notorious?) for the vast variety of plug-ins available to enhance its already robust capabilities. FileMaker, too, supports these application-specific modules that allow you to extend FileMaker's power. (You have to pay for most of them, but a few are free.)

Troi Automatisering

www.troi.com

One of the largest and best-known developers of FileMaker Pro plug-ins and utilities, this Dutch company has been developing FileMaker databases and utilities since 1995. They are always revising and augmenting their product line, and you can find a current catalog at www.troi.com/software/index.html.

All their plug-ins are available as demo versions so that you can try them out before you decide to buy.

24U Software

www.24usoftware.com

Since around 2000, 24U has established itself as a leading vendor of FileMaker Pro plug-ins. Included among their offerings are both commercial and freeware plug-ins and example databases. Two of the more interesting examples, from a layout designer's perspective, are freeware — scripting tab controls and nesting tab controls.

WorldSync

www.worldsync.com

If you want your database to operate in a distributed environment, where synchronization of multiple copies is a fact of life, you'll really want to check out WorldSync's SyncDek product. SyncDek won Macworld's 2004 "Best of Show" award and has only gotten better with new releases. It offers users one-click synchronization and developers the ability to control synchronization from within their application via a scripted plug-in.

Expanding Your Themes

www.scriptology.com/theme-library

Are you artistically challenged? Do your user interfaces look a little drab? If so, you really should check out Matt Petrowsky's Scriptology Theme Library (yes, the same Matt mentioned earlier from FileMaker Magazine).

By simply dragging and dropping, you can create layouts that use elements from a vast library of graphics and other layout elements. You can find out what the product can do by checking out the free demo version, and you'll also find a six-minute online video infomercial for the product on the theme library's Web page. If you like what you see, you can buy the full copy for $80.

Not Just Scripting, but AppleScripting

FileMaker Pro offers external scripting control on both Mac (via AppleScript) and Windows (via Visual Basic). For whatever reason, Mac-based FileMaker developers and users have embraced this scripting functionality far more than have their Windows-based brethren (and sistren?). (I think it is because Apple has promoted a consistent, system-wide approach to AppleScript, whereas Microsoft hasn't been nearly so evangelistic of VB except where it applies to their own applications.) One evidence of this disparity is that the Mac version of FileMaker Pro includes a sample database extolling the capabilities of FileMaker's scriptability — the Apple Events Reference database found in the FileMaker application directory's English Extras subdirectory. However, the Windows side doesn't have a similar, sample database.

FileMaker Pro was one of the first applications on the Mac platform to embrace AppleScriptability, back in the early 1990s. Not only can you control FileMaker via AppleScripts, but your FileMaker scripts (created in ScriptMaker) can invoke AppleScripts via the Perform AppleScript script step.

For an excellent introduction to FileMaker's AppleScript interface, check out an article by Ben Waldie in the April 2006 issue of *MacTech Magazine.*

You can find ready-to-use AppleScripts from various sources on the Internet — in particular, MacScripter (`http://macscripter.net`). At this repository of useful AppleScripts, you can find some that are meant specifically for use with FileMaker. Here are a few examples of the scripts you can find:

- A script that tells your iSight camera (assuming you have one, either external or built-in) to take a picture and store that picture in a container field in your database. An instant photo-ID badge generator for your company, all without leaving FileMaker, is just a script away! (`http://macscripter.net/articles/400_0_1_0_C`)
- A few other possibilities that come to mind are using AppleScript to obtain address information from OS X's Address Book application (or send such data from FileMaker to the Address Book), interfacing with iCal's calendar information, or retrieving photos from iPhoto.

Writing your own AppleScript is beyond the scope of this book, but if you're interested in exploring this topic, check out *AppleScript For Dummies,* 2nd Edition, by Tom Trinko (Wiley Publishing).

Appendix

Scripting Reference

● ●

*T*his is the designated, dog-eared, paper-clipped, sticky-note-targeted section of the book. I expect you to put a bookmark here and to keep referring to this section as you need it. While it is not as complete or extensive as I would like (I would love to do an 800-page FileMaker language reference guide), it is enough to get you going and assist you with your journeys with FileMaker script programming. You can also use the FileMaker online help system for getting more information about the available script steps and Calculation Editor functions that you'll employ to specify script step parameters.

The following is an explanation of the format used throughout this reference. Each entry begins with the script step function name and continues with the following categories:

- ✔ **Web:** Yes, if compatible with the Web; No if not compatible with the Web. You publish to the Web with the Instant Web Publishing feature, covered in detail in Chapter 12.

- ✔ **Purpose:** A description of what this statement does.

- ✔ **Prototype:** Format of the statement.

- ✔ **Parameters:** Describes the parameters that the statement uses.

- ✔ **Results:** The results, if any, that the statement returns after execution.

- ✔ **Comments:** Additional comments about using this statement.

- ✔ **Example:** An example of how to use the statement.

Add Account

Web: Yes

Purpose: Adds a new account, password, and privilege set. The account ID and password can be generated via calculations built in the Calculation Editor, or hard coded (typed directly).

Prototype: Add Account [Account Name: "*account name*";
Password: "*password*"; Privilege Set: "*privilege set*";
Expire password]

Parameters:

- *Account Name:* The name for the new account.
- *Password:* The password for the new account.
- *Privilege Set:* Select an existing privilege set or you can create a new privilege set. The use of the Full Access privilege set is not permitted. If you need full access rights, create a new privilege set with full rights.
- *User Must Change Password On Next Login:* Select this if you want to force the user to change the password the next time they log in.

Comments: You have to have Full Access privilege in order to perform this script step. If you want users without full access to execute this script, set the Run Script With Full Access Privileges option.

Adjust Window

Web: No

Purpose: Hides or changes the size of the currently active window.

Prototype: Adjust Window [*specify option*]

Parameters: Use Specify to chose one of the following:

- *Resize To Fit:* Sets the window size to the smallest possible size while keeping all the layout items visible.
- *Maximize:* Sets the window to the maximum size.
- *Restore:* Sets the window to its previous size.
- *Hide:* Hides the window.

Example:

```
Go to Layout ["ImportDetails"]
Adjust Window [Hide]
```

Allow Toolbars

Web: No

Purpose: Hides or shows the toolbars and the menu items associated with the toolbars.

Prototype: `Allow Toolbars [On/Off]`

Parameters:

- ✔ *On:* Makes the toolbars and associated menu items visible.
- ✔ *Off:* Hides the toolbars and associated menu items.

Comments: Toolbars do not appear in Kiosk mode.

Allow User Abort

Web: Yes

Purpose: Allows or prevents the user from stopping a script from executing by pressing either Esc or Cmd +. (Mac).

Prototype: `Allow User Abort [On/Off]`

Parameters:

- ✔ *On:* Permits the user to halt script execution.
- ✔ *Off:* Prevents the user from halting script execution.

Comments: The default setting is Off.

Example:

```
Allow User Abort [Off]
Go to Record/Request/Page [First]
Loop
  Set Variable [$newSequence; Value: $newSequence + 1]
  Set Field [tblUsers::Sequence; $newSequence]
```

```
      Exit Loop If [$newSequence    Get(TotalRecordCount)]
      Go to Record/Request/Page [Next]
End Loop
```

This example loops through a table and sets a sequential value in the `Sequence` field — and prevents the user from interrupting the script.

Arrange All Windows

Web: No

Purpose: Sets the location and the size of all the currently open windows.

Prototype: `Arrange All Windows [Specify option]`

Parameters:

- ✔ *Tile Horizontally:* Places the windows in a left-to-right sequence and resizes to fit adjacent to each other.
- ✔ *Tile Vertically:* Places the windows in a top-to-bottom sequence and resizes to fit adjacent to each other.
- ✔ *Cascade Window:* Places the windows in atop-left-to-bottom-right sequence and each sequential window overlaps the previous.
- ✔ *Bring All To Front (Mac):* Places all the windows to the front without any resizing.

Beep

Web: No

Purpose: Plays an audible system beep.

Prototype: `Beep`

Example:

```
If [IsEmpty ( tblUsers::LastName )]
   Beep
```

```
   Show Custom Dialog ["Warning"; "Last Name is empty!"]
   Go to Field [tblUsers::LastName]
End If
```

This example plays a beep if the `LastName` field is empty.

Change Password

Web: Yes

Purpose: Changes the password on the current account.

Prototype: Change Password [Old Password: *oldpassword*; New Password: *newpassword*; No dialog]

Parameters:

- ✔ *Old Password:* The current password on the current account. Can be generated via the Calculation Editor or entered directly.
- ✔ *New Password:* The new password to assign to the current account. Can be generated via the Calculation Editor or entered directly.
- ✔ *Perform Without Dialog:* When not checked, FileMaker lets the user enter the old and new password. Otherwise, the script parameters are used.

Comments: The user has to have password-change privileges in order to perform this script step. If you want users without this privilege to execute this script, select the Run Script With Full Access Privileges option.

A user gets five attempts to change her password, unless the Set Error Capture option is `On`, which then gives the user just one attempt.

Example:

```
Allow User Abort[Off]
If [$$changeDate = true]
  Change Password []
End If
```

In this example, if the global variable `changeDate` has a value of `true`, the user has to change his password.

Check Found Set

Web: No

Purpose: Uses the spelling checker on each field in the Find result after performing a Find.

Prototype: `Check Found Set`

Check Record

Web: No

Purpose: Checks the spelling in each field of the current record.

Prototype: `Check Record`

Check Selection

Web: No

Purpose: Checks the spelling of the currently selected text.

Prototype: `Check Selection [`*`table::field`*`]`

Parameters:

- ✔ *Table::Field:* Use Select to pick the `table::field` to check.
- ✔ *Select Entire Contents:* If not checked, you need to select the field prior to execution of this script step.
- ✔ *Go To Target Field:* Sets focus on the selected `table::field`.

Clear

Web: Yes

Purpose: Removes the contents of the specified table::field.

Prototype: Clear [*table::field*]

Parameters:

- ✔ *Table::Field:* Use Select to pick the table::field to clear.
- ✔ *Select Entire Contents:* If not checked, select the field prior to execution of this script step.
- ✔ *Go To Target Field:* Sets focus on the selected table::field.

Comments: Does not copy the contents to the Clipboard. When using with Web publishing, use the Commit Record/Request step after a Clear to make sure the record is updated.

Close File

Web: No

Purpose: Closes the selected file — or if no file is selected, closes the current file and halts the currently active script.

Prototype: Close File [*file*]

Parameter:

File: Use Select to pick the file to close.

Close Window

Web: Yes

Purpose: Closes the currently active window or the selected window.

Prototype: Close Window [*Window*]

Parameter:

Window: Use Select to pick the window to close.

Comment

Web: Yes

Purpose: Puts a comment in the script to document the script code.

Prototype: # *text*

Parameter:

> *Text:* The text to place into the comment.

Example:

```
Set Variable [$State]
# Check for valid address data, Warn user if not valid.
If [IsEmpty (Users::Street) = True]
  Show Custom Dialog ["Warning"; "Street not valid."]
  Go to Field [Users::Street]
  Exit Script []
End If
```

Commit Records/Requests

Web: Yes

Purpose: Ensures that the current record changes are written to the database.

Prototype: Commit Records/Requests [No dialog]

Parameters:

> ✔ *Skip Data Entry Validation:* Skips any validation options for this field, unless the field is set to Always Validate.

> ✔ *Perform Without Dialog:* Does not ask the user for confirmation.

Example:

```
If [$$webActive = True]
  Commit Records/Requests [No dialog]
End If
```

Constrain Found Set

Web: Yes

Purpose: Examines the current Find result set and applies the specified constraints to that result.

Prototype: `Constrain Found Set [Specify]`

Parameter:

> *Specify Find Requests:* If checked, adds the specified criteria to the previous Find Request, else the previous Find criteria is applied again.

Example:

```
If [Get(FoundCount)> 0]
  Constrain Found Set [Restore]
End If
```

The example checks if the number of records from the previous Find are greater than 0; if so, that result set is constrained further with the `Constrain Found Set` criteria.

Convert File

Web: No

Purpose: For converting a file from a supported type into a FileMaker file.

Prototype: `Convert File ["filename"]`

Parameters:

- ✔ *Specify Data Source:* For selecting the file, or the input source, for the data to be imported. If no file is specified, an Open File dialog box appears for user input.
- ✔ *Perform Without Dialog:* When checked, doesn't display the associated dialog boxes.

Copy All Records/Requests

Web: Yes

Purpose: Copies all the records to the Clipboard.

Prototype: `Copy All Records/Requests`

Results: The copied text fields are kept on the Clipboard in a tab-delimited structure, in plain text. If the copied field is from a repeating field, each repetition is separated with a group separator character.

Comments: If the step is executed after a Find, only the text from the Find request is copied. Includes any text in container fields.

Copy Record/Request

Web: Yes

Purpose: Copies the values from the current record or Find request result to the Clipboard.

Prototype: `Copy Record/Request`

Results: If the copied text is from a repeating field, each repetition is separated with a group separator character.

Example:

```
Go to Record/Request/Page [Next]
Copy Record/Request
Go to Layout ["Archive List"]
New Record/Request
Paste [Select; Archive List::Transaction]
Commit Records/Requests []
```

This example copies the text from the next record, opens a layout, and then pastes the Clipboard contents into a new record.

Copy

Web: Yes

Purpose: Copies the current field value to the Clipboard.

Prototype: Copy [*option*]

Parameters:

> ✔ *Select Entire Contents:* Highlights and copies the entire contents of the field. If not checked, only the currently highlighted values are copied.
>
> ✔ *Go To Target Field:* Forces the step to copy the values in the designated table::field.

Correct Word

Web: No

Purpose: Activates the FileMaker spelling checker for correcting the spelling.

Prototype: Correct Word

Comments: The Check Spelling As You Type option must be turned on, by choosing File⇨File Options⇨Spelling. Only words that FileMaker is able to identify as misspelled can be corrected.

Cut

Web: Yes

Purpose: Cuts the contents of the current field and saves the values to the Clipboard.

Prototype: Cut [*Select; table:field*]

Parameters:

> ✔ *Select Entire Contents:* Highlights and cuts the entire contents of the field. If not checked, only the currently highlighted values are cut.

    ✔ *Go To Target Field:* Forces the step to cut the values in the designated table::field.

Comments: If the database is published to the Web, you should follow the Cut step with a Commit Record/Request step to update the changed record.

Delete Account

Web: Yes

Purpose: For deleting the specified user account.

Prototype: Delete Account [*account name*]

Parameter:

    Account Name: Name of the account to be deleted.

Comments: You cannot delete a full access user account with this function. You need to use FileMaker's File⇨Define⇨Accounts & Privileges command for managing full access accounts.

Delete All Records

Web: Yes

Purpose: Deletes all the records in the current table or all the records in the current Find result set.

Prototype: Delete All Records [*option*]

Parameter:

    Perform Without Dialog: Doesn't display a confirmation dialog box when checked.

Comments: Use with caution. If you enable this with the Perform Without Dialog option, you give the user the ability to delete all the records in a table without warning.

Delete Portal Row

Web: Yes

Purpose: Deletes the data in the currently selected portal row.

Prototype: Delete Portal Row [*No dialog*]

Parameter:

Perform Without Dialog: Doesn't display a confirmation dialog box when checked.

Comments: If there are no portal rows selected, this step is skipped. You can use the Go to Portal Row statement for selecting a row.

Example:

```
Go to Portal Row [Last]
Delete Portal Row [No dialog]
```

Delete Record/Request

Web: Yes

Purpose: Deletes the current record when in Browse mode and deletes the current Find request when in Find mode.

Prototype: Delete Record/Request [*No dialog*]

Parameter:

Perform Without Dialog: Doesn't display a Confirmation dialog box when checked.

Comments: If you have a portal row selected and the Enable Deletion Of Related Records option is selected in the Portal Setup dialog box, FileMaker asks you if you want to delete the parent record or the related portal record.

Dial Phone

Web: No

Purpose: Dials the specified phone number.

Prototype: `Dial Phone [`*`No dialog; phone number`*`]`

Parameters:

- ✔ *Perform Without Dialog:* Doesn't display the dialog box for requesting the phone number.
- ✔ *Phone Number:* Predefines the phone number to be called. Use the Calculation Editor for generating the phone number or selecting the number from a `table::field`.

Comments: A useful feature; for example, in a Contacts database when you want the computer to dial the phone for you (assuming you have your phone line configured for computer dialing).

Duplicate Record/Request

Web: Yes

Purpose: Makes a copy of the current record in Browse mode or makes a copy of the current Find request while in Find mode.

Prototype: `Duplicate Record/Request`

Comments: If there are fields configured for automatic entry, such as serial values, the new record contains the next value for the field and not a duplicated value for that field.

Edit User Dictionary

Web: No

Purpose: Displays the User Dictionary dialog box so that the user can make changes to his dictionary for spell checking.

Prototype: Edit User Dictionary

Else If

Web: Yes

Purpose: Evaluates a logical condition within the body of an If statement and executes the associated steps if the evaluation is true. The Else If can only follow an If or another Else If statement.

Prototype: Else If [*logical condition*]

Parameter:

Specify: Use the Specify button to bring up the Calculation Editor for entering a logical calculation that can result in a true or false condition.

Results: If the condition is true, pass control to the following indented statements. If the condition is false, pass control to the next Else, Else If, or End If statement.

Example:

```
If [JobTasks::Status = "Done"]
    Show Custom Dialog ["Status"; "Task completed."]
Else If [JobTasks::Status = "Pending"]
    Show Custom Dialog ["Status"; "Task is pending."]
Else If [JobTasks::Status = "Assigned"]
    Show Custom Dialog ["Status"; "Task has been
            assigned."]
Else
    Show Custom Dialog ["Status"; "No status for this
            task."]
End If
```

This example checks the contents of the JobTasks::Status field, and then shows the appropriate message based on the contents.

Else

Web: Yes

Purpose: Executes the following indented statements if the preceding If statement resulted in a False.

Prototype: Else

Example:

```
If [User:Rights = 1]
    Perform Script ["Enable Admin Menus"]
Else
    Perform Script ["Enable User Menus"]
End If
```

Enable Account

Web: Yes

Purpose: Enables or disables the specified user account.

Prototype: Enable Account [Account; Activate/Deactivate]

Parameters: Use the Specify button to access the parameters.

  ✔ *Account:* The name of the account that you want to activate or deactivate.
  ✔ *Activate:* Turns on the account.
  ✔ *Deactivate:* Turns off the account.

Comments: The user must either have Full Access rights to be able to execute this statement or you must select the Run Script With Full Access Privileges option all allow users to execute this statement. Accounts with Full Access rights (privileges) cannot be deactivated with this statement.

End If

Web: Yes

Purpose: This signifies the end of an If statement structure.

Prototype: End If

Comments: The FileMaker ScriptMaker environment automatically adds an End If statement when you select the If statement.

End Loop

Web: Yes

Purpose: This signifies the end of a Loop statement structure.

Prototype: End Loop

Comments: The FileMaker ScriptMaker environment automatically adds an End Loop statement when you select the Loop statement.

Enter Browse Mode

Web: Yes

Purpose: Selects the Browse mode for viewing and entering data.

Prototype: Enter Browse Mode [*pause*]

Parameter:

> *Pause:* Temporarily pauses the script to allow the user to view or enter data.

Enter Find Mode

Web: Yes

Purpose: Selects the Find mode for searching for records that match the entered criteria.

Prototype: `Enter Find Mode [specify; pause]`

Parameters:

- *Specify Find Requests:* Defines the Find requests.
- *Pause:* Temporarily pauses the script to allow the user to enter the Find request criteria.

Comments: You can define the Find request in the Specify Find Requests dialog box.

Enter Preview Mode

Web: No

Purpose: Selects the Preview mode for doing a Print Preview of the currently active layout.

Prototype: `Enter Preview Mode [pause]`

Parameter:

Pause: Temporarily pauses the script to allow the user to view the layout.

Execute SQL

Web: No

Purpose: Send a SQL statement to any SQL-compatible external database via the use of the ODBC interface.

Prototype: Execute SQL [*No dialog; Specify*]

Parameters:

↳ *Perform Without Dialog:* Executes the statement without displaying the associated dialog boxes.

↳ *Specify:* Use the Specify button to select the ODBC Data Source options and the SQL statement to execute.

Comments: While this statement lets you send SQL statements to an external database, it does not let you receive SQL results. You need to use the Import Records statement to receive data from an external database via SQL. Use the Get(LastODBCError) function via the Calculation Editor for checking for SQL errors.

Example:

```
UPDATE Accounts SET Balance = 134.99 WHERE CustomerID =
        'SmithLawrence02'
```

This is a sample SQL statement you could enter in the Calculation Editor as the argument to an Execute SQL script step.

Exit Application

Web: Yes

Purpose: Exits FileMaker after closing all open files.

Prototype: Exit Application

Exit Loop If

Web: Yes

Purpose: Causes an exit of a Loop if the specified logical criteria is True.

Prototype: Exit Loop If [*logical criteria*]

Parameter:

> *Specify:* Use the Specify button to open the Calculation Editor for defining the required logical criteria.

Example:

```
Set Variable [$$Active; 0]
Go to Record/Request/Page [First]
Loop
    If [Customer::Status = "Active"]
        Set Variable [$$Active; + 1]
    End If
    Exit Loop If [Get(RecordNumber)
            Get(TotalRecordCount)]
    Go to Record/Request/Page [Next]
End Loop
```

This example counts the number of records in the table with a status of `Active`. When the last record is examined, the `Exit Loop` criteria is `true`.

Exit Script

Web: Yes

Purpose: Halts execution of the currently active script and returns to the calling script (if any).

Prototype: `Exit Script [Specify]`

Parameter:

> *Specify:* Use the Specify button to define a return value via the Calculation Editor.

Results: Passes the value specified via the Calculation Editor back to the calling script, which is retrieved via the use of the `Get(ScriptResult)` function.

Export Field Contents

Web: No

Purpose: Takes the contents of the designated or currently active field and exports to a new file.

Prototype: Export Field Contents [*table::field; "filename"*]

Parameters:

- *Table::field:* Click Specify Target Field to select the table::field to export.
- *Filename:* Click Specify Output File to select the file for receiving the exported field.

Example:

```
Go to Layout ["Document Details"]
Export Field Contents [Documents::TextContainer;
          "MyDoc.txt"]
```

Export Records

Web: No

Purpose: Exports all the records being browsed or all the records in a Find result to a designated file.

Prototype: Export records [*No dialog; "filename"; options*]

Parameters:

- *Perform Without Dialog:* Executes the statement without displaying the associated dialog boxes.
- *Specify:* Use Specify Output File to define the file and file type for exporting.
- *Specify:* Use Specify Export Order to define the desired format and order for the export.

Extend Found Set

Web: Yes

Purpose: Expands the criteria of the current, or stored, Find request.

Prototype: `Extend Found Set [option]`

Parameter:

> *Specify:* Define a Find request with which to OR the existing Find request.

Flush Cache to Disk

Web: No

Purpose: This causes FileMaker to flush the current cache in memory to the hard drive.

Prototype: `Flush Cache to Disk`

Comments: FileMaker normally does this when there have been a lot of changes made to the database or when FileMaker is idle. Forcing this process just helps to increase data integrity in situations where there might be computer hardware problems or power failures. Using this statement frequently can impact performance.

Freeze Window

Web: No

Purpose: Prevents updates from visually occurring in the currently active window.

Prototype: `Freeze Window`

Comments: This is a good way to improve performance if you're updating a lot of records. Use the `Refresh Window` statement to force an update to the window.

Go to Field

Web: Yes

Purpose: Places focus on a specific field.

Prototype: `Go to Field [select/perform; table::field]`

Parameters:

➤ *Select/Perform:* If the field is a container, the associated action is performed for the type of file contained in the field (movie, sound, OLE document); or if the field is text, the text is selected.

➤ *Specify:* Defines the specific table::field to direct focus to.

Example:

```
Go to Field [Select/Perform; Sounds::SContainer]
Example plays the sound file contained in the
        Sounds::SContainer field.
```

Go to Layout

Web: Yes

Purpose: Loads and displays the specified layout form.

Prototype: `Go to Layout [layout name]`

Parameter:

Specify: Define the layout name that you want to display.

Go to Next Field

Web: Yes

Purpose: Sets the focus on the next field in the tab order on the currently displayed layout.

Prototype: `Go to Next Field`

Comments: If there is no currently active field on the layout, the focus is placed on the very first field in the tab order.

Go to Portal Row

Web: Yes

Purpose: Sets the focus on a specific row in the currently active portal.

Prototype: `Go to Portal Row [`*`specify`*`]`

Parameters:

- ✔ *Specify:* Select the First row, Last row, Previous row, Next row, or use the Calculation Editor to specify the row to select.
- ✔ *Select Entire Contents:* When checked, highlights the entire contents of the selected portal row.

Go to Previous Field

Web: Yes

Purpose: Sets the focus on the previous field in the tab order on the currently active layout.

Prototype: `Go to Previous Field`

Comments: If there is no currently active field on the layout, the focus is placed on the very last field in the tab order.

Go to Record/Request/Page

Web: Yes

Purpose: Goes to the specified record in the currently active table, or to a Find request if it's in Find mode.

Prototype: `Go to Record/Request/Page [`*`specify`*`]`

Parameter:

> *Specify:* Select the First record, Last record, Previous record, Next record, or use the Calculation Editor to specify the record to go to.

Go to Related Record

Web: Yes

Purpose: Goes to the related record in the specified layout.

Prototype: `Go to Related Record [`*`from table; layout name`*`]`

Parameters: Use Specify to define any of the following options:

- ✔ *Get Related Record From:* Select the table to use for showing the related record.
- ✔ *Show Record Using Layout:* Select the layout to use for showing the record.
- ✔ *Use External Table's Layouts:* Check if you want to use the layouts from an external table.
- ✔ *Show In New Window:* Define the attributes for a new window to use.
- ✔ *Show Only Related Records:* Uses a newfound set to show the related record, or shows all the related records.

Halt Script

Web: Yes

Purpose: Immediately halts the execution of all scripts.

Prototype: `Halt Script`

Comments: This can be handy if you have disabled the use of the Esc key via the `Allow User Abort` statement.

If

Web: Yes

Purpose: Examines a logical calculation and executes the following indented statements if the calculation result is `true`; or executes statements related to `Else` and `Else If` statements (if any), if the calculation result is `false`.

Prototype: `If [logical calculation]`

Example:

```
If [User:Rights = 1]
   Perform Script ["Enable Admin Menus"]
Else
   Perform Script ["Enable User Menus"]
End If
```

Import Records

Web: No

Purpose: For importing records from an external file or data source.

Prototype: `Import Records [No dialog; specify]`

Parameters:

- ✔ *Perform Without Dialog:* Executes the statement without displaying the associated dialog boxes.
- ✔ *Specify:* Use Specify Data Source to define the file source, camera source (Mac), or ODBC data source for importing the data.
- ✔ *Specify:* Use Specify Import Order to define the desired format and order for the import.

Insert Calculated Result

Web: Yes

Purpose: Places a calculation result into the currently active field.

Prototype: `Insert Calculated Result [table::field; calculation]`

Parameters:

> ✔ *Select Entire Contents:* When checked, highlights the entire contents of the selected field.
>
> ✔ *Specify Target Field:* Defines the specific table::field to direct focus on for the calculated result.
>
> ✔ *Calculated Result:* Use the Calculation Editor for entering a calculation. The result of the calculation is placed in the specified field.

Comments: If nothing is selected in the current, or selected, field, the calculated result is inserted at the current cursor location in the field.

Example:

```
Insert Calculated Result [Customers::FullName;
        Customers::LastName & ", " &
        Customers::FirstName]
```

This example gathers the full name of the customer, formats it, and places it into the `FullName` field.

Insert Current Date

Web: Yes

Purpose: Places the current system date into the current or defined target field.

Prototype: `Insert Current Date [table::field]`

Parameters:

> ✔ *Select Entire Contents:* When checked, highlights the entire contents of the selected field.
>
> ✔ *Specify Target Field:* Defines the specific table::field to direct focus on for the inserted date.

Comments: If nothing is selected in the current or selected field, the date is inserted at the current cursor location in the field.

Insert Current Time

Web: Yes

Purpose: Places the current system time into the current or defined target field.

Prototype: `Insert Current Time [table::field]`

Parameters:

> ✔ *Select Entire Contents:* When checked, highlights the entire contents of the selected field.
>
> ✔ *Specify Target Field:* Defines the specific table::field to direct focus on for the inserted time.

Comments: If nothing is selected in the current, or selected, field, the time is inserted at the current cursor location in the field.

Insert Current User Name

Web: No

Purpose: Places the current logged-in username into the current or defined target field.

Prototype: `Insert Current User Name [table::field]`

Parameters:

> ✔ *Select Entire Contents:* When checked, highlights the entire contents of the selected field.
>
> ✔ *Specify Target Field:* Defines the specific table::field to direct focus on for the inserted username.

Comments: If nothing is selected in the current, or selected, field, the username is inserted at the current cursor location in the field.

Insert File

Web: No

Purpose: Places an imported file or a reference to the file in the currently selected container field.

Prototype: `Insert File [reference; table::field]`

Parameters:

> ✔ *Store Only A Reference:* Instead of storing the actual file, a reference (link) to the file is stored.
>
> ✔ *Specify Target Field:* Defines the specific table::field to direct focus on for the inserted file or reference.
>
> ✔ *Specify Source File:* Selects the file to be inserted.

Comments: When using the Store Only A Reference option, if the file is moved or deleted, the reference is broken and FileMaker isn't able to display the associated file.

If a source file is not specified, FileMaker uses a dialog box to ask the user for a file.

Example:

```
Go to Field [Parts::Video]
Insert File ["AutoliteA734.mov"]
```

Insert From Index

Web: No

Purpose: Displays a dialog box with a list of all the values used by the field. The user can select one of the values, which is then placed into the currently selected, or target, field.

Prototype: `Insert From Index [select; table::field]`

Parameters:

- *Select Entire Contents:* When checked, highlights the entire contents of the selected field.
- *Specify Target Field:* Defines the specific table::field to direct focus on for the inserted index.

Comments: An Index can be defined when the field is defined. When enabled, this builds a list of values that are used in the field. This statement can be used only if indexing is turned on for the field.

Insert From Last Visited

Web: Yes

Purpose: Places the data from a field from the last active record into the target field in the currently active record.

Prototype: `Insert From Last Visited [select; table::field]`

Parameters:

- *Select Entire Contents:* When checked, highlights the entire contents of the selected field.
- *Specify Target Field:* Defines the specific table::field to direct focus on for the inserted field.

Example:

```
New Record/Request
Go to Field [ActionDate]
Insert From Last Visited[]
```

Insert Object (Windows)

Web: No

Purpose: Inserts an OLE object or creates a link for an OLE object in the currently selected container field.

Prototype: `Insert Object [object]`

Parameters: Use Specify Object to define the following options:

- *Object Type:* The type of object that you want to access.
- *Create New:* Creates a blank object of the selected type, which then allows creation of the object with the related application.
- *Create From File:* Select or enter the name of the file to be inserted or linked.
- *Display As Icon:* Shows the inserted or linked object as an icon instead of displaying the actual object.

Insert Picture

Web: No

Purpose: Places a selected picture into the currently active container field.

Prototype: `Insert Picture [select; table::field]`

Parameters:

- *Store Only A Reference To The File:* When checked, stores a link to the file rather than the actual picture file.
- *Specify Source File:* Defines the specific picture file to be placed into the field.

Insert QuickTime

Web: No

Purpose: Places a QuickTime file into the currently active container field.

Prototype: `Insert QuickTime [filename]`

Parameter:

> *Specify Source File:* Defines the specific QuickTime file to be placed into the field.

Insert Text

Web: Yes

Purpose: Places text into the current, or selected, field.

Prototype: `Insert Text [select; table::field; "text"]`

Parameters:

- ✔ *Select Entire Contents:* When checked, highlights the entire contents of the selected field.
- ✔ *Specify Target Field:* Defines the specific table::field to direct focus on for the inserted text.
- ✔ *Specify:* Defines the text to be inserted.

Install Menu Set

Web: No

Purpose: Defines the menu set to be utilized in the current database.

Prototype: `Install Menu Set [set name]`

Parameters:

- ✔ *Use As File Default:* Replaces the current default menu with the specified menu.
- ✔ *Specify:* Select the name of the menu set to be used.

Loop

Web: Yes

Purpose: Begins a loop of repeatable statements to be executed until an Exit Loop If statement is executed as True, or the After First/Last option is used in a Go to Record/Request/Page statement or a Go to Portal Row statement.

Prototype: Loop

Comments: ScriptMaker automatically adds a matching End Loop when the Loop statement is selected.

Example:

```
Set Variable [$$Active; 0]
Go to Record/Request/Page [First]
Loop
    If [Customer::Status = "Active"]
        Set Variable [$$Active; + 1]
    End If
    Exit Loop If [Get(RecordNumber)
            Get(TotalRecordCount)]
    Go to Record/Request/Page [Next]
End Loop
```

This example counts the number of records in the table with a status of Active. When the last record is examined, the Exit Loop criteria is true.

Modify Last Find

Web: Yes

Purpose: Makes changes to the last Find request criteria.

Prototype: Modify Last Find

Example:

```
If [Get(FoundCount) < 1]
    Modify Last Find
    Pause/Resume Script[Indefinitely]
    Perform Find[]
End If
```

This example allows changing the last Find Request if no records were found.

Move/Resize Window

Web: No

Purpose: Makes adjustments to the attributes of the current, or selected, window.

Prototype: `Move/Resize Window [window name; current file; height; width; top; left]`

Parameters:

- *Current Window:* Uses the current window.

- *Window Name:* Specifies an open window.

- *Current File Only:* Only allows window selections in the current file.

- *Height:* The pixel height of the window.

- *Width:* The pixel width of the window.

- *Distance From Top:* The pixel distance from the top of the FileMaker window (in Windows), or from the top of the screen (in Mac).

- *Distance From Left:* The pixel distance from the left of the FileMaker window (in Windows), or from the left of the screen (in Mac).

Comments: The window position and size attributes do not have to be entered. You can enter only the values that you want to change. You can also use negative values for moving the window off-screen.

New File

Web: No

Purpose: Opens the dialog box for creating a new FileMaker database.

Prototype: New File

New Record/Request

Web: Yes

Purpose: Creates a new record in Browse mode, or a new Find Request in Find mode.

Prototype: New Record/Request

Example:

```
New Record/Request
Go to Field [ActionDate]
Insert From Last Visited[]
```

New Window

Web: Yes

Purpose: Creates a new window with the same attributes as the current foreground window and the same current record.

Prototype: New Window [*name; height; width; top; left*]

Parameters:

- ✔ *Window Name:* The name that you want to give the new window.
- ✔ *Height:* The pixel height for the new window.

- *Width:* The pixel width of the new window.
- *Distance From Top:* The pixel distance from the top of the FileMaker window (in Windows), or from the top of the screen (in Mac).
- *Distance From Left:* The pixel distance from the left of the FileMaker window (in Windows), or from the left of the screen (in Mac).

Comments: The window position and size attributes do not have to be entered. You can enter only the values that you want to use. You can also use negative values for creating the window off-screen.

Omit Multiple Records

Web: Yes

Purpose: Omits a number of records from the current Found Set, starting with the current record.

Prototype: `Omit Multiple Records [no dialog; number]`

Parameters:

- *Perform Without Dialog:* Executes the statement without displaying the associated dialog boxes.
- *Specify:* Indicate the number of records that you want to omit. If no number is entered, only the current record is omitted.

Omit Record

Web: Yes

Purpose: Omits the current record from the current Found set.

Prototype: `Omit Record`

Open Define Database

Web: No

Purpose: Displays the Define Database dialog box, for managing the creation and editing of databases and tables.

Prototype: `Open Define Database`

Comments: The current user account must have Full Access privilege in order to execute this statement or use the Run Script With Full Access Privileges option.

Open Define File References

Web: No

Purpose: Displays the Define File References dialog box for creating and editing external file references.

Prototype: `Open Define File References`

Comments: The current user account must have Full Access privilege in order to execute this statement or use the Run Script With Full Access Privileges option.

Open Define Value Lists

Web: No

Purpose: Displays the Define Value Lists dialog box for creating or editing value lists.

Prototype: `Open Define Value Lists`

Comments: The current user account must have Full Access privilege in order to execute this statement, or use the Run Script With Full Access Privileges option.

Open File Options

Web: No

Purpose: Displays the File Options dialog box for allowing the user to change the associated options.

Prototype: `Open File Options`

Open File

Web: No

Purpose: Opens a specific FileMaker database file.

Prototype: `Open File [Open hidden; filename]`

Parameters:

- ✔ *Open Hidden:* Hides the database after it has been opened.
- ✔ *Specify:* For selecting the FileMaker database file to be opened. If no file is defined, the Open File dialog box is displayed to allow the user to select a file.

Open Find/Replace

Web: No

Purpose: Displays the Find/Replace dialog box.

Prototype: `Open Find/Replace`

Open Help

Web: No

Purpose: Displays the FileMaker help system.

Prototype: `Open Help`

Open Preferences

Web: No

Purpose: Displays the Preferences dialog box.

Prototype: `Open Preferences`

Open Record/Request

Web: Yes

Purpose: Sets the current record, or find request, for editing, which locks the record and prevents other users from making changes to the record.

Prototype: `Open Record/Request`

Comments: This normally, automatically occurs when you try to modify data on the currently displayed record.

Open Remote

Web: No

Purpose: Displays the Open Remote dialog box for selecting a shared database via a local area network.

Prototype: `Open Remote`

Open ScriptMaker

Web: No

Purpose: Displays the Define Scripts dialog box for creating or editing a script program.

Prototype: `Open ScriptMaker`

Open Sharing

Web: No

Purpose: Displays the Network Settings dialog box for setting up a database for sharing on a local area network.

Prototype: Open Sharing

Comments: The current user must have a privilege set that allows changes to the sharing settings, or select the Run Script With Full Access Privileges option if you want users with lesser privileges to execute this step.

Open URL

Web: Yes

Purpose: Opens the default web browser with the specified URL.

Prototype: Open URL [*no dialog; URL*]

Parameters:

- ✔ *Perform Without Dialog:* Executes the statement without displaying the associated dialog boxes.
- ✔ *Specify:* Shows the Open URL options box for entering the desired URL. The URL supports the following prefixes: http:, file:, mailto:, and fmp7: (for using a shared FileMaker database).

Example:

```
Open URL [No dialog; "http://www.timothytrimble.info"]
```

Paste

Web: Yes

Purpose: Inserts the contents of the system Clipboard into the target field.

Prototype: `Paste [select; style; table::field]`

Parameters:

- *Select Entire Contents:* Highlights the entire area to paste into, thus replacing the entire contents of the field.
- *Link If Available:* Selects a link from the Clipboard if it is available. When an OLE object is in the Clipboard, this option pastes the link for that object.
- *Paste Without Style:* Ignores the special formatting (`font style`, and so on) for the text.
- *Specify Target Field:* Defines the specific table::field to direct focus on for the inserted text.

Pause/Resume Script

Web: Yes

Purpose: Places the currently executing script on hold for a designated amount of time or indefinitely. This allows viewing or action to take place on the current layout.

Prototype: `Pause/Resume Script [duration]`

Parameters: Use the Specify button to define the following options:

- *Indefinitely:* Pauses the script until the Continue button is clicked or the Enter key is pressed.
- *For Duration:* Specify the number of seconds to place the script on hold, or the Calculation Editor can be used for calculating the desired seconds.

Example:

```
Go to Layout ["Transfer Status"]
Pause/Resume Script [Duration (seconds): 5
Go to Layout ["Main Screen"]
```

Perform AppleScript (Mac OS)

Web: No

Purpose: Performs generated or specific AppleScript steps.

Prototype: `Perform AppleScript [script]`

Parameters: Use the Specify button to define the following options:

- *Calculated AppleScript:* Uses the Calculation Editor to generate the desired steps.
- *Native AppleScript:* For entering the AppleScript directly.

Comments: Can be used for Mac systems only. Windows systems ignore this statement.

Perform Find

Web: Yes

Purpose: Places FileMaker into Find mode and performs a Find on the specified criteria, or performs a Find on the last Find request.

Prototype: `Perform Find [criteria]`

Parameters: Use the Specify button to create, edit, and/or manage the Find request criteria.

Example:

```
If [Get(FoundCount) < 1]
    Modify Last Find
    Pause/Resume Script[Indefinitely]
    Perform Find[]
End If
```

This example allows the changing of the last Find Request if no records are found.

Perform Find/Replace

Web: No

Purpose: Performs a Find and Replace of data throughout the Found Set.

Prototype: `Perform Find/Replace [No dialog; criteria]`

Parameters:

- ✔ *Perform Without Dialog:* Executes the statement without displaying the associated dialog boxes.
- ✔ *Specify:* Use the Specify button to create, edit, and/or manage the Find request criteria.

Example:

```
Perform Find/Replace [No dialog; "818"; "760"; Replace &
        Find]
```

Perform Script

Web: Yes

Purpose: Executes a script module.

Prototype: `Perform Script ["scriptname"; parameter]`

Parameters:

- ✔ *Specify:* For selecting a script from the list of existing scripts.
- ✔ *Optional Script Parameter:* For passing data to the script that is being executed.

Comments: If you're passing data via the Option Script Parameter, use the `Get(ScriptParameter)` function in the called script to retrieve the passed value.

Example:

```
Perform Script ["Error Handler"; Parameter: $$ErrCode]
```

Print Setup

Web: No

Purpose: For setting the Printer options within the options or launching the Print Setup Options dialog box for the user.

Prototype: `Print Setup [Specify; No dialog]`

Parameters:

- ✔ *Perform Without Dialog:* Executes the statement without displaying the associated dialog boxes.
- ✔ *Specify:* Use for defining the various options for the printer.

Print

Web: No

Purpose: Prints the currently displayed layout and all specified associated data.

Prototype: `Print [Specify; No dialog]`

Parameters:

- ✔ *Perform Without Dialog:* Executes the statement without displaying the associated dialog boxes.
- ✔ *Specify:* Displays the Printer Options dialog box for defining how you want to print the data.

Recover File

Web: No

Purpose: For attempting to recover a damaged FileMaker file.

Prototype: `Recover File [No dialog; filename]`

Parameters:

  ✔ *Perform Without Dialog:* Executes the statement without displaying the associated dialog boxes.

  ✔ *Specify:* For selecting the file that you want to recover.

Refresh Window

Web: No

Purpose: Refreshes the entire contents of the currently displayed window.

Prototype: `Refresh Window`

Re-Login

Web: Yes

Purpose: Allows the user to re-log in to the current database with a different user account without reopening the database.

Prototype: `Re-Login [account; password; No dialog]`

Parameters:

  ✔ *Perform Without Dialog:* Executes the statement without displaying the associated dialog boxes.

  ✔ *Specify:* For selecting the account name and password to use.

Comments: Useful for logging into the database with a different set of privileges without having to close and reload the database.

Relookup Field Contents

Web: Yes

Purpose: Grabs new data from the `lookup source` field and places the data into the `match` fields of the records in the current Found set.

Prototype: `Relookup Field Contents [No dialog; table::field]`

Parameters:

- *Perform Without Dialog:* Executes the statement without displaying the associated dialog boxes.
- *Specify Target Field:* Defines the target match table::field that you want to use for the relookup.

Replace Field Contents

Web: Yes

Purpose: Replaces the data of a specific field in all the records with the value of the specified field or a specified/calculated value.

Prototype: `Replace Field Contents [No dialog; table::field; Specify]`

Parameters:

- *Perform Without Dialog:* Executes the statement without displaying the associated dialog boxes.
- *Specify target field:* Specifies the field for the replace.
- *Specify:* Sets the criteria of field replacement(s).

Reset Account Password

Web: Yes

Purpose: For resetting the password of a specific account.

Prototype: `Reset Account Password [account; new password; specify]`

Parameters: Use the Specify button to define the following settings:

- ✔ *Account Name:* The name of the account to be reset.
- ✔ *New Password:* The new password for the account.
- ✔ *User Must Change Password On Next Login:* Forces the user to select a new password the next time she logs in.

Comments: Requires that either you have Full Access privilege, or that the script is running with full access privileges.

Revert Record/Request

Web: Yes

Purpose: Performs a rollback on the current record or Find request, thus canceling any recent data changes.

Prototype: Revert Record/Request [*No dialog*]

Parameter:

Perform Without Dialog: Executes the statement without displaying the associated dialog boxes.

Save a Copy as

Web: No

Purpose: For saving a copy of the current database.

Prototype: Save a Copy as [*filename; Specify*]

Parameters:

- ✔ *Specify:* Specifies the new filename for the copy.
- ✔ *Specify Format:* Can be saved as a copy, a *compacted copy* (compressed and smaller), or a *clone* (without any records).

Save Records As Excel

Web: No

Purpose: Saves the records as a Microsoft Excel spreadsheet.

Prototype: `Save Records As Excel [No dialog; filename; Specify]`

Parameters:

- *Perform Without Dialog:* Executes the statement without displaying the associated dialog boxes.
- *Specify Output File:* Defines the filename and path to save to, with the option for automatically opening the file or e-mailing the file after saving.
- *Specify Options:* Selects all records, current record, and spreadsheet description options.

Save Records As PDF

Web: No

Purpose: Saves the records as a PDF file.

Prototype: `Save Records As PDF [No dialog; filename; Specify]`

Parameters:

- *Perform Without Dialog:* Executes the statement without displaying the associated dialog boxes.
- *Specify Output File:* Defines the filename and path to save to, with the options for automatically opening the file or e-mailing the file after saving.
- *Specify Options:* Defines the view options, security options, and document description options for the PDF file.

Scroll Window

Web: No

Purpose: For scrolling the current window.

Prototype: Scroll Window [*option*]

Parameter:

Specify: Defines a directional scroll (Home, End, Page Up, or Page Down), or a scroll to a selection.

Example:

```
Go to Field [Contacts::Fax Number]
Scroll Window [To Selection]
```

Select All

Web: Yes

Purpose: Highlights the entire currently active field.

Prototype: Select All

Select Dictionaries

Web: No

Purpose: Displays the Select Dictionaries dialog box for allowing the user to select a specific dictionary for spelling.

Prototype: Select Dictionaries

Select Window

Web: Yes

Purpose: Selects a specific window and brings it to the foreground.

Prototype: `Select Window [window name; current]`

Parameters:

- ✔ *Current Window:* Selects the window that contains the currently active script program.
- ✔ *Specify:* For selecting the name of the window to select.
- ✔ *Current File Only:* Limits the window matches to the windows in the currently active database file.

Send DDE Execute (Windows)

Web: No

Purpose: Calls another Windows application and passes DDE (Dynamic Data Exchange) commands to that application.

Prototype: `Send DDE Execute [application; topic; commands]`

Parameters:

- ✔ *Service Name:* The name of the application to receive the DDE commands.
- ✔ *Topic:* Describes the topic that the target application executes the commands on. Specific to each individual application.
- ✔ *Commands:* Text or Calculation Editor values specific to the application for execution.

Comments: Mac systems ignore this statement.

Send Event (Mac OS)

Web: No

Purpose: Sends an Apple event to an application that is specific to that application.

Prototype: `Send Event [application; class; id; text]`

Parameters:

- ✔ *Send The <value> Event With:* Provides the ability to launch an application, open a document, perform a script associated with the target application, or send Apple events with the `class` and `Event ID`.

- ✔ *Bring Target Application To Foreground:* Does exactly what it says!

- ✔ *Wait For Event Completion Before Continuing:* FileMaker waits until the event is done before continuing.

- ✔ *Copy Event Result To The Clipboard:* Places the results of the event onto the Clipboard.

- ✔ *Specify Application:* Select the target application.

- ✔ *Document:* Select the document to be used with the target application.

- ✔ *Specify Calculation:* Generate values to send with the event.

Send Event (Windows)

Web: No

Purpose: For running an application, opening a document in another application, or printing a document.

Prototype: `Send Event [application; event name, filename]`

Parameters: Use the Specify button to select any of the following options:

- ✔ *Send:* Defines what is to receive the `Event` message.

- ✔ *File:* Select a file to launch or load.

    ✔ *Calculation:* Use the Calculation Editor to generate the `Event` message.

    ✔ *Text:* Direct entry of the `Event` message.

    ✔ *Bring Target Application To The Foreground:* Does just what it says!

Send Mail

Web: No

Purpose: For sending an e-mail message with the option of including a file attachment.

Prototype: `Send Mail [No dialog; to; subject; message; attachment]`

Parameter:

    ✔ *Perform Without Dialog:* Executes the statement without displaying the associated dialog boxes.

    ✔ Use the Specify button to define any of the following options:

- *One E-mail:* For sending a single e-mail with data from current record.

- *Multiple E-mails:* For sending multiple e-mails with data from multiple records — one record per e-mail.

- *To, CC, BCC:* Who to send to. Can be directly entered or selected from a field.

- *Subject:* The subject of the e-mail.

- *Message:* Contents of the e-mail.

- *Attach File:* When selected, a file can be selected as an attachment.

Comments: Uses the default e-mail application on the system.

Set Error Capture

Web: No

Purpose: Turns on or off the ability to intercept errors.

Prototype: `Set Error Capture [on/off]`

Parameters:

> ✔ *On:* Hides alert messages and some dialog boxes.
> ✔ *Off:* Allows all alerts and dialog boxes to appear.

Comments: When on, use the `Get(LastError)` function for determining when and what errors are occurring.

Set Field

Web: Yes

Purpose: Places a new value in the designated table::field via the use of the Calculation Editor.

Prototype: `Set Field [table::field; value]`

Parameters:

> ✔ *Specify Target Field:* Specify the table::field that you want to place the new value into.
> ✔ *Specify:* Use the Calculation Editor to define the value that you want to place into the designated field.

Example:

```
Set Field [Dicey::Result; Round(Random*(6-1)+1;0)]
```

Example generates a random number between 1 and 6 and places the value into the `Dicey::Result` field.

Set Multi-User

Web: No

Purpose: Sets or disables network access to a database.

Prototype: `Set Multi-User [option]`

Parameters: Use Select to pick any of the following options:

- *On:* Permits network access to the database via FileMaker Network Sharing.
- *On (Hidden):* Permits network access to the database via FileMaker Network Sharing, but does not show the database in the Open Remote File dialog box. Users need to know the specific name of the database in order to connect.
- *Off:* Disables network access to the database.

Set Next Serial Value

Web: Yes

Purpose: For use with fields that have been defined with auto-entry serial numbers. Defines the next value to be used for the serial number.

Prototype: `Set Next Serial Value [table::field; value]`

Parameters:

- *Specify Target Field:* For defining the table::field to receive the new serial number value setting.
- *Specify Value:* Use the Calculation Editor to enter or calculate the new next serial number value.

Set Selection

Web: Yes

Purpose: Sets the beginning and ending position of selection (highlighting) within the designated table::field.

Prototype: `Set Selection [table::field; start; end]`

Parameters:

- *Select Target Field:* For defining the table::field to use for the selection.
- *Specify:* For selecting the start and ending positions of the selection.

Comments: Position location includes spaces and symbols.

Example:

```
Set Field [contacts::phone; "(800) 555-1212"]
Set Selection [contacts::phone; Start Position: 2; End
         Position: 4]
Copy[]
```

This example copies the area code from the contacts::phone field.

Set Use System Formats

Web: No

Purpose: Selects if FileMaker is to use the current system formats or use the formats saved with the database file.

Prototype: Set Use System Formats [*on/off*]

Parameters:

- *On:* Use the current system formats.
- *Off:* Use the formats stored with the database file.

Comments: The system formats include the formats for dates, time, and numbers.

Set Variable

Web: Yes

Purpose: Defines a local or global variable and/or sets its value.

Prototype: `Set Variable [variable name; value]`

Parameters:

⊳ *Name:* Name of the variable. A prefix of $ is for local variable, and a prefix of $$ is for global variables.

⊳ *Value:* The value to place into the variable.

⊳ *Repetition:* Index number of the variable to create.

Comments: Declared Local variable values are only available within the currently executing script. Declared Global variables can be used anywhere within a database file.

Example:

```
Set Variable [$$AppPath; "C:\Program Files\FileMaker Pro"]
```

Set Window Title

Web: Yes

Purpose: Sets the title text of a specific window.

Prototype: `Set Window Title [window; file; new name]`

Parameters: Use Specify to set the following options:

⊳ *Window To Rename:* Select which window to rename.

⊳ *Current File Only:* Will only display windows in the current database file.

⊳ *Rename Window To:* Define the new name for the window.

Comments: Is not case sensitive.

Set Zoom Level

Web: No

Purpose: Sets the screen zoom level.

Prototype: `Set Zoom Level [Lock; level]`

Parameters:

 ↙ *Lock:* Prevents the user from making zoom level changes.

 ↙ *Specify:* Defines the zoom level.

Show All Records

Web: Yes

Purpose: Makes all the records in the table available for viewing.

Prototype: `Show All Records`

Comments: Useful after working with a limited number of records from a Found set.

Show Custom Dialog

Web: No

Purpose: Displays a custom dialog box for providing the display of messages and providing for user input.

Prototype: `Show Custom Dialog [title; message; input]`

Parameters:

 ↙ *Title:* The title of the dialog box.

 ↙ *Message:* The message to display to the user.

 ↙ *Button Labels:* You can use from one to three buttons at the bottom of the dialog box.

 ↙ *Show input field (n):* Activates an input field.

 ↙ *Specify:* For selecting the table::field to target for input.

    ✔ *Use password character (*):* Masks entered text with the asterisk as it is being entered.

    ✔ *Label:* Assigns a label to an input field.

Comments: To receive input from the buttons, use the `Get(LastMessageChoice)` function. The values that are returned by the buttons are:

    ✔ 1 for the right button (left box in the Dialog Options).

    ✔ 2 for the middle button (middle box in the Dialog Options).

    ✔ 3 for the left button (right box in the Dialog Options).

The right button is also used for writing data from the input fields.

Example:

```
Show Custom Dialog ["Warning";"Delete all records?"]
If [Get(LastMessageChoice)= 1]
   Delete All Records [No dialog]
End If
```

Show Omitted Only

Web: Yes

Purpose: Shows only the records that are not a part of the current Found set.

Prototype: Show Omitted Only

Show/Hide Status Area

Web: Yes

Purpose: Shows or hides the status area.

Prototype: Show/Hide Status Area [*Lock; option*]

Parameters:

- ✔ *Lock:* Prevents the user from clicking the status area button at the bottom of the layout.
- ✔ *Show:* Shows the status area.
- ✔ *Hide:* Hides the status area.
- ✔ *Toggle:* Toggles between Hide and Show.

Show/Hide Text Ruler

Web: No

Purpose: Shows or hides the Text Ruler on the layout.

Prototype: Show/Hide Text Ruler [*option*]

Parameters:

- ✔ *Show:* Shows the text ruler.
- ✔ *Hide:* Hides the text ruler.
- ✔ *Toggle:* Toggles between Hide and Show.

Sort Records

Web: Yes

Purpose: Performs a sort on the current set of records.

Prototype: Sort Records [Select; No dialog]

Parameters:

- ✔ *Perform Without Dialog:* Executes the statement without displaying the associated dialog boxes.
- ✔ *Specify:* For selecting the sort order.

Speak (Mac OS)

Web: No

Purpose: Generates computer-generated speech from the designated text.

Prototype: `Speak [text]`

Parameters: Use the Specify button to set the following options:

- *Calculation Editor:* Use for entering the text to be spoken or create a calculation to generate the text.
- *Use Voice:* Select the type of voice to use.
- *Wait for speech completion before continuing:* Does just what is says.

Comments: Works with speech-enabled Mac computers only.

Spelling Options

Web: No

Purpose: Displays the Spelling Options dialog box.

Prototype: `Spelling Options`

Undo

Web: Yes

Purpose: Cancels the latest actions performed in FileMaker.

Prototype: `Undo`

Unsort Records

Web: Yes

Purpose: Returns the currently sorted records back to their original creation order.

Prototype: `Unsort Records`

Update Link (Windows)

Web: No

Purpose: Performs an update on the OLE link in the currently active or defined container field.

Prototype: Update Link [*table::field*]

Parameter:

Select Target Field: For defining the table::field to update.

View As

Web: Yes

Purpose: Defines how to view the current layout.

Prototype: View As [*option*]

Parameters:

- ✔ *View As Form:* Use the form view for the layout.
- ✔ *View As List:* Use the list view for the layout (rows and columns).
- ✔ *View As Table:* Use the table view for the layout, just like a spreadsheet grid.
- ✔ *Cycle:* Cycle through the various views.

Index

Notes

Notes

Notes

Notes

BUSINESS, CAREERS & PERSONAL FINANCE

0-7645-5307-0

0-7645-5331-3 *†

Also available:
- Accounting For Dummies †
  0-7645-5314-3
- Business Plans Kit For Dummies †
  0-7645-5365-8
- Cover Letters For Dummies
  0-7645-5224-4
- Frugal Living For Dummies
  0-7645-5403-4
- Leadership For Dummies
  0-7645-5176-0
- Managing For Dummies
  0-7645-1771-6

- Marketing For Dummies
  0-7645-5600-2
- Personal Finance For Dummies *
  0-7645-2590-5
- Project Management For Dummies
  0-7645-5283-X
- Resumes For Dummies †
  0-7645-5471-9
- Selling For Dummies
  0-7645-5363-1
- Small Business Kit For Dummies *†
  0-7645-5093-4

HOME & BUSINESS COMPUTER BASICS

0-7645-4074-2

0-7645-3758-X

Also available:
- ACT! 6 For Dummies
  0-7645-2645-6
- iLife '04 All-in-One Desk Reference
  For Dummies
  0-7645-7347-0
- iPAQ For Dummies
  0-7645-6769-1
- Mac OS X Panther Timesaving
  Techniques For Dummies
  0-7645-5812-9
- Macs For Dummies
  0-7645-5656-8

- Microsoft Money 2004 For Dummies
  0-7645-4195-1
- Office 2003 All-in-One Desk Reference
  For Dummies
  0-7645-3883-7
- Outlook 2003 For Dummies
  0-7645-3759-8
- PCs For Dummies
  0-7645-4074-2
- TiVo For Dummies
  0-7645-6923-6
- Upgrading and Fixing PCs For Dummies
  0-7645-1665-5
- Windows XP Timesaving Techniques
  For Dummies
  0-7645-3748-2

FOOD, HOME, GARDEN, HOBBIES, MUSIC & PETS

0-7645-5295-3

0-7645-5232-5

Also available:
- Bass Guitar For Dummies
  0-7645-2487-9
- Diabetes Cookbook For Dummies
  0-7645-5230-9
- Gardening For Dummies *
  0-7645-5130-2
- Guitar For Dummies
  0-7645-5106-X
- Holiday Decorating For Dummies
  0-7645-2570-0
- Home Improvement All-in-One
  For Dummies
  0-7645-5680-0

- Knitting For Dummies
  0-7645-5395-X
- Piano For Dummies
  0-7645-5105-1
- Puppies For Dummies
  0-7645-5255-4
- Scrapbooking For Dummies
  0-7645-7208-3
- Senior Dogs For Dummies
  0-7645-5818-8
- Singing For Dummies
  0-7645-2475-5
- 30-Minute Meals For Dummies
  0-7645-2589-1

INTERNET & DIGITAL MEDIA

0-7645-1664-7

0-7645-6924-4

Also available:
- 2005 Online Shopping Directory
  For Dummies
  0-7645-7495-7
- CD & DVD Recording For Dummies
  0-7645-5956-7
- eBay For Dummies
  0-7645-5654-1
- Fighting Spam For Dummies
  0-7645-5965-6
- Genealogy Online For Dummies
  0-7645-5964-8
- Google For Dummies
  0-7645-4420-9

- Home Recording For Musicians
  For Dummies
  0-7645-1634-5
- The Internet For Dummies
  0-7645-4173-0
- iPod & iTunes For Dummies
  0-7645-7772-7
- Preventing Identity Theft For Dummies
  0-7645-7336-5
- Pro Tools All-in-One Desk Reference
  For Dummies
  0-7645-5714-9
- Roxio Easy Media Creator For Dummies
  0-7645-7131-1

* Separate Canadian edition also available
† Separate U.K. edition also available

Available wherever books are sold. For more information or to order direct: U.S. customers visit www.dummies.com or call 1-877-762-2974.
U.K. customers visit www.wileyeurope.com or call 0800 243407. Canadian customers visit www.wiley.ca or call 1-800-567-4797.

SPORTS, FITNESS, PARENTING, RELIGION & SPIRITUALITY

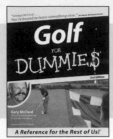

0-7645-5146-9

0-7645-5418-2

Also available:
- Adoption For Dummies
  0-7645-5488-3
- Basketball For Dummies
  0-7645-5248-1
- The Bible For Dummies
  0-7645-5296-1
- Buddhism For Dummies
  0-7645-5359-3
- Catholicism For Dummies
  0-7645-5391-7
- Hockey For Dummies
  0-7645-5228-7

- Judaism For Dummies
  0-7645-5299-6
- Martial Arts For Dummies
  0-7645-5358-5
- Pilates For Dummies
  0-7645-5397-6
- Religion For Dummies
  0-7645-5264-3
- Teaching Kids to Read For Dummies
  0-7645-4043-2
- Weight Training For Dummies
  0-7645-5168-X
- Yoga For Dummies
  0-7645-5117-5

TRAVEL

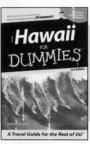

0-7645-5438-7

0-7645-5453-0

Also available:
- Alaska For Dummies
  0-7645-1761-9
- Arizona For Dummies
  0-7645-6938-4
- Cancún and the Yucatán For Dummies
  0-7645-2437-2
- Cruise Vacations For Dummies
  0-7645-6941-4
- Europe For Dummies
  0-7645-5456-5
- Ireland For Dummies
  0-7645-5455-7

- Las Vegas For Dummies
  0-7645-5448-4
- London For Dummies
  0-7645-4277-X
- New York City For Dummies
  0-7645-6945-7
- Paris For Dummies
  0-7645-5494-8
- RV Vacations For Dummies
  0-7645-5443-3
- Walt Disney World & Orlando For Dummies
  0-7645-6943-0

GRAPHICS, DESIGN & WEB DEVELOPMENT

0-7645-4345-8

0-7645-5589-8

Also available:
- Adobe Acrobat 6 PDF For Dummies
  0-7645-3760-1
- Building a Web Site For Dummies
  0-7645-7144-3
- Dreamweaver MX 2004 For Dummies
  0-7645-4342-3
- FrontPage 2003 For Dummies
  0-7645-3882-9
- HTML 4 For Dummies
  0-7645-1995-6
- Illustrator CS For Dummies
  0-7645-4084-X

- Macromedia Flash MX 2004 For Dummies
  0-7645-4358-X
- Photoshop 7 All-in-One Desk Reference For Dummies
  0-7645-1667-1
- Photoshop CS Timesaving Techniques For Dummies
  0-7645-6782-9
- PHP 5 For Dummies
  0-7645-4166-8
- PowerPoint 2003 For Dummies
  0-7645-3908-6
- QuarkXPress 6 For Dummies
  0-7645-2593-X

NETWORKING, SECURITY, PROGRAMMING & DATABASES

0-7645-6852-3

0-7645-5784-X

Also available:
- A+ Certification For Dummies
  0-7645-4187-0
- Access 2003 All-in-One Desk Reference For Dummies
  0-7645-3988-4
- Beginning Programming For Dummies
  0-7645-4997-9
- C For Dummies
  0-7645-7068-4
- Firewalls For Dummies
  0-7645-4048-3
- Home Networking For Dummies
  0-7645-42796

- Network Security For Dummies
  0-7645-1679-5
- Networking For Dummies
  0-7645-1677-9
- TCP/IP For Dummies
  0-7645-1760-0
- VBA For Dummies
  0-7645-3989-2
- Wireless All In-One Desk Reference For Dummies
  0-7645-7496-5
- Wireless Home Networking For Dummies
  0-7645-3910-8

EALTH & SELF-HELP

Diabetes
FOR DUMMIES

0-7645-6820-5 *†

Low-Carb Dieting
FOR DUMMIES

0-7645-2566-2

Also available:

- Alzheimer's For Dummies
  0-7645-3899-3
- Asthma For Dummies
  0-7645-4233-8
- Controlling Cholesterol For Dummies
  0-7645-5440-9
- Depression For Dummies
  0-7645-3900-0
- Dieting For Dummies
  0-7645-4149-8
- Fertility For Dummies
  0-7645-2549-2

- Fibromyalgia For Dummies
  0-7645-5441-7
- Improving Your Memory For Dummies
  0-7645-5435-2
- Pregnancy For Dummies †
  0-7645-4483-7
- Quitting Smoking For Dummies
  0-7645-2629-4
- Relationships For Dummies
  0-7645-5384-4
- Thyroid For Dummies
  0-7645-5385-2

DUCATION, HISTORY, REFERENCE & TEST PREPARATION

Spanish
FOR DUMMIES

0-7645-5194-9

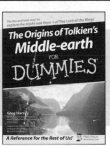

The Origins of Tolkien's Middle-earth
FOR DUMMIES

0-7645-4186-2

Also available:

- Algebra For Dummies
  0-7645-5325-9
- British History For Dummies
  0-7645-7021-8
- Calculus For Dummies
  0-7645-2498-4
- English Grammar For Dummies
  0-7645-5322-4
- Forensics For Dummies
  0-7645-5580-4
- The GMAT For Dummies
  0-7645-5251-1
- Inglés Para Dummies
  0-7645-5427-1

- Italian For Dummies
  0-7645-5196-5
- Latin For Dummies
  0-7645-5431-X
- Lewis & Clark For Dummies
  0-7645-2545-X
- Research Papers For Dummies
  0-7645-5426-3
- The SAT I For Dummies
  0-7645-7193-1
- Science Fair Projects For Dummies
  0-7645-5460-3
- U.S. History For Dummies
  0-7645-5249-X

Get smart @ dummies.com®

- **Find a full list of Dummies titles**
- **Look into loads of FREE on-site articles**
- **Sign up for FREE eTips e-mailed to you weekly**
- **See what other products carry the Dummies name**
- **Shop directly from the Dummies bookstore**
- **Enter to win new prizes every month!**

Separate Canadian edition also available
Separate U.K. edition also available

vailable wherever books are sold. For more information or to order direct: U.S. customers visit www.dummies.com or call 1-877-762-2974.
K. customers visit www.wileyeurope.com or call 0800 243407. Canadian customers visit www.wiley.ca or call 1-800-567-4797.